Web-Weaving
Intranets, extranets and strategic alliances

With love to my children – Thomas and Katie –
the Web-Weavers of the future. *PL*

With love to Mary and John Boyle, and Mark
and Will Stoddard. *PB*

Web-Weaving

Intranets, extranets and strategic alliances

Edited by

Peter Lloyd and Paula Boyle

OXFORD BOSTON JOHANNESBURG MELBOURNE NEW DELHI SINGAPORE

Butterworth-Heinemann
Linacre House, Jordan Hill, Oxford OX2 8DP
225 Wildwood Avenue, Woburn, MA 01801-2041
A division of Reed Educational and Professional Publishing Ltd

A member of the Reed Elsevier plc group

First published 1998

British Library Cataloguing in Publication Data
Web-Weaving: intranets, extranets and strategic alliances
   1. Business – Computing networks
   I. Lloyd, Peter   II. Boyle, Paula
   658'.05'46

ISBN 0 7506 3866 4

Typeset by Avocet Typeset, Brill, Aylesbury, Bucks
Printed and Bound in Great Britain

Contents

Contents

Figures

Contributors

Abramson, Frank
After a successful career in industry and financial services, Frank Abramson joined the late Graham Telford as a founding director of the Relationship Consulting Group Limited working with progressive service industry organizations who recognize the value of developing long-term relationships with their customers and, in appropriate cases, with compatible business partners. His particular strengths include a rigorous approach to business strategy development, facilitating change and, most importantly, developing and implementing customer-led marketing strategies. He is a regular speaker and frequently chairs retail and financial conferences.

Belbin, Meredith
Meredith Belbin gained his first and second degree at Cambridge to which he later returned after holding various academic and industrial appointments to become, in turn, Chairman of the Industrial Research Unit and Director of the Employment Development Unit. Dr Belbin is the author of the widely read *Management Teams: Why They Succeed Or Fail, The Job Promoters, Team Roles At Work, The Coming Shape Of Organization* (1996) and *Changing The Way We Work* (1997) all published by Butterworth-Heinemann. He currently works as a Partner in Belbin Associates, producers of INTERPLACE, a computer-based Team Role Expert System used worldwide and is now engaged in developing WorkSet, a new way of organizing and setting up work.

Berners-Lee, Tim
A graduate of Oxford University, UK, Tim is now with the Laboratory for Computer Science (LCS) at the Massachusetts Institute of Technology (MIT). He directs the W3 Consortium, an open forum of companies and organizations with the mission to

realize the full potential of the Web. With a background of system design in real-time communications and text processing software development, in 1989 he invented the World Wide Web, an Internet-based hypermedia initiative for global information sharing while working at CERN, the European Particle Physics Laboratory.

Birnbaum, Joel

Joel Birnbaum is Hewlett-Packard's Senior Vice President of Research & Development and Director of HP Laboratories (the company's central research and development organization), a position he assumed in 1991. He reports to the Chairman and CEO and serves as the company's chief technology officer with responsibility for the coordination of worldwide activities in research and development. Throughout his career he has been involved in the management of diverse activities in measurement, computing and communication technologies. His personal contributions are in the areas of distributed computer system architecture, real-time data acquisition, analysis and control, and RISC processor architecture.

Boyle, Paula

Paula Boyle is a Senior Analyst with Kinetic Information (www.kineticinfo.com) a research and consulting firm in the USA dedicated to studying how organizations are transforming the way they move, manage and share information. Known for her ability to synthesize many different industry perspectives, she has worked with users, vendors and venture capitalists to clarify issues ranging from technology adoption and integration to new product development, to business partnerships, mergers and acquisitions. Ms Boyle is an internationally renowned public speaker, has featured on Internet radio programmes and is quoted regularly in *The Wall Street Journal, PC Week, Computer Shopper, Computerworld* and *Infoworld*.

Brown, John Seely

John Seely Brown is the Chief Scientist of Xerox Corporation and the Director of its Palo Alto Research Center (PARC). At Xerox, Brown has expanded the role of corporate research to include such topics as organizational learning, ethnographies of the workplace, complex adaptive systems and techniques for unfreezing the corporate mind. His personal research interests include digital culture, ubiquitous computing, user-centering design, organizational and individual learning. A major focus of Brown's research over the years has been in human learning and in the management of radical innovation.

Chow, John

John Chow is the Deputy Director of Parsons Brinckerhoff's Office of Professional Practice, which sponsors the Practice Area Networks and a number of the other programmes. John is an environmental project manager who has worked in PB's corporate headquarters in New York since 1982.

Duguid, Paul

Paul Duguid is an independent researcher who holds long-term consultant positions at the University of California at Berkeley and Xerox Palo Alto Research Center (PARC). He was formerly a member of the Institute for Research on Learning. His work has been published in journals of anthropology, computer science, education, history and organization science. He is currently engaged in a National Endowment for the Humanities funded, historical study of eighteenth and nineteenth-century trading companies. With John Seely Brown, he is expanding ideas set out in 'Organizing Knowledge', the article published here, for a book, *The Knowledge Continuum*, to be published by Harvard Business School Press.

Espejo, Raul

Raul Espejo is currently Director of the Centre for Systems Research at the Lincoln School of Management (University of Lincolnshire and Humberside, UK). His current research is in second order cybernetics and Computer Supported Cooperative Work (CSCW). He has been published extensively in books and journals and is co-editor and co-author of several books, most recently *Organizational Transformation and Learning: a cybernetic approach to management* (Wiley, 1996) and *To Be and Not to Be, That is the System* (Karl-Auer Verlag, 1997). In 1985 he created Syncho Ltd a management consultancy in the field of organizational cybernetics which operates from the University of Aston Science Park, Birmingham, UK.

Evans, Lilly

Lilly Evans is Programme Director of Strategic Learning Web ☺ and a founder member of Global Consulting Group (GCG). She brings into management thinking and action a unique blend of multidisciplinary and multicultural knowledge and understanding from her own experience and from continuous involvement with new developments in sciences, art and business. Head of Organizational Engineering at BP Exploration, Lilly was responsible for introducing systems thinking and other learning organization principles at the top levels in the company. Dr Evans has been associated with MIT OLC since 1991. She is also a Consultant member of the Society for Organizational Learning (SOL) in Boston, USA and is a founding member of SOL-UK.

Flint, David

David Flint is a Principal of Wentworth Research, the provider of the IT Management Programme. He has twenty-five years' IT experience, having joined the Post Office Data Processing Service in 1972. He then worked for Butler Cox as a consultant to government and major businesses and contributed to much of the Butler Cox Foundation's research on IT. In 1993 he was one of the team that created the IT Management Programme. Recent publications have dealt with local area networks, the design of 'IT-friendly' buildings, E-commerce, customer-focus and the assessment of IS performance.

Friedman, Lawrence G.

Lawrence G. Friedman is a Senior Vice President at Oxford Associates, a go-to-market strategy and research firm based in Bethesda, Maryland, USA. He has also held executive positions with Andersen Consulting and with the sales research and training firm Huthwaite, Inc. He was a co-author of *Getting Partnering Right* (McGraw Hill, 1996) and is currently working on his next book, *The Strategy of Going to Market*. His focus over the last decade has been on helping clients make the transition from sales force-centric selling models to indirect, alternative channels such as alliances and business partners. His clients have included almost all of the large hardware, software and integration firms, as well as a variety of Fortune 500 companies outside of high-technology.

Gates, Bill

William H. (Bill) Gates is Chairman and Chief Executive Officer of Microsoft Corporation, the leading provider of software for personal computers worldwide. Gates began his career in personal computer software when he started programming at the age of 13. In 1974, while an undergraduate at Harvard University, he developed BASIC for the first microcomputer, the MITS Altair. Led by the belief that the personal computer would ultimately be a valuable tool on every office desktop and in every home, Gates formed Microsoft with Paul Allen in 1975 to develop software for personal computers. Gates' early foresight about personal computing and his continuing vision have been central to Microsoft and the software industry.

Hills, Mellanie

Mellanie Hills is an internationally known expert on intranets and extranets. She is the author of two intranet best-sellers, *Intranet Business Strategies* and *Intranet as Groupware*, published by John Wiley and Sons. She is a frequent speaker at Internet, intranet, and extranet conferences worldwide, and writes for various computer trade publications. Ms Hills is Founder and President of Knowledgies, a Plano, TX-based consulting firm, which provides strategic Internet consulting, helping companies create and use intranets, extranets and groupware for competitive advantage.

Holtham, Clive

Clive Holtham is Bull Information Systems Professor of Information Management and Head of the Department of Management Systems and Information at City University Business School, London, UK. He is the inventor of the BFS (Business Facilitation System) – an intensively computer supported environment for executive workgroups, supported by DTI/EPSRC. He co-founded the Multimedia Research Group which reviews the convergence of broadcasting, publishing, telecomms, computing and music industries. He has been published widely and lectures, broadcasts and consults in the UK, USA and continental Europe.

Judge, Peter

Peter Judge is an industry commentator and consultant covering intranets and electronic commerce. He edits Web Open

Technologies (http://www.wot.co.uk) and the Corporate Intranet Forum Report (http://www.corporate-intranet.com). He has written numerous books and reports on the web revolution.

Kim, Anthony H.

Tony Kim is a Senior Business Analyst with Oxford Associates, a sales and marketing strategy firm with offices in Washington, DC, San Francisco and London. With cross-industry experience in critical sales and marketing issues, his focus has been to understand the 'Go-to-Market' business process and the emergence of low-cost channels as an increasingly important component of hybrid marketing. Mr Kim has worked with clients to determine which type of model will maximize process improvements while containing costs. He has had relationships with Bristol-Myers Squibb, UPS and Tandem Computers.

Klineberg, Arnaud M.

Arnaud Klineberg is a Consulting Manager at Oxford Associates, a sales and marketing strategy firm with offices in Washington, DC, San Francisco and London. As an industry consultant, Arnaud has completed some ground-breaking work over the last three years with 'early adopters' who have invested heavily to achieve e-commerce leadership. He has worked inside these companies to incorporate the Web into their channel mix to improve coverage and service levels at reduced costs. Arnaud has most recently worked with Xerox, IBM, Microsoft, American Express and GE.

Lipnack, Jessica

President of the Networking Institute Inc., Jessica Lipnack is a journalist who began her career as a reporter for the *Pottstown (Pennsylvania) Mercury* when she was sixteen and has written for many publications since, including *The Boston Globe, The Christian Science Monitor, Esquire, The New York Times, The Futurist* and *Mothering*. In 1985 Ms Lipnack helped found the Electronic Networking Association. She has moderated and participated in numerous online computer conferences using a variety of software.

Lloyd, Peter

Peter Lloyd is the founder of Frontiers, a consultancy dedicated to all aspects of strategic alliances and partnerships. He is chairman of Team IT – the forum for Computer Supported Collaborative working – which was set up and funded by the UK Government Department of Trade and Industry. He is a regular speaker and chairman at international conferences and has organized several high-profile conferences himself on Collaborative Technology and Groupware. He has written and edited several books including *Groupware in the 21st Century* (Admantine/Praeger, 1994) and *Transforming Organizations through Groupware: Lotus Notes in action* (Springer Verlag, 1996). He also runs Trading Post which is a closed network of IT and organizational development visionaries and champions within large and complex organizations.

Malone, Michael

Michael Malone has been called 'the Boswell of Silicon Valley' (*San Jose Mercury-News*). Malone was raised in Silicon Valley and holds a bachelors in Combined Sciences and an MBA from Santa Clara University. In his eclectic career he has been an instructor on moral values at the Santa Clara Law School, a rock record reviewer, B-movie critic, even a saloon reviewer. He is currently host of *Malone*, a half-hour interview programme seen on PBS stations throughout the US that is now in its ninth season. Besides the television programme, Malone is best known as an author. His first book, *The Big Score: The Billion Dollar Story of Silicon Valley* (Doubleday) was named one of the top-ten business books of 1985 by *Business Week* magazine.

McIntyre, John

Following over twenty years with IBM in a number of strategic management positions in the UK and Paris, John McIntyre set up the company's Personal Computer Business in the UK. He left IBM in 1984 and held executive positions in UK and international systems and software companies until 1992 when he took up consulting to business. His experience in assisting enterprises to achieve sustained high performance led him to become involved with the Centre for Tomorrow's Company, of which he is an Honorary Member. He divides his time between working with the Centre to 'inspire and enable' its clients to apply Tomorrow's Company principles, and consulting in business strategy, development and performance in the 'de-jobbed' world of work.

Martin, James

James Martin is the Chairman of James Martin and Co, a world-wide consulting group. He is one of the world's best attended lecturers, founder of several successful companies and a futurist, correctly predicting business and technology trends for over thirty years. He has written more textbooks than any other living person and has been nominated for a Pulitzer Prize. *Cybercorp*, released in October 1996 was Martin's one-hundredth book and he was named by *Computerworld* as fourth out of twenty-five People Who Have Most Influenced the Computer Industry. In addition to his nineteen years working for IBM, he has conducted studies at top-management level for companies such as AT&T, Honeywell, Texas Instruments, Xerox and GTE. He also advised the UK Government on how to restructure telecommunications in Britain.

Opper, Susanna

Susanna Opper heads the consulting firm she founded in 1983 to help organizations use networked computers to achieve competitiveness and improve profitability. Clients include major US and multinational companies, consultants, associations and small businesses. She is co-author of *Technologies for Teams: enhancing productivity in networked organizations* (Van Nostrand Reinhold, 1991). Ms Opper is the Executive Director of The Shawenon Center which she and her husband founded in 1998. The Center provides an environment in which teams can address key strategic issues. Located in an idyllic rural environment, Shawenon offers state-of-the-art meetingware technology and skilled facilitation.

Potterf, Katheryn

Katheryn Potterf works for Oracle Corporation, in the System Products, Alliances Marketing Division. She is the Online Editor of the What's New section of Alliance Online, as well as a key contributor to the content of the Partner section of www.oracle.com. Prior to migrating to the web, she was News & Associate Editor of the (now-defunct) *Oracle Alliance Journal*, a print publication for and about Oracle's Alliance partners. She has authored, edited, or compiled several technology focus sections and third-party success stories. At present, she is also completing a doctorate in Comparative Literature at Stanford University. Her speciality is Chinese fiction of the Ming dynasty.

Roberts, James

Appointed Editor of *Intranet Communicator* magazine in June 1997, James Roberts has quickly come to grips with what is a rapidly evolving market. He helped to mastermind the US launch of the magazine in late 1997 and has recently overseen the launch of the Intranet Communicator website, which incorporates a cutting edge online subscription service. James is also involved in communications and management consultancy work, with a focus on knowledge management.

Saveri, Andrea

Andrea Saveri works in two core areas at IFTF – emerging technologies and strategic planning. Her research in these areas focuses on identifying and understanding long-term trends – social, demographic and technological – shaping the transformation of work and the household. Andrea leads IFTF's research on the Future Work Space which examines key shifts in the patterns of work among the US workforce, such as mobile, remote, home-based and other types of work settings. Her research involves exploring the evolving set of alternative work relationships (such as flexible staffing, contracting and outsourcing) as well as emerging forms of the virtual office and their implications for companies in the long term.

Siebel, Tom

Tom Siebel is the founder, Chairman and Chief Executive Officer of Siebel Systems, Inc. (www.siebel.com), the world's leading provider of enterprise-class sales, marketing and customer service information systems. Siebel Enterprise Applications address the requirements of call centre operations, field sales, distribution and Internet based sales and service and has become, since its founding in 1993, the fastest growing application software company in history. Siebel Systems is a global corporation providing sales, marketing and customer service application software systems to many of the world's leading corporations including: Compaq Computer, Dow Chemical Corporation, NationsBanc, Charles Schwab Corporation, Nationwide Insurance, Siemens, Kellogg's and Cisco Systems. Siebel, a frequent industry spokesman, is the author of *Virtual Selling: going beyond the automated sales force to achieve total sales quality*, published by the Free Press.

Skyrme, David J.
David Skyrme is a strategic analyst and management consultant whose consultancy company, David Skyrme Associates, participates in several virtual organizations, including the ENTOVATION International network. He has extensive experience in the IT industry, including the post of UK Strategic Planning Manager at DEC. He is a world-recognized authority on knowledge management, having co-authored the 520 page report *Creating the Knowledge-based Business* (Business Intelligence, 1997). He is currently writing a book on knowledge networking, to be published later this year by Butterworth-Heinemann.

Stamps, Jeffrey
Director of Research for The Networking Institute, Jeffrey Stamps is a systems theorist and the author of *Holonomy: a human systems theory* (Intersystems, 1980) based on his doctoral dissertation with a foreword by Professor Kenneth Boulding, one of the founders of General Systems Theory. Originally studying mathematics as an Alfred P. Sloan Scholar under John Kemeny at Dartmouth College, he has a BA in Political Science, was a Woodrow Wilson Fellow and a Fulbright Scholar, has an Mlitt in Political Philosophy from Oxford University and received his PhD in Human Systems from Saybrook Institute in 1980.

Tapscott, Don
Don Tapscott is Chair of the Alliance for Converging Technologies, which is currently conducting a multimillion dollar investigation into the information highway and its impact on business. An internationally sought consultant, speaker and writer on the topic of information technology, he is the author of the best-selling books *Growing Up Digital*, *The Digital Economy* and co-author of *Paradigm Shift*, plus three other widely read books. He is President

of New Paradigm Learning Corporation (www.mtnlake.com/para-digm), a consulting firm that specializes in helping organizations manage the transition to the Digital Economy.

Tea, Kevin

Kevin Tea trained as a journalist and held senior positions with the regional press and international magazine groups before turning to public relations and working for some of the largest blue chip companies in Europe. For the past five years he has been advising small to medium-sized enterprises on the benefits of Internet technologies and electronic communications. Projects involve electronic marketing consultancy and the design and maintenance of World Wide Web sites.

Telford, Graham

The late Graham Telford was a founding Director with Frank Abramson of the Relationship Consulting Group Limited. The Group works with progressive service industry organizations who recognize the value of developing long-term relationships with their customers and, in appropriate cases, with compatible business partners.

Thall, Nelson

Nelson Thall is recognized as one of the world's leading authorities on communication/media theory and process analysis. His work is devoted to an understanding of the relationship between communications, technology and culture. He became the Research Director of The McLuhan Center for Media Sciences, a non-profit media research organization, in 1995. He has consulted to both government, courts and business organizations and has written and published widely. He has been interviewed and quoted in over 100 major newspapers, magazines and books including *The New York Times*, *The Telegraph*, *USA Today*, *Wired Magazine*, *Paris Match* and *Time Magazine*.

Weissman, Steven B.

Steven B. Weissman is the founder and president of Kinetic Information (www.kineticinfo.com), a US-based research and consulting firm dedicated to studying how organizations are transforming the way they move, manage and share information. Weissman is known for his strong business sense, marketing savvy and innate ability to pinpoint critical success factors for clients who are both vendors and users of information technology. Weissman is a popular public speaker and frequently participates in leading industry forums. Well known for his pragmatic analyses, he is routinely quoted in national periodicals such as *Business Week* and the *New York Times* and the trade publications such as *Computerworld* and *Infoworld*. He also has many broadcast media appearances to his credit including the *Financial News Network* and *Entertainment Tonight*.

Willshaw, Isabel

Isabel Willshaw creates learning cafés and trains people to be effective network hosts and participants. Poolside Learning Café at the Edinburgh Festival takes place every August. Isabel welcomes contact from fellow networkers and explorers.

Wolff, Michael

Michael Wolff is the principal of Ki Net Limited which specializes in the provision of business intelligence services. He has been engaged in the telecoms and information industries for over twenty years. In 1976 he founded Lydiastar Telecoms Ltd, a company specializing in the international refile of telex and fax messages. In 1989 Lydiastar was merged with Comtext International. The combined entity is now the acknowledged global leader in its field. Since 1991 he has been involved in the research, development and launch of several information-based businesses. He is currently engaged in the development of KiLink™, a web-based business process management system to support distributed teams of independent knowledge professionals.

Wood, Robin

Robin Wood is the Managing Director of Genesys, a strategy consulting boutique applying the new sciences to organizations. Genesys is a strategic partner with Ernst & Young, working with them to develop a complexity-based approach to strategic management for the twenty-first century. The work of Genesys involves the use of collaborative technologies to accelerate learning and realize innate human potential and sustainability of organizations. Dr Wood has co-authored several articles and books including *Tactical Engineering for Rapid Results – a modular approach to organizational design* and *Financial Futures*. His latest book, *Complexity in Action – the new sciences, entrepreneurship and value in the 21st Century* will be published by Economist Books in 1999.

Zdravkovic, Nada

Nada Zdravkovic is an Information Manager with Halliburton/ Brown and Root with eighteen years' business experience in the project management, implementation and delivery of integrated information systems and associated working practices. She has worked on major projects for BP, Stat Oil, British Gas and Conoco, among others. In addition to consulting experience gained with a document management solutions provider, she is currently undertaking a thesis in Information Management and is a qualified neuro-linguistic programming (NLP) practitioner. This gives a unique view and passion, for implementing focused and business driven information strategies and solutions, which meet the highly technical and failsafe requirements of the oil and gas industry – experiences she shares with others, as a visiting lecturer at Cranfield and Kingston universities.

Foreword

Having worked with a number of clients on electronic collaboration and knowledge management, I have come to realize that what starts as a technical project almost inevitably ends with a focus on people, so I was glad to see that most of the authors in this volume deal with both people and technology. I have been a proponent of the concept that although technology is a critical enabler, people are generally the problem, as it is they who have to use this technology successfully. This theme runs through both of my earlier books on groupware as well as my next book, which is on knowledge networks.

In intranet-based organizations the concepts of electronic collaboration and knowledge sharing are as much about behaviour and culture as they are about the technology. As these markets have matured, and those dealing with these technologies become more sophisticated, so they begin to deal more with the intangible. The concepts of trust and relationship are as critical as servers and transport protocols. Web-weaving encompasses both people and technology – which is admirably demonstrated in this volume. The scope of this book is enormous. It includes chapters on technologies and their applications (intranets, extranets and electronic commerce) in the first section, as well as looking at people as nodes in the web and how they use these technologies.

A web is a social structure as well as a technological implementation. In reality we have been weaving this web throughout the history of man. The technologies of web-weaving have not made relationships any less valued, but rather have made them even more critical because of the rapidity with which they can be formed and the low cost with which they can be maintained. The ability to communicate and engender trust is critical in developing sustainable, topic-oriented relationships (now called on-line or virtual communities).

Interestingly, the strands of the web are identified by a variety of authors. They are of all types – wires, wireless, relationships, financial transactions, etc. The relationship strands can take the form of customer intimacy, electronic commerce, electronic selling, partnerships, alliances, mergers, acquisitions, hostile take-overs, virtual teams, knowledge networks, etc. The web speaks the language of business and organization as well as technology.

Although the book has a mix of academics, consultants, users and vendors contributing to it, the editors have managed to strike a fine balance between theory and practical applications of that theory, including case studies. I found the first section to be an excellent primer for those who need to get up to speed on all these issues and technologies. I would point out John Seeley Brown and Paul Duguid's chapter as particularly thoughtful and cogent as they attempt to deal with not only knowledge that individuals have, but also knowledge that forms in groups.

The second section of this volume looks at practical applications or case studies of web-weaving. It examines everything from virtual libraries to consulting companies and from disease detection to the building of mobile oil drilling platforms. It is clear to me that intranets and extranets, the strands of the web, are being strung in an ever widening arc, tying all of us together in a myriad of ways. I particularly liked Steve Weissman's humorous accounts of how kinks in the strands of the web can affect all of us, even in the most mundane of interactions. He does a very good job of keeping a body count.

These reports are consistent with my own experience of working with a global drug development company which consists of nine people. They are coordinators for a variety of projects and functions that get drugs to market 2–3 years earlier at 40 per cent lower cost. This virtual organization of nine does 100 per cent outsourcing. Besides logging innumerable air miles they are developing a collaborative web site to support each drug development team and thus increase the efficiencies by enabling the sharing of knowledge across projects. They have already begun weaving their web of efficiency and profitability.

The third and final section of the book looks at the future of web-weaving. What do many of the esteemed authors see in our future …? In some visions, everything (not just everyone) has a web page (a URL) and the ability to locate information on that object at the touch of a key. How could, or would, this transform society? Bill

Gates uses the metaphor of a nervous system for a business or organization in his vision of the future, where the cost of computing has dropped (again) a million times. In this computationally cheap environment, where 'information appliances' are readily available, he sees the network tying people together into an organism. This organism can react much the same way a person does, but on a much larger scale. What are the implications for society here? Tim Berners-Lee believes that the future of the web is not technology, but relationships. It is not hyperlinks, but trust networks.

In this world of the future metadata, or data about data, will become just as important as the data itself. For example, the metadata on me writing this Foreword is just as important as what I say. Who am I? When did I write it? Do I have an axe to grind? What is my knowledge about each of the authors or chapters in the book? Did I read the chapters? What is my relationship to the editors or publisher? All of these questions could comprise the metadata on what you are reading and they are just as important. What many of the futurists see is a web that not only carries the data, but also one that supports the metadata needed for trustful interactions.

Many of the authors in this section use ecological or biological metaphors for the role of the intranet and its implications on human behaviour. I agree with these analogies and would even take them one step further. Our information systems today reflect our organizational mindsets. Look at any organization's network and you can determine how willing they are to share (security), how important communication is to them (bandwidth), what their level of collaboration is (e-mail), and even what is important to them in terms of values (what content goes up first in the web sites). After all, the intranet is just an extension of your nervous system, which provides us with four socio-biological functions: communication, collaboration, coordination and corporate memory. These four functions so ably provided by our nervous systems are now being projected along the invisible wires of the web. How we construct this web, our assumptions, beliefs, etc. make up our mindset, and this mindset is reflected in not only the type of web we weave, but also how we walk the web.

Many of these authors point out that if you change the way people communicate and you change the way they access/share information, you have changed the corporate structure. Whether this emergent structure is more effective remains to be seen. Meredith Belbin points out that 'networking should radically affect collective intelligence within large and complex organizations'.

Since communities are composed of groups and groups of communities with common goals make up an organization, and organizations make up a society, the fact that these technologies are radically changing corporate structures means that societal structural changes are already in the works. The ability of affinity groups to form in the past was limited by their ability to find each other, bind together around a common idea or issue and then act in concert. With the web, today, not only are all these functions now easy, but cheap!

These affinity groups or communities will not only become more specific (e.g. black, wheelchair veterans living in Maui who are into kayaking) but they will also become a political force in our culture as soon as they begin to voice their preferences and wants (which again the web makes it easy for them to do). The web potentially provides a way to change the political process. For the first time, the common man has the ability to not only see, but vote on every piece of legislation available. I don't know anyone, not even a politician, who would want to do this, but it is now possible.

How will you feel communicating not only with 'intelligent agents' that do your bidding on the net, but intelligent appliances that scan and re-order the food in your refrigerator before you run out? The interactivity provided by the strands of the web we have woven has only just begun to show its effects on our rapidly changing culture. I believe this far-reaching volume helps to prepare you for a radically different future that is close at hand. Remember, the only inoculation against future shock is an imaginative, informed and open mind!

David Coleman
Managing Director
Collaborative Strategies

Preface

Yesterday: the book's thread – following something bigger

When we began working on this book, the intention was to pick up from an earlier book, *Groupware in 21st Century* (ed. Peter Lloyd, Praeger/Adamantine Press, 1994), and explore intranets and the role of virtual teams in business today. But it soon became clear that these themes were just one part of something *else*, something much bigger was going on that just could not be ignored. That something, we believe, is 'web-weaving'.

The first thread for this book, though it was barely seen at the time we started, was painted in graphic detail in the last chapter of the above book, 'Groupware for a small planet', by Peter and Trudy Johnson-Lenz. In it there was a fictitious character named Aziz Abdul Wahhab whose job, of all things, was to be a 'WEB Weaver' – 'one who sees patterns and makes connections'. When they wrote this back in 1993, they had a vision of a web connecting the planet earth (in fact they thought WEB would stand for Worldwide Electronic Brain!) and indeed it is becoming very real today with the WorldWide Web.

Another inspiration for this book was Peter Russell, who is well known for his prescient book, *The Awakening Earth – the Global Brain* (ARK, 1984). In it he compares the growth of interconnected computers on the planet with the stages of development of the human brain in the embryo. The first phase is a massive population of nerve cells; the second is billions of individual nerve cells making connections with each other. He points out that: 'As worldwide communication capabilities become increasingly complex, society is beginning to look more like a planetary nervous system. The global brain is being activated.' Twelve years before the Internet and the WorldWide Web became mainstream, he suggested that:

'the global telecommunications network could equal the brain in complexity by the year 2000 ... the changes that this will bring will be so great that their full impact may well be beyond our imagination. No longer will we perceive ourselves as isolated individuals; we will know ourselves to be part of a rapidly integrating global network, the nerve cells of an awakening global brain.'

And one of his inspirations was Pierre Teilhard de Chardin, who decades before him believed that humanity was headed towards unification and a single thinking group. He coined the term 'noosphere', from the Greek word for mind – *noos* – to describe the cumulative effect of interconnected minds around the world and 'noogenesis' as the 'planetisation of Mankind [sic] ... [into] a single, major organic unity'.

These threads indicated that what we were calling web-weaving was something really big. It is not just spiritually and figuratively big, but literally big. In fact, in practical applications we found it is being woven into some *very* big connections, from global leaders and world trade to outer space.

For example, the Davos community, which comprises global leaders from business, government and academia (who gathered together for a meeting in Switzerland) are being connected through a visual communication network called WELCOM. The founder of the World Economic Forum (WEF), Klaus Schwab, calls this a 'visual hotline of global decision-makers' (http://www.weforum.org).

Another example is a plan to replace all the paper documents involved in global trade with electronic forms. The 'Bolero Service' will offer guaranteed and secure delivery, regardless of technological platforms, within the context of a binding legal environment, which will provide the contractual framework for trading partners and drive a consistent international legal approach (http://www.boleroproject.com).

A further illustration is how the people at the SETI Institute are 'harnessing the power of hundreds of thousands of Internet connected computers in the Search for Extra-Terrestrial Intelligence (SETI)'. They have created a distributed application which behaves as a screensaver and leverages the downtime on volunteers' personal computers in order to process an enormous amount of information in a distributed fashion. 'When active, the program automatically downloads a small chunk of radio-telescope data, processes it for few hours or days, and returns a result to the server' (http://www.seti-inst.edu).

Now that is BIG!

<u>Tomorrow: the end of the thread – something still bigger yet?</u>

So we followed the threads of web-weaving as we produced this book. But we were surprised to find that, while web-weaving is being used in very big ways and is having significant impact on work and society, there is no real 'end in sight' and it is still being woven. We are still in the process, still travellers on the journey – there is no 'one thing' yet revealed that is the cumulative result of this weaving process.

The Internet and the WorldWide Web (WWW) have been integral to accelerating the web-weaving process, so the seeing of patterns and making new connections has had a much greater impact than the technology on its own. As weavers, we can only speculate about the structure and the form and the potential for the web-weaving to produce a significant transformation to something even bigger yet.

Shh. Can you hear it? Listen carefully for the sound of the spider meticulously preparing to ensnare its next victim. This subtle silence of web-weaving is both frightening and beautiful. The spider's invisibly thin, soft but strong web, is deadly only to those victims that fail to see it coming and are too weak to untangle themselves in time.

While it is frightful to be stuck inside a web, or to be blindly outside on a course to get snarled, it is powerful to be part of one. By being one of the threaded nodes, connected but disparate parts create a beautiful pattern.

… A pattern that is transcendent and translucent. A pattern that is both thin and wide, both sticky and leaky, both broad and near. A pattern that is woven inside, and outside and in-between. A pattern that is as important to its purpose as a pause is to music, as silence is to sound. *A pattern that is the recorded reflection of having been, having done.*

Perhaps, it is not a web being woven, but a cocoon. Perhaps, the silent spinning forms a shroud and after time will reveal a new form. Perhaps, because we are the only being on earth that can record its own actions, we will be the only butterfly to know, that once, it could not have flown.

Shh. Listen. Can you hear the harmony in the recording of the web-weaving?

Today: the book – just patterns and connections

We are entering an era when the quiet, invisible but powerful technology of the Internet and the Web will reveal its beautiful structure by creating patterns in business and our lives. This book is the result of following threads and listening to the voices of our time, to those who are learning from and influencing these patterns as they are revealed.

The criteria we used to organize these voices into chapters includes answering how and why the web is being used inside organizations, outside organizations, and in-between them; forming systems such as intranets, extranets and strategic alliances. In addition, we have gone beyond the comfort of these designs of today and cast a line out loosely into the future. We conclude this book, not with resolutions to the fears that web-weaving may cause, but with the potentially dissonant voices of leaders, whose writings explore what tomorrow may bring.

We hope that in the quiet time you spend reading this, you will bring these ideas and insights into the context of your own life and work, resonate with them and enjoy the patterns ahead.

Paula Boyle and Peter Lloyd

In the future science will gradually free us from the optical illusions that restrict our view of reality (Scott Adams, the creator of Dilbert, from his book *The Dilbert Future*).

Acknowledgements

I would like to thank the following: my wife and life partner, Ruth, for her unconditional love and belief in me, Caroline Struthers and Deena Burgess of Butterworth-Heinemann for their faith and flexibility, Peter and Trudy Jonson-Lenz for their inspiration and pointing out what has become my path, all the chapter contributors, without whom this book would not have been possible and special thanks to Paula Boyle, who has been a joy to work with.   *PL*

Utmost of thanks to all my family and friends without whose support nothing worth doing would get done – and for this project particularly, thanks to Molly, Evelyn and Heather. With gratitude to a few great teachers who inspired me to reach – particularly the Hardins, D. Anderson and S. Sanders. And a special thanks to S. Weissman for giving me guidance and time and to Peter Lloyd for being a great role model and partner.   *PB*

Abbreviations

ABC	Audit Bureau of Circulation
ACD	automated call distribution
AES	Applied Energy Services
Amex	American Express
ASI	aggregated statement of importance
ATM	automatic teller machine
BL	British Library
BP	British Petroleum
BPR	business process re-engineering
BT	British Telecommunications [British Telecom]
CAD	computer-aided design
CCO	Cisco Connection Online
CDD	Centre for Disease Protection
CEO	chief executive officer
CFO	chief finance officer
CGI	common gateway interface
CIBER	computer-interactive based electronic retailing
CIO	chief information officer
CMM	Competency Maturity Model
CSCW	computer supported cooperative work
CSI	consolidated statement of importance
e-commerce	electronic commerce
e-mail	electronic mail
EDI	electronic data interchange
EPA	Environmental Protection Agency
EU	European Union
FedEx	Federal Express
FMCG	fast-moving consumer goods
FSI	final statement of importance
FTP	file transfer protocol
GATT	General Agreement on Tariffs and Trade
GE	General Electric

Abbreviations

GIS	Global Information Solutions
GON	Global Office Network
GUI	graphical user interface
HALWEB	Halliburton's WorldWide Web
HR	human resources
HTML	hypertext markup language
IPC	Internetworking Products Centre
IS	information systems
ISDN	integrated services digital network
ISP	Internet service provider
ISV	independent software vendor
IT	information technology
IUMA	Internet Underground Music Association
IVANS	Insurance Value Added Network Services
LAN	local area network
MBA	Masters Degree in Business Administration
MIS	management information system
MIT	Massachusetts Institute of Technology
NC	network computer
NLP	neuro-linguistic programming
P&R	planning and resources
PAN	practice area network
PART	Part Analysis and Requirement Tracking
PB	Parsons Brinckerhoff
PC	personal computer
PDF	portable document format
PICA	Partner-Initiated Customer Access
PR	public relations
QA	quality assurance
R&D	research and development
RDF	resource description framework
ROI	return on investment
SETI	Search for Extra-terrestrial Intelligence
SGI	Silicon Graphics
SI	statement of importance; system integrator
SONIC	Spares Ordering Nonstop Inventory System
TCP/IP	transmission control protocol/Internet protocol
TP	Trading Post
TPN	Trading Process Network

TQM	total quality management
UN	United Nations
URL	universal request locater
VAN	value-added network
VAR	value-added reseller
VCR	video cassette recorder
VP	vice-president
VT	Virtual Teamwork
W3C	WorldWide Web Consortium
WAN	wide area network
WEF	World Economic Forum
Womex	World Merchandise Exchange
WRC	Wing Responsibility Centre
WWW	WorldWide Web

The Elements of Web-Weaving

Part One defines and explores the elements of web-weaving. Chapters 1–4 focus *inside* the organization on intranets, knowledge management, 'the cybercorp' and learning organizations. Chapters 5–9 focus *outside* the organization on extranets, electronic commerce, electronic consumerism, competitive advantage through information and sales force automation. Finally, Chapters 10–13 focus *in-between* organizations on alliances, virtual teams and market communities.

Web-weaving is about more than the Internet and the Web. It is about making electronic connections that add a new dimension to the fabric of life and work. It is about understanding how the behaviours of people and the processes of work are *changing* because of networked access to the globe. This section addresses the elements of this *change* – inside, outside and in-between organizations.

After defining intranets in Chapter 1, Mellanie Hills looks at how intranets improve competitiveness and enable a culture of information sharing. In Chapter 2, James Martin describes the 'cybercorp' and how intranets are an integral part of the 'corporate nervous system'. He also looks at the economic issues surrounding knowledge as a resource and the need for the cybercorp to do 'learning-intensive' work. Then John Seely Brown and Paul Duguid fully examine the complex issues of organizing knowledge in Chapter 3 and Lilly Evans covers some basics of the learning organization in Chapter 4.

Chapter 5 moves outside the organization, with a definition of extranet solutions provided by OneSoft Corporation. It describes the uses of extranets for purposes such as building customer support systems. David Flint, in Chapter 6 on electronic commerce, describes how the Internet has severely changed the nature of competition so that 'in an electronic market your every move is visible to every other player'. In such a market, he describes the intimacy with the customer as critically important in order to escape 'commodity corner'. The cus-

1

tomer is the centre of Chapter 7 on electronic consumerism, which details the changes in markets through computer interactive-based electronic retailing. The consumer is emphasized once again in Chapter 8 where Frank Abramson and Graham Telford summarize how every transaction is 'an opportunity for relationship information to be obtained, given or stored'. How to exploit this information from a sales point of view is the focus of Tom Siebel and Mike Malone's 'Automating the virtual sales force' in Chapter 9.

The final chapters in Part One consider the *in-between* issues, such as the dynamics of successful alliances between organizations and how they all contain vision, impact and intimacy (Chapter 10 by Lawrence Friedman). Since alliances can get much from the technology and techniques of virtual teams, Jessica Lipnack and Jeffrey Stamps detail the virtues of being virtual in Chapter 11. This is followed on in Chapter 12 where David Skyrme gives twenty-five principles of proven practice based on his hypothesis on what makes virtual teams work. But teams and alliances are not the only form of in-between organization. Communities of interest can make up market systems, as is described by the Institute for the Future in Chapter 13.

Chapter 1

The definition and dynamics of intranets[1]

Mellanie Hills

What is an intranet?

Imagine for a moment that you are the chief information officer (CIO) of a company that has locations spanning the globe. The director of communications comes to you with a problem. She has to communicate company news and corporate policy changes to employees in 2,000 locations in fifty countries around the world. She also has to help these employees feel like they are part of the company family. She needs a better way to do this.

Right now, none of her options is ideal. They are:

1. Mail – much too slow.
2. E-mail – time-consuming to keep up with the changing names and e-mail addresses at all these locations.
3. Telephone – expensive and time-consuming. Besides, who can keep up with the constantly changing contact names and phone numbers?
4. Fax – expensive and time-consuming. Same problems as telephone when it comes to keeping up with changing contacts.
5. Overnight letters and packages – too expensive for 2,000 locations.
6. Video conference – much too expensive.

How can you help her? You already made her job much easier in communicating with people outside the company by putting the earnings' reports and press releases on your Website. Now the media and analysts can obtain information from the Website whenever they need it. Can you do the same kind of thing for her in order to reach employees?

The answer is yes, you can, with an *intranet*. An intranet allows you to post on an internal web site information that everyone should see. In fact, the intranet is all about communications *inside* your organization.

So what is this intranet thing anyway? By now you are probably familiar with, and may have used, the Internet. An intranet is simply a small-scale version of the Internet inside your organization. A firewall keeps out intruders from the outside. The intranet typically is a network based on the Internet's transmission control protocol/Internet protocol (TCP/IP). It also uses WorldWide Web (WWW or the Web) tools, such as hypertext markup language (HTML), common gateway interface (CGI) programming and Java. You can get all the functionality of the Internet on your own private intranet inside your company.

The Web tools, which primarily make up the intranet, make any information just a few mouse clicks away. On the Internet, you can click on WWW links that connect you to almost any place in the world. That is much like a telephone, where you enter a *phone number* to connect you to almost any place in the world. The big difference is that the Web is probably easier to use. You do not even have to remember a phone number, you simply point and click.

Not only are intranets easy for your users, they are easy for you as well. An intranet may be just the solution you need. With an intranet, you can bridge your islands of information and provide that information to everyone, so making it easier for them to make decisions and to serve customers.

Does this sound great? Of course it does! So what is the catch? It must be expensive – anything that comes along to help solve your problems is always expensive. The good news is, it is not! In fact, it is cheap. The components of an intranet range from relatively inexpensive to free. If you want, you can do it *on the cheap*.

The intranet

Some of the earliest organizations to adopt the use of intranets were Lockheed, Hughes and the SAS Institute. Each of these organizations had someone on board from an academic environment who was familiar with Internet tools. They already knew about gopher, file transfer protocol (FTP), the Web and lots of others. They were aware of what these tools could do, and they decided to try a pilot programme to see if there was any value in using these tools in a commercial environment. Sure enough, they found the tools to be useful. Word of their experiences started leaking out just as companies were starting to take an interest in the Internet itself.

Based on these successes, many companies started experimenting with the Internet. Most probably began by putting up an Internet gateway to hook their e-mail systems to the rest of the world. They soon added Web servers and Web browsers for accessing the Internet itself. It became obvious that they could use those same browsers to access internal information, such as policy manuals and documentation. Soon they added access to Internet newsgroups, and realized they could create their own internal newsgroups as well. It all just happened.

We started calling the internal use of Internet technology by many different names. Some companies called them internal webs, while others called them internet clones, corporate webs or private webs. Sometime in 1995, someone in the media called them *intranets* and the name stuck. There are lots of differing stories about the source of the term *intranet*. One version which has been heard more times than any other is that Amdahl started using the term in 1994, and the media picked it up from them. Others have said that they were using the term even earlier. It is easy to believe that it was one of those good ideas that pops up simultaneously in different places. Once the media picked up on it, everyone started using the term.

Why and how did companies create their intranets?

From talking with a variety of companies, it is clear that a lot of intranets started as grassroots efforts, though some were formal initiatives. Many started with the information technology (IT) group, and some started in research and development (R&D), engineering and human resources (HR).

There is no one right way to create an intranet. The right way for you is the one that suits your organization and its culture.

Reasons for creating intranets include:

- because of the power and possibilities for the tools to solve business problems
- to meet communications needs
- to access information
- to share information and support mobile users.

What are the uses of intranets?

Once you get your intranet started, you will find the uses for it are almost limitless. Some of the uses are quite simple, requiring nothing more than internal web pages created using HTML. Others are very sophisticated and require links to databases, while still others may require extensive programming to create full-fledged applications. Some of the uses are:

- e-mail
- directories
- organization charts
- memos
- personnel manuals
- benefits information
- newsletters and publications
- systems user documentation
- training
- newsgroups
- news extracts
- job postings
- sales reports
- financial reports
- customer information
- quality statistics
- vendor information
- product information
- marketing brochures, videos and presentations
- product development information and drawings
- supply and component catalogues
- inventory information
- network management

- asset management.

What changes will occur?

For most of the companies, intranets did indeed yield the results for which they built them. The results fit two major scenarios, with a lot of dimensions within each:

1. Improved competitiveness through operational efficiency and productivity by:
   (a) improved access to up-to-date information
   (b) cost savings
   (c) time savings
   (d) improved productivity
   (e) improved operational efficiency and effectiveness
   (f) improved decision-making
   (g) improved ability to respond to customers and to be proactive
   (h) empowered users
   (i) leveraged intellectual capital
   (j) provided new business and revenue-generating opportunities
   (k) improved service to customer.

2. Broke down walls and built a culture of sharing and collaboration, because they:
   (a) improved communication
   (b) enabled sharing of knowledge and collaboration
   (c) empowered people
   (d) facilitated organizational learning
   (e) facilitated organizational bonding
   (f) improved the quality of life at work.

Improved competitiveness through operational efficiency and productivity

When everyone can have an intranet, how does a company use an intranet for competitive advantage? It comes from integrating your databases and applications into the intranet. This allows your employees to leverage that information through improved decision-making, productivity and service to your customers. This also stimulates creativity and innovation. The value that your employees add becomes your competitive advantage. This is a natural by-product of the things you do with your intranet.

Improved access to up-to-date information

Intranets are fast becoming the primary distribution and communications vehicles in many companies. Some are even extending the types of information available to users. For instance, the impact so far at EDS has been so great that it is committed to getting even more information delivered via the intranet. Using PointCast I-Server on its intranet, employees select from categories of information to receive personalized news and other information directly on their computer screens. This includes not only outside information, but also internal EDS news and announcements. This will allow EDS to immediately communicate bulletins to those who need that specific information.

Cost savings

Another frequently cited result is the cost savings. This is the result of most interest to executives. Most of the companies studied replaced any paper that they could with an intranet to save money on printing, warehousing, and distributing documents. They also saved money by eliminating faxes and memos. Since the intranet includes the network, some companies found cost savings through eliminating redundancy in their networks. One company, AT&T, estimated that through consolidating its individual networks into a single global intranet it has saved about $30 million per year. This resulted from reducing duplication of people, equipment and other costs.

One other large area of cost savings relates to the cost of proprietary solutions. With browsers and servers cheap or free, nothing else competes on price for so much functionality.

Time savings

Time savings are another often cited result. When the information they need is only a mouse click away, employees do not waste time trying to hunt things and verify their accuracy. This efficiency turns into greater productivity.

Improved productivity

EDS reported improved efficiency and productivity because the intranet provides faster communication of information and a more intuitive user interface, which improves people's comprehension.

Silicon Graphics (SGI) is progressively implementing applications that increase organizational productivity. An example is its electronic requisition system, which it uses to manage purchase orders and the associated approval process. This workflow application reduces the time it takes to process and track requisitions.

Improved operational efficiency and effectiveness

Intranets allow users to do things more efficiently, which allows them to use the time they save to do things more effectively. Turner Broadcasting feels that each employee who learns to use the intranet will be more effective. EDS even provides job aids through the intranet to assist employees in doing their work more efficiently. Workgroups at AT&T communicate electronically, which improves their efficiency.

The efficiency does not just apply to users. Intranets are a welcome relief to IT groups as well. They are easy to maintain and so require fewer people. For instance, SGI with over 2,000 servers, has a staff of only five to handle their intranet.

Many companies said that the Web is now their platform of choice for applications development and to modernize their legacy systems. The intranet even lets them reuse software components.

The end result of all of this for IT is that intranets stretch their budgets further. You can now do more with the same budget.

Improved decision-making

Intranets provide timely access to people and information in order to help you make better decisions. Often, when trying to get answers, you play telephone tag. It is even worse when employees and work groups span time zones, especially on opposite sides of the globe. If employees do not have information available to them, they may make bad decisions. Even worse, they may make no decision at all because they cannot get the information they need. Things happen slowly until the information becomes available and, in this fast-paced world, not having the right information at the right time can lead to lost opportunities.

With an intranet, the answers are at your fingertips and you can act quickly to make a decision. Decisions based on facts will inevitably be better than those made without facts.

Improved ability to respond to competitors and to be proactive

The Internet is particularly effective for situations where the competition has just come out with a new product. For instance, if Sun Microsystems brings out a new product, SGI can have a video on Silicon Junction in just twenty-four hours to enable salespeople to respond. By putting videos and sales information on the intranet, their selling can be more proactive.

Empowered users

Intranets have provided a lot of good news for IT. Since they are inexpensive to deploy and maintain, companies have saved money over other solutions. Even better, users now take control of their own information. Information technology simply provides the infrastructure and services. At Texas Instruments, intranets empower the end users to provide their own information management solutions. This means that they have less dependence on the IT department. With absolutely no work other than to register their server, they can make the information available to anyone in the organization. As if this was not good enough already, as better tools come along it will be even easier for end users to do almost everything themselves.

Leveraged intellectual capital

Booz Allen and EDS both said precisely the same thing: that their intranet allowed them to leverage their intellectual capital. It has changed the way they think about knowledge and information. The second of these, EDS, puts its customer profiles and project outlines on its internal web to capitalize on the intellectual capital available within the corporation.

Provided new business and revenue-generating opportunities

The intranet also opened up new business opportunities for several companies' products and services. Another interesting twist is that several companies are generating revenue from vendors who pay to advertise to employees on the internal web. These are ways these companies have tapped into the power of intranets. What could you do with your intranet?

Improved service to customers

The end result of all this should be improved service to customers. If intranets cause you to do things faster, cheaper or better, then customers benefit. Happy customers translate into profits and happy shareholders.

Breaking down walls: building a culture of sharing and collaboration

While all the operational results are important, the most valuable results may come from the culture changes the intranet will cause. Intranets facilitate communication and collaboration among employees, flattening of the hierarchy, and organizational bonding.

Improved communication

Improved communication was one of the two most often cited results from intranets. Some of the ways that intranets improved communications within these companies were:

- *Speed*. EDS has an on-line news service to supplement its paper news. It allows for immediate distribution of information and provides more complete news than can be delivered on paper.
- *Comprehension*. The message was easier to understand because the interface was more intuitive.
- *Consistency*. Leaders can communicate directly to all rather than going through layers of management. This avoids distorted messages with each subsequent delivery.
- *Free flow of information*. Intranets, by their very nature, stimulate free-flowing conversations with other people, with whom

you do not normally work or make contact. This helped break down barriers within organizations. SGI, for instance, found that its intranet facilitates its open culture.

- *Cross-organization.* The intranet facilitated communication and sharing between and among organizations. It helped to break down the barriers between different parts of an organization.
- *Universality.* Intranets make communications available to everyone at the same time.
- *Availability.* Intranets make communications available when you need them.

Some companies have started to expand this communication beyond the corporate walls. They are giving suppliers and customers access to their intranets to facilitate communication and coordination.

Enabled sharing of knowledge and collaboration
A large number of the companies reported a major result of their intranets is the enabled sharing of information across the enterprise. This then became critical to their operations.

One of these companies, AT&T, has geographically dispersed teams that use the intranet as their virtual meeting place. Also, widely dispersed ad hoc interest groups have formed to share knowledge on various technical issues. The company currently runs a corporate-wide project that impacts all 280,000 employees. Teams post their status on the internal web for the entire organization to view. The field deployment teams use the intranet to communicate about the project and coordinate their scheduling.

Empowered people
Intranets make it easy for leaders to share their vision with everyone. When people have access to information and share the vision, they have a powerful yardstick against which to measure their decisions and to take action. This can be a potent force for change or for empowering the whole organization to meet the needs of customers.

Facilitated organizational learning

Intranets provide a variety of tools to enable people to learn. Some of the ways intranets enable organizational learning include:

- *Career development.* The intranet can serve as a repository of career development information to allow employees to be proactive in their development. Career path information can include moves that are available and the training that is available or necessary for them.
- *Training programs.* Web-based multimedia is perfect for just-in-time training and is far more likely to be up to date. These programs usually combine the richness of sound, pictures, animations and videos for maximum impact. Multimedia greatly increases learning speed and retention.
- *Scheduling of training.* For those classes that are best taught in a classroom setting, you can post training schedules on the intranet and let people sign up directly for them.
- *Documentation.* The internal web is also a great repository for documentation and support materials for existing systems and for new applications.
- *Newsgroups.* Newsgroups, both internal and external, provide access to knowledge and information.

Facilitates organizational change: breaking down bureaucracy

The first step in organizational change is for the leader to share his or her vision with the troops. The intranet facilitates this communication directly to everyone so that it does not become garbled along the way. This helps develop the shared vision and commitment necessary to propel the organization forward.

The intranet also provides a forum upon which you can champion your risk-takers and make them role models for the rest of the organization. They are the ones who will drive the organizational change.

Facilitated organizational bonding

One somewhat unexpected result from having an intranet is that it helps build what the folks at Rockwell call a *corporate con-*

sciousness. The Turner Broadcasting intranet has made their employees in other locations around the world feel part of the team. Intranets promote bonding of employees and bonding to the organization. People feel a lot closer and know that they are part of a team. When the organization communicates its vision, goals and strategies, people know and understand what is happening and why, and become part of making it happen.

Improved the quality of life at work

Intranets have even gone so far as to improve the quality of life at work. The SAS intranet has made the atmosphere around the workplace more open. People are more satisfied because they can easily find what they need. At SGI, the intranet has changed the way people work and how they feel about their work. The intranet has helped to facilitate an open culture and communication.

How culture changes: a new information community

These changes will be some of the slowest in coming because cultures do not change overnight. Changing a culture, other than by brute force, takes a lot of time. Here are some of the ways intranets will cause cultures to change:

1. *Sharing and cooperation will become the norm.* People will stop hoarding information.
2. *Managers will manage results, not people.* Extra layers of management will go away, if they have not already. The role of the new manager is to coach and empower the team. Some of the things managers will do include:
   (a) Help the team formulate their vision.
   (b) Acquire resources for them, including any necessary training.
   (c) Remove roadblocks.
   (d) Encourage, guide, and support the team.
   (e) Act as a sounding board for them.
   (f) Stay out of the team's way as they achieve their results.
   (g) Reward the team for their accomplishments.
3. *Empowered people are not afraid to try new things.* Most people are self-motivated. Empowerment, enabled by shared

vision and access to knowledge, will help people feel more confident and self-sufficient. They will feel empowered to take care of customers and solve problems. This will make them feel more in control, which is very gratifying.

4. *Cross-functional teams will become the way of doing projects in the future.* They already appear to be the norm for building intranets. This is not just a project for the techies. These teams have representation from several functional areas. Several companies commented that these cross-functional teams were so successful that they have become the prototype for future projects.

   These cross-functional teams start the communication between employees and areas that normally would not come in contact with each other. The intranet provides the mechanism to support this communication. These evolving relationships start breaking down the functional walls and create more communication among areas. This free-flowing communication serves to further empower employees.

5. *Political power used to mean having information and knowledge.* When everyone has information, the power structure changes. This access to information, coupled with a shared vision throughout the organization, will move the whole organization purposefully in a single direction. Different departments will no longer negatively affect the organization's results to produce good results for themselves. *Shared power will propel organizations forward into the future.*

Note

1. This chapter has been published previously in *Intranet Business Strategies* (Wiley, 1996).

Chapter 2

The cybercorp[1]

James Martin

Electronic organisms

In the year that the Kinsey Report on sexual behaviour was first published another book rivalled its success. It went through four printings in its first six months. It was about organisms not orgasms. Most of the public could barely comprehend the book, but its title, *Cybernetics*, caught on in the popular press. It compared behaviour in creatures with behaviour in machines. Norbert Weiner, a Massachusetts Institute of Technology (MIT) professor, showed, with much mathematics, how electronic or mechanical devices could have control mechanisms like creatures.

During the Second World War, Weiner worked on servomechanisms which could steer ships and weapons. After the war he steadily extended his work to more complex situations, using the flexibility of electronic circuits and then computers. Weiner had an assistant who was a neurologist and together they applied the theories of servomechanisms to experiments with animals. They could predict the behaviour of muscles under different loads. Weiner's ideas caught the attention of the mass media when he generalized them into a universal principle: lifelike self-control could be done with electronic circuits.

Weiner defined *cybernetics* as *'the science of control and communication* in the animal and the machine'.[2] We should extend that to 'control and communication in the corporation'. The modern enterprise can be thought of as an organism, rather like a biological organism, except that it consists of people and electronics, organized to achieve certain goals. It has a nervous system going to every employee's desk. A corporation, like an animal, is exceedingly complex and cannot be described with simple equations. The mechanisms for corporate control and communications are changing greatly as we race into the era of information highways and complex software.

New forms of corporation have been referred to with terms such as 'Virtual Corporation', 'Adaptive Corporation', 'Learning Enterprise', but such terms describe only one aspect of the cybernetic corporation. We need a word that encompasses all of them. Corporations now emerging have a vast web of electronic links to other corporations. They will have virtual operations worldwide, be designed to adapt rapidly and continually to changing environments, and learn and evolve constantly at all levels. We will refer to this human-electronic organism as a *cybernetic corporation – cybercorp* for short. Today's ubiquitous networks are making the cybercorp reality.

The word *cybernetics* derives from the Greek word for 'steersman' which was also used in ancient Greece to denote a governor of a country. The Latin version of the word *kubernetes* means *governor*. The famous physicist Ampère described cybernetics as the science of governance.

The prefix *cyber* became popular when hackers started to discover that roaming the world on computer networks was very different from roaming the world physically. Personal computer users could connect to anywhere almost instantly and explore complex realms of software. The traditional sense of geographic space was replaced by *cyberspace*.

'Cyberspace' refers to the universe behind the computer screen. As tens of millions of computers become interlinked worldwide a form of global collective consciousness is being created. Cyberspace explorers can find themselves in a world in many ways richer and more complex than their physical world. The modern enterprise exists in cyberspace (whether or not it takes advantage of it).

Managers, executives, change agents and creative people everywhere need to ask: 'What should their corporation look like if it takes maximum advantage of cyberspace, cybernetics and superhighways?' For many in traditional corporations the answers are startling.

Cybercorp characteristics

It does not usually make much sense to say, 'Is such-and-such a corporation a cybercorp or not?' Corporations may be thought of as having cybercorp characteristics or mechanisms. Some have extensive cybercorp characteristics; some have just a touch of cybercorp. Almost all corporations would benefit from having more cybercorp characteristics than they have today.

Cybercorp *(sì´ber-kôrp)* noun
(From Greek *kubernêtês*, governor, from *kubernan*, to govern.)
A corporation designed using the principles of cybernetics. A corporation optimized for the age of cyberspace. A cybernetic corporation with senses constantly alert, capable of reacting in real time to changes in its environment, competition and customer needs, with virtual operations or agile linkages of competencies in different organizations when necessary. A corporation designed for fast change, that can learn, evolve and transform itself rapidly.

Society's massive institutions are manifestations of the technology of their age. Cyberspace brings new ways of thinking about business which affect managers everywhere (whether they know it or not).

The corporation that can compete best in the Internet era has an architecture quite different from the corporations of the 1980s. Ordered hierarchies of the 1980s are doomed; new organizational structures are taking their place. A designer in London interacts with a designer in Tokyo as though they were in the same room. New teams with new technology deliver new results. Jobs are being reinvented so that all employees are challenged to improve the corporate know-how. Agile networks of corporations can share competencies so that they can quickly seize new opportunities.

While mass production is being replaced by agile networks of producers, mass marketing is giving way to individualized marketing and the ability to deliver customized solutions. Standardized long-lived products and services are giving way to constantly changeable products and services. The entire nature of enterprises and employment is at the start of a massive historical transformation.

The Internet is causing a chain reaction of technology feeding technology and people stimulating people, worldwide. In aggregate it spells a momentous change which will affect the whole planet. The cybercorp world is characterized by intense competition bypassing national frontiers and unions. It brings dynamic computerized relationships among corporations using worldwide networks, with electronic reaction times, virtual operations and massive automation. It is a bloodless revolution (one hopes) that by the time it has run its course will have brought deeper changes worldwide than most violent revolutions.

In such an environment managers need to concentrate on how to delight their customers. How can we understand customer needs better? How do we make exciting products? How do we eliminate defects and improve quality? How do we cut costs? How do we cope with a world of rapidly rising complexity and climb learning curves more rapidly?

Designing the creature

The cybercorp, a creature designed to prosper in the corporate jungle, needs many parts that work together to make it creature-like, constantly alert, ready to spring into action.

Russell Ackoff describes corporations as complex systems. He describes an important property of such systems: 'If each part of a system, considered separately, is made to operate as efficiently as possible, the system as a whole will not operate as effectively as possible.'[3]

Ackoff comments that if many types of car were examined by engineers, and engineers identified which components were the best designed and then assembled a car from those best components, that car would not work. The parts would not operate well together. The performance of a system depends more on how its parts interact than on how well they work independently of one another.

In a corporation which consists of many departments, we could try to make each department work as efficiently as possible, using the most advanced computer systems for that department. But this would not make the corporation as a whole efficient. This is especially true in an era of great reinvention such as today. When machines or corporations are reinvented many of the old parts are scrapped.

Optimizing the parts of a corporation independently can be

highly inefficient compared with optimizing the whole. If the
designer of a jungle creature perfected the stomach without
thinking about the teeth, or optimized the ability to run without
thinking about the senses, the creature would not survive long.
Unfortunately most corporations do that. An enormous amount
of money has been spent on localized redesign, personal computers, ISO 9000 applied to existing processes, departmental client-
server systems, and so on, without redesigning the end-to-end
behaviour. If total quality management or ISO 9000 is applied
within an obsolete organization structure, it has the effect of optimizing and polishing procedures which ought to be scrapped. It
is a waste of money to automate or re-engineer departments that
ought to be replaced because the overall cybercorp architecture
needs to be different. Builders of the cybercorp must be concerned with end-to-end streams of activities.

The nervous system

To be creature-like, the cybercorp needs a *nervous system*. The
1990s is a decade of explosive growth in worldwide networks. As
well as the Internet, the world is laced with private networks like
those of McDonalds and American Express, and multicorporate
networks like those handling funds transfer, travel bookings,
stock market trading, goods distribution and so on.

The Internet, however, had one very important effect: computers of all types could use it. Prior to that different computers
had often been incompatible and could not 'talk' to one another.
Suddenly there was a way for all the world's computers to inter-
communicate. The WorldWide Web, its bulletin boards, and
software for easily browsing its contents with a mouse-clicking
dialogue, made it easy for people to interact with computers
anywhere. An astonishing worldwide nervous system came into
place and the stage was set for rapid evolution in corporate
behaviour.

Intranets

A cybercorp should have two nervous systems: an *internal* one
which is private and secure, and the *external* public one linking
it to customers, suppliers and the public at large.

When the Internet became high fashion it became clear that

the easiest way to build an *internal* corporate network was to use the same technology and software. Corporations around the world began to build their own private versions of the Internet, called 'intranets'. It steadily became understood that all manner of valuable information should be made usable on the corporate intranet. Before long far more money was being spent on intranets than on the public Internet.

The corporate intranet has closed borders. It uses 'firewall' software to keep unwanted visitors out. Computer users inside the corporation can access both the public Internet and the private intranet, but security measures keep the internal network sealed from intruders.

Not all corporate networking needs can be met with Internet-like facilities. A corporation may have separate networks for functions such as high-volume transaction processing, or video interaction. Collectively these networks provide the cybercorp nervous system.

Firewalls

Some systems are highly secure, for example, in banks and the military. Nobody has stolen a hydrogen bomb. However, in many organizations computer security measures are feeble, and this invites misuse. A corporate network should be designed to have tight security, and should not be connected to the Internet without protection. There must be airlocks between public networks and private internal networks.

The term *firewall* describes a small computer through which traffic has to pass to travel from an insecure network to a secure network. It may be used to authenticate messages from the Internet before passing them to the corporate intranet. Messages are taken into a filter and subjected to various tests before they are put on the internal corporate network. Some systems automatically translate internal network addresses, so that the internal systems are shielded, and allow only certain types of packets to reach certain machines. Sometimes multiple firewalls are used within an organization to isolate separate security domains. The software and hardware facilities designed to provide protection are constantly being improved.

As in real cities, security in the global city is never likely to be perfect, but the dangers can be reduced to an acceptable level. The value of the Internet far outweighs the risks. The simplest form of protection is to ensure that personal computers connected to the Internet are *not* connected to the internal corporate network. This is often done when the use of the Internet is that of one department or team. To make full use of the Internet, however, it is desirable for machines on the corporate network to be able to use Internet without inconvenience to the user.

Cryptography

An essential technique in achieving good security is *cryptography*. Cryptography is used to encode traffic so that messages cannot be read by unauthorized eyes, and phony messages cannot masquerade as genuine. It is also used for trustworthy identification of a machine or credit card.

Stories of breaking enemy codes are among the legends of past warfare. However code-breakers have a difficult time when chips are very powerful. In the battle between cryptographers and code-breakers, an inexpensive processor chip can scramble a message so formidably that no code-breaker is likely to unscramble it. A common misconception is that any cryptography can be broken. There are much publicized instances of Internet security violation and the press says 'The Internet is not secure.' It should be understood that *if a cryptography code is cracked it can be made immensely more secure by doubling the size of the key.* Computers can handle *very* large keys and they do not need to be very large to stop code-breaking. Some transmissions that have been cracked have used a 40-bit key; the KGB used a 100-bit key which was probably never cracked; computers can easily use a 1,000-bit key or much larger if necessary.

Widespread use is made of *public key* encryption. This relies on each party having a *private key*, which no one else knows, and a *public key* which is made available to chosen recipients of messages. These keys work in tandem. Messages encoded with the private key can be decoded by recipients using the public key of the sender. In effect the sender 'signs' messages with the private key and recipients can check the signature with the public key.

Private cryptography can be made far more secure than

public key encryption. Powerful cryptography is essential for cyberspace security, but it is not sufficient by itself. It must be used in conjunction with other security techniques.

Security servers

Cryptography works well if the sender and recipient have agreed ahead of time about what key will be used. However, the user may need to communicate securely with a new party with whom they have never dealt before. In such a situation cryptography can be used if both parties use a common security service. A server computer on the Internet is used to provide security; only this server knows the keys of all parties.

The user's machine enciphers the message and sends it to the security server which knows the user's public key. The security server decodes the user's message and then re-enciphers it so that it can be sent securely to the destination computer. This security procedure is inexpensive, and transparent so that the user is not aware of it; it all occurs under the covers.

Social engineering

However good the firewalls, cryptography and other measures, ingenious hackers have sometimes violated security by human techniques. Hackers use the term 'social engineering' to describe ingeniously talking their way into having changes made which enable them to bypass security:

' Hello, I'm Tony Boyle. Henry told my password has been compromised and that I must call you immediately to get it fixed. I haven't used it for some time and a hacker may be using it. Henry says we must fix it like pronto.'
'OK. What do you want me to do?'
'Just change the password for my login on your machine. Make it real secure. Change it to YINOFEAP7260 and make sure it's hashed.'
'Can you give me that again?'

Tight security needs tight administrative procedures. People responsible for security need to understand that they must not be talked into bypassing the correct procedures.

The cybercorp economy

Peter Drucker points out that a new form of capitalist society has evolved which he calls 'post-capitalist'.[4] The classical resources of capitalism described by economists are capital, equipment, labour, land and natural resources. Today the most important resource is none of these. It is *knowledge.* Value is created by applying knowledge to work.

An era in which the key economic resource is *knowledge* is startlingly different from an era when the key resources were capital, raw materials, land and labour. Most knowledge, unlike traditional economic resources, is replicable endlessly. It can reside in computers and on disks; it may reside in exceedingly complex software. It can be transmitted worldwide in a fraction of a second. Customs officials have no idea that the most valuable economic resource has just flitted past them.

A corporation should employ all the knowledge it can muster. If this knowledge is not shared with other corporations it provides a unique advantage. We might say, 'Unshared knowledge is money'. However, it must be fully shared *within* the corporation. 'Intellectual property rights' can protect little corporate knowledge (with a few striking exceptions) because most knowledge leaks to other corporations. Therefore, learning which creates new knowledge provides the primary competitive advantage.

The total worldwide investment in information and communication technologies is now more than a trillion dollars per year. An ongoing investment of this magnitude on technologies so potent is bound to change the world economy. We are heading towards a totally different type of economy. Terms like *information economy* are repeatedly used, but these do not fully describe what is happening. What is evolving is a *cybercorp economy*, with corporations designed for worldwide real-time interaction over information superhighways and an interlaced mesh of virtual and agile operations. Such corporations will increasingly be *non-national*, with capital, management, talent and resources coming from around the planet. In various ways there will be a *separation of state and economy*.[5]

This is not simply a speeding up of the old economic environment but a fundamentally new kind of economic environment.

Learning-intensive work

The great rate of change means that cybercorp work must be *learning-intensive*. If an employee has spent ten years doing routine work he or she has probably lost the ability to do learning-intensive work. The corporation with its eye on the future keeps its employees constantly learning. All employees should be encouraged to think creatively about how their procedures can be improved.

The most successful corporations spend more than one percent of gross revenue on training and education. In its great days, IBM spent almost 2 per cent on internal education and customer education. Motorola requires many of its employees to spend a total of one month per year of their time on training. At Chaparral Steel, at any given time 85 per cent of its personnel are in part-time training courses and all personnel take an educational sabbatical during which they visit customers' plants, other steel companies or universities. This is the price that must be paid to succeed with high levels of technology.

We must grow human potential as fast as we grow technological potential. As computerized tools, robot machinery and automated processes become ever more powerful, people tend to move into jobs requiring higher skills. Humans no longer need to act like robots on a relentlessly moving production line; robot-like jobs are done by robots. Book-keepers no longer add up columns of figures. Staffs of many types, working with data warehouses and decision-support tools, are expected to make better and larger-scale decisions. Designers have tools of great power that enable them to be more creative. In many jobs, computers should do the drudgery work and people should do work that is uniquely human. The annual revenue generated per person is often several times higher in highly automated corporations than in corporations with little automation. Automated corporations demand greater skill for greater pay. *The computer should be an intellect amplifier.*

The cybercorp is the culmination of the twentieth-century journey from treating employees as dumb slaves who must be made to obey orders, to challenging every employee to use his or her wits in devising new ways to add value. The twentieth century started with Kafka-like bureaucracy and contempt for employees, with Frederick Taylor timing every motion of workers with a stopwatch. It ends with the challenge of regarding the entire corporation as a cybercorp which must climb the steepest learning curve, where everybody is challenged to strive for their full potential.

In the past what was good for the corporation was often bad for the individual. We created soul-destroying jobs. The best corporations today are creating a work environment where difficult challenges energize and excite people. They are reinventing work so that what is good for the corporation is good for the individual. They aim for the highest of Maslow's hierarchy of human needs so that everybody tries to achieve their full potential. Most boring jobs can be abolished (but not quite all). The dehumanizing methods of early mass production are gone. The intense competition and emphasis on quality mean that we can buy far more interesting goods and services. Unlike with Adam Smith's revolution, the wealth of nations is maximized by maximizing the value added by everybody.

Unexpected competition

In the traditional economy, corporations knew who their competitors were. In the cybercorp economy totally unexpected competition can come from anywhere because it depends on knowledge which can be transmitted anywhere. In 1995 Microsoft tried to buy the financial software company, Intuit. The acquisition was blocked by the Justice Department, because the financial industry was worried. *Fortune* commented 'Microsoft would become, in effect, a nationwide consumer bank.'[6] Microsoft wanted its customers to pay bills, buy stocks, manage investments and carry out other banking functions from their personal computer (PC) screen. The Intuit deal was blocked but it is inevitable that other newcomers will provide Internet banking. Other Internet-based companies will attack the services of travel agents, insurance brokers and almost all service organizations. Newcomers can compete with shops, for example, by having software which searches the Internet for the lowest prices.

Simple operations which have been profitable in the past may generate little profit in the future because of the new forms of competition with computers and networks. Computers are being used to find the lowest price of goods and services on the

Internet, so when corporations each say 'We will not be under-sold', vicious price wars may ensue. Profits will come from doing more complex work that is less easy to emulate. High profits will come from unique skills. Many service or intermediary organizations will have to move higher up the food chain in order to survive.

This reshuffling of the cybercorp economy has been described as being like the early days of the universe after the big bang, before the galaxies started to congeal. New corporations will congeal, some with extremely high growth rates. *Management everywhere will need much understanding and vision if they are to be among the winners.*

Notes

1. This chapter has been published previously in *Cybercorp: the New Business Revolution* (AMACOM, 1996). Reproduced by permission of AMACOM, a division of American Management Association, http://www.amanet.org. All rights reserved.
2. Weiner, N. (1948) *Cybernetics*. Wiley.
3. Ackoff, R. (1981) *Creating the Corporate Future*. Wiley.
4. Drucker, P. (1993) *Post-Capitalist Society*. Harper Business.
5. Holland, K. and Cortese, A. (1995) The future of money. *Business Week*, 12 June.
6. Pan, T. P. (1995) Why the banks lined up against Bill Gates. *Fortune*, 19 May.

Chapter 3

Organizing knowledge

John Seely Brown and Paul Duguid

Discussions of organizing knowledge concern themselves primarily with one of three issues:

1. How to produce or generate something almost intangible.[1]
2. How to manage and coordinate something that in von Hippel's term is 'sticky'.[2]
3. How to enter the market with something that is, on the one hand, hard to commodify, yet on the other hand often 'leaky'.[3]

Together, these three appear incoherent. It is hard to imagine anything that is simultaneously intangible, sticky, and leaky. From the perspective we present here, however, *these differences reflect less incoherence than different stages in the production, development and use of knowledge.*[4] They also reflect distinct perspectives on those different stages. Issue one reflects the problem of locating useful knowledge production – a problem of particular interest to the folks in R&D; two reflects the problems of strategic management and IT in dealing with such inchoate knowledge; while three reflects the organizational and economic challenges of controlling knowledge as it becomes progressively more robust. Recognizing all three together – and the feedback loops and tensions they produce – are among the central demands of organizing knowledge.

Social knowledge

Some knowledge is inextricably communal in its production. Knowledge-based arguments about the firm lean heavily on Polanyi's notions of 'personal knowledge', and in particular, 'tacit knowledge'.[5] This sort of knowledge, similar to 'know how' rather than to 'know what',[6] emerges not through detached reflection so much as through action and participation. The dynamic process of *knowing* has both epistemological and organizational significance.[7]

Implicit, tacit and dynamic, this sort of knowledge resists explication, commodification and exchange – either in or out of the market. It cannot simply be parcelled up and passed from those who know to those who learn. From an individual's perspective, the process of acquiring knowledge involves not ingesting or receiving objective knowledge, but becoming a member of a community of practice and coming simultaneously to share and participate in its collective knowledge.[8]

In terms of learning, moreover, practice is not simply a method for inducting new members into community membership. It is also the way communities learn about the world – the way they produce new knowledge. Given humanity's social character and the way people divide labour among themselves, the bulk of new human knowledge arises through *social* practice as people work together on shared, collective and coordinated, but divided tasks. Here, then, we depart somewhat from Polanyi or Nonaka and Takeuchi[9] in suggesting that not all knowledge has its origin in individuals. Important knowledge and knowing are collectively produced and held.

This social process of knowledge production involves collective sense-making and judging as people, by engaging in densely shared practice, develop collective background assumptions and methods of investigation and validation. Developing practice changes a community's world view, which in turn provides new perspectives on the practice. The process is a dialectical one, with the new practice being shaped by the community's assumptions and vice versa. In a parallel fashion, the community shapes the practice and, reciprocally, the practice shapes the community. The practice, the perspective and the community are, in certain ways, mutually defining, inseparable and dynamic.

Consequently, the complex new behaviours of particular communities can, on the one hand, be almost impossible to replicate outside the community and, from outside, easily appear abstruse, absurd or trivial. Von Hippel suggests the problem is that 'one does not know in advance which subset of ... information will be relevant to anticipating potential failures'.[10] To which we would add, that such behaviours can be so profoundly implicit that they do not even emerge as information, relevant or irrelevant. They are simply practice. In developing knowledge, the routes a community of practice follows, the standards it sets, and the warrants it uses are inextricable from practice. When the knowledge is inchoate, it is often inexplicable without engaging in the practice.

Overall, as communities develop new practices, knowledge develops – but not as an aggregate of individual contributions, like adding bricks to a wall. It is more like the mixing of colour, where the outcome requires several contributions, but the process and product dissolve individual contributions indivisibly. Organizational synthesis of knowledge, then, may not begin with a step from individuals to groups or communities. Rather, it may begin with communities. Synthesis involves the articulation into a larger whole of the knowledge of distinct communities – going from palette to composition, to continue our painting metaphor.

Organizational learning in practice

The ways that organizations go about learning vary dramatically. Many look on the challenge as one of gathering information about a detached set of circumstances. They conduct market surveys or they monitor incoming customer service calls. They analyse the results, build them into databases and pass these out to the people in production, sales and service, for instance, who then modify their routines to reflect the customer needs. This centralized, detached information-gathering and top-down dissemination, while clear and simple in plan, places too much faith in individuals and information as the focus of learning. Social practice, with its awkward dynamics is almost entirely missing.

Yet organizations are never detached from their environment

and that environment is rarely static. Indeed, a great deal of organizational activity or 'enacting'[11] aims directly at engaging in and stirring up its environment. The same organizations that attempt to monitor the customer base are usually involved in simultaneously influencing it through new products, better service, marketing, advertising and sales.

Moving from a top-down, centralized to a bottom-up, diffused approach turns things around in several ways. It may limit the scope of inquiry, but it can increase the depth dramatically. Instead of starting by detaching information from the context that makes it valuable, this approach tries to develop knowledge out of engagement. It also relies on the people who are actually engaged in the practice to develop the knowledge.

Eureka

Xerox's 'Eureka' project illustrates a process of organizational knowledge production *in situ*. It not only relies on situated knowledge of customer activity, but it deploys the very people who must work in those situations to develop that knowledge.

Previously, Xerox had taken an *ex ante* approach to customer service. It provided service technicians with detailed instructions of how to deal with machine behaviour. Unfortunately, the machines did not obey company procedures and, in the end, the only way for the technicians to operate was to disobey them too. The technicians developed their own creative, non-canonical practices to handle the emergent and unanticipated in the machine and the needs of the customer's community.[12]

The Eureka project has helped consolidate this turn around from top down to bottom up.[13] It has provided a dynamic central database of problems and service tips to capture new problems as they have emerged. Such databases are not uncommon. But often they flood with information of varied provenance and value. Once they do, the use value of the database as a whole drops precipitously. By contrast, with Eureka, technicians themselves build and validate what goes into their database. As a consequence of this filtering, content reflects the leading edge of the collective understanding of a broad community of technicians all engaged in shared practice, with a shared background and shared belief in what is useful and what is not. The database contains the gems of understanding without the dross amongst which those gems are originally found. The value of Eureka – and it has provided immensely valuable – lies in the way it reflects not 'information' in general, which can be infinitely varied, but the local, specific knowledge produced by participants.

Reach and reciprocity in organizational learning

We characterize the different approaches here in terms of reach and reciprocity. New technologies have dramatically extended the reach of information gatherers. The reach of conventional customer relations, for example, is now extensive. New software often demands that we send detailed customer profiles electronically to manufacturers before we even consider using their technology. Customer help lines threaten to record our every word. But this reach renders a good deal of the information gathered thoroughly anaemic and unreflective of users' actual dilemmas.

To provide something richer requires reciprocity – the give and take of interaction and shared practice through which shared meanings and understanding develops. Reach allows people to pluck information out of context and interpret it how they will. It also allows people to deliver instructions and canonical practices. Reciprocity, by contrast, allows people to provide context for the information and to negotiate instructions. In both cases, reciprocity makes learning a two-way, mutual process.

This notion of reciprocity reflects our understanding of what Lave and Wenger call 'legitimate peripheral participation'.[14] In particular, they suggest that people learn by being on the periphery of practice, able both to observe and to join in. The Eureka database draws on the knowledge of those who live in the communities both of the corporation and the customers. They have reciprocity in two worlds. Moreover, it supports collective participation (rather than just information extraction) among a third world – the community of the technicians. Consequently, the technicians participate fully in making, using and giving meaning and value to the database contents. Reciprocity helps hone input into dense, rich and valuable knowledge.

At issue here are two approaches to technology: information-centred and participation-centred. Information- rather than participation-centred approaches allow extensive reach. Too often, though, they lack any sort of intensive reciprocity. Reach for gathering data, as both these examples suggest, may be primarily a technological matter. The reciprocity required for developing knowledge is significantly social.

<u>Organizational divisions</u>

Stickiness

When, as the adage has it, organizations do not always know what they know, cross-organizational synthesis confronts the problem of the stickiness of knowledge.[15] Discussions of such stickiness often assume that new knowledge does not travel to where it is needed primarily because the need is not recognized, the knowledge cannot be found, or the information channels are not in place. To deal with the problem, search-and-retrieval mechanisms are introduced. We claim, however, that the problem of stickiness requires a more complex understanding of the boundedness of knowledge.

If knowledge were easily relocated, then the conventional producer–customer interactions would not only be invaluable, but also relatively effortless. That they are not reflects the difficulty of transforming local knowledge into something more widely useful. New knowledge, we have been arguing, is situated, implicit, locally embedded. It takes discernment to understand what of local knowledge is worth disembedding and what is not, and it takes effort to re-embed it in broader communities.

Assumptions

Knowledge is divided because labour is divided. This claim does not entail, of course, that knowledge is therefore sticky. The division of labour also divides the production of material objects, but it does so on the premise (well supported by the history of mass production) that the parts produced are anything but sticky. Furthermore, the idea of stickiness runs against the perception, much enhanced by information technology, that information is anything but sticky.

We contend, however, that newly produced knowledge is sticky because, unlike widgets, knowledge travels differently *between* communities from the way it travels *within* them. Community members share knowledge as they share practice. People outside the community, who do not share the practice, have trouble sharing the knowledge, because new knowledge does not make much sense without the practice that brought it to light.

Leakiness

Organizations must work to overcome the stickiness that develops *between* their constituent communities. Organizations do not only face the internal problem of stickiness. They also face the external problem of leakiness. The explanation we have just given helps to explain why knowledge can often travel more easily between organizations than it does within them.

While the division of labour erects boundaries within firms, it also results in communities extending across the external boundaries of firms. Interfirm relations among participants with similar practices can thus be comparatively easy. Shared practice in a field allows ideas to spread. So in this direction it is often harder to stop ideas spreading than to spread them.

Paradoxically then, *inter*organizational work, both formal and informal, leads to enrichment and consolidation *within* disciplines or professions. Collective contributions from diverse organizations help these to consolidate. Whereas, the *intra*firm work leads to productive synthesis *between* disparate specialties and professions. These relations and impediments throw light on the role of organizations. They also suggest that organizations have more to gain than to lose by loosening boundaries to the ecology around them.

Synthesis and synergy

Community members often find it much easier to work among themselves rather than with other communities. Hence, they will work across organizational boundaries rather than within them.

35

This allows them to tap into the emerging direction of their field directly. Inevitably, this raises the question: *Why do we need organizations at all?*

Communities of practice can be highly insightful. They can also be remarkably narrow minded. In a detailed analysis of high-technology research, Garud and Rappa show how communities can fall victim to behaviour that reinforces their prejudices and blinds them to their own limits or to changes elsewhere in society.[16]

Organizations develop around explicit plans and aim for certain established goals. Communities, by contrast, are highly fluid, informal arrangements that develop around practice. *Tension is inevitable.*

Together the two create a powerful (if occasionally explosive) mixture. Organizations can channel the energies and insights of communities. Communities, by contrast, can challenge an organization's strategies, goals and tactics. Organizations can give communities direction and stability. Communities provide organizations with dynamism and fresh insight. Formal organization provides standard business endeavour, emergent community practice may engage in the speculation that explores and exploits the cracks left by those endeavours. Formal organizations developed the Internet; emergent communities have given it its vibrant diversity.

The two play off one another in a relationship of structure and spontaneity. Structure can produce stability and coherence; for that very reason it can be conservative and domineering. Spontaneity can be dynamic; for that very reason it can be disruptive, incoherent and ephemeral. But together each can help overcome the other's limitations, producing coherence within diversity rather than either chaos or rigidity.

From this perspective, the organizational challenge is to understand divisions and boundaries, not to try to obliterate them. Instead of pursuing uniformity, hegemony or boundaryless information societies, the productive way seems to be to exploit heterogeneous combinations of overlapping communities of practice, firms, networks, social worlds and regions that can engage both the strengths of organization and the dynamism of evolution. Getting the balance right, achieving the right level of coor-

dination and coupling among heterogeneous groups is a complex
challenge.

The end of organization

In contrast to what we have just argued, the success of small,
volatile start-ups in high-technology areas such as Silicon Valley
suggest to many that the conventional firm is dead. Start-ups do
not, however, point inescapably to the disappearance of organization. In particular, in complex sectors such as high-technology,
focusing on the size of individual start-ups may be quite mis-
leading.

Many small start-ups are inextricably part of complex
'knowledge ecologies'. The latter provide a 'social structure for
innovation'[17] whereby small, new firms remain intricately
dependent on large established ones through partnerships, both
formal and informal.[18] Large organizations underpin the
'embeddedness' that is often particularly critical for the survival
of smaller firms and start-ups.[19] Evidence, we are suggesting,
shows a systemic relationship between the large and the small
rather than a progression from larger to smaller.

Still, many believe that information technology and formal
organization are inimical.[20] The firm is essentially hierarchical.
Cyberspace, it is countered, is profoundly antihierarchical.[21] Yet
the relation of information technology to organizational structure
is less straightforward. Certainly IT has produced flatter organizations. But the rise of these does not show that hierarchical
control is in decline. Flatter organizations do not necessarily relin-
quish control. Often, with the help of powerful, technologically
mediated reach, they simply centralize it.[22] As Fukyama shows,
Walmart and Benetton built commercial empires by removing
decision-making authority from their periphery in this way.[23]

Even communities of practice which are fundamentally self-
organizing seem to militate against formal organization. Self-
organizing systems[24] or catallaxies[25] back some of the strongest
arguments against formal organization. Yet while such systems
help reveal the folly of such things as planned economies, they do
not reject planning on a more local scale. Arrow, for example,
merely points to the 'limits' to organization, not its complete lack
of utility; while Hayek allowed that within spontaneous catallax-

37

ies, goal-oriented, organizational planning is important. The undeniable power of spontaneous organization does not prove that formal organization should be abandoned. Rather, it calls for a better understanding of the relation – one of 'structure and spontaneity' – between the two.

Significantly, those who argue for self-organization often sound less economical or sociological than entomological: bees, ants and termites (as well as bats and other small mammals) provide much of the self-organizing case.[26] In a related vein, others like to draw examples from 'artificial life'.[27]

Such parallels undoubtedly reveal many similarities between humans and insects. But they mask some important differences, too. In particular, all these examples of complex adaptive systems, particularly those of artificial life, overlook the importance to human behaviour of deliberate social organization. To pursue these analogies much further, we would need to know what will happen when bugs or artificial agents decide to form a committee, pass a law or organize a strike.

Ants moving across a beach, for example, do exhibit elaborate, collective patterns that emerge as each individual adjusts to the environment. In this way, they undoubtedly reflect certain aspects of people – of, for example, the uncoordinated synchronicity of sunbathers on the same beach seeking the sun or trying to keep the blown sand out of their sandwiches. But, unlike the sunbathers, ants do not construct beachfront supermarkets to provide food, or coastal highways to reach the supermarket, or farms to supply the supermarket, or coastal commissions to limit supermarkets, highway building, and farming, or supreme courts to rule on the infringement on constitutionally protected private property rights of coastal commissions or, indeed, constitutions or property rights at all.

It is often recognized that humans distinguish themselves from most other life forms by the increasingly sophisticated technologies they design. It is less often recognized that they also design sophisticated social institutions. With organization, people have learned to produce more food out of the same areas of land, to deploy known energy resources and search for new ones, to establish new regions for human endeavour and to design the very technologies that are now paradoxically invoked as the end of organization. Organization has also helped to foster and focus humanity's most valuable resource: its infinitely renewable knowledge base.

Perhaps most significantly of all, humanity has relied on organization not merely to harness, but to ward off disasters produced by the downside of self-organizing behaviour. For example, establishing and continually adjusting socially acknowledged property rights have limited the 'tragedy of the commons'. Such constraints can channel self-organizing behaviour and knowledge production in productive rather than destructive directions. This ability may be one of society's greatest skills.

It seems to us, then, that it makes no more sense to demonize institutions than it does to demonize the ecology. The challenge is to deploy each to moderate the other's worst excesses. That challenge is profoundly difficult, facing as it must the complex feedback loops that social institutions create. These make human organization quite different from that of other species. As Buckley and Chapman – an anthropologist and an economist – put it:

Human systems are not like [non-human ones]. The individuals within them are defined by the system, but they are also its creators and definers; they define themselves, their own terms of existence, their own relevant objectives … they can self-monitor, self-reflect, amend, or retain. Systems of this kind are not susceptible to determinate study; they are constantly in flux, and their changes are not predictable on the basis of past performance.[28]

Yet as the sociologist Giddens argues in a discussion of human reflexivity: 'the chronic revision of social practices in the light of knowledge about those practices is part of the very tissue of modern institutions'.[29] And institutions, as many, including institutional economists acknowledge,[30] are part of the very tissue of modern society.

Such institutional structures play these complex roles in what we call 'knowledge ecologies', too. Like natural ecologies, these knowledge ecologies are, in the large, ungovernable. But again like natural ecologies, they are most productive when subject to local husbandry.[31] This is the role of organizations.

We can see the contribution organization can make if we glance back to the nineteenth century. The era gave us the telegraph, the train, the car, the telephone, the airplane, the cinema, and much more. Yet Williams contends that the incredible creative energies of the nineteenth century are evident less in the arts or in industry and engineering than in the of new kinds of social institution it developed (among which are the limited liability corporation, the research university, and the union).[32] Indeed, North suggests that an absence of suitable husbanding organizations caused a century-long lag between the dawn of industrial revolution and the late-nineteenth century's dramatic economic expansion.[33] Chandler claims that half of this expansion resulted from organizational, not technological innovation.[34] One clue to today's 'productivity paradox'[35] may well be that we have simply failed to develop knowledge organizations adequate for a knowledge economy.[36]

In all, the agricultural image of husbandry we borrow from Spender and Grant strikes us as particularly apt.[37] Society developed out of hunter-gatherers into its modern state not by simply awaiting the spontaneous evolution of its resources, but by developing farms and markets to accelerate certain ecological shifts (crops, domestic animals and the like) and to hold at bay others (resource depletion, species and habitat degradation). Firms, we suggest, are the farms of a knowledge ecology.

Conclusion

The virtual should extend and transcend the limits of the social while at the same time honouring its salient features of division and boundedness. In the light of a social theory of knowledge production, not only do organizations and their role need reappraising, but so do technologies. In designing organizations, people consider not simply individuals and information, but also communities, communication and knowledge. Technology design must face the same demands, though today it often avoids them. Once communities, communication and knowledge come into consideration, for example, the implicit claim, often made, that technologies can replace social institutions looks extremely dubious. More often than not, such arguments are merely a sleight of hand, a quick confusion of social systems with technological systems.

It is confusion over social systems and technological systems that has allowed many firms to conclude that an intranet will meet the challenge of synthesizing knowledge. For genuine synthesis, technology will be vital. But design must engage directly with the social institutions it hopes to address. Too often it assumes these can simply be bypassed.

Here, the issue of reach and reciprocity comes back again. Social factors, we argue, demand reciprocity, though this inevitably serves to check the implicit paradigm of limitless reach implicit in a good deal of technology design. The increasing reach of technologies is unquestionably of colossal importance. It is equally important, however, that striving for reach does not disrupt the social need for reciprocity.

Reciprocity is difficult to handle. It involves not just simple tit-for-tat, but rather the means for all participants in technologically linked interactions to participate fully. It remains a common lament on the Web that most design there only simulates interaction.

Some emerging technologies suggest richer possibilities for reciprocity are under development. New forms of multicasting over the Internet, such as the 'M-Bone', offer much denser forms of interaction (without needing the infinite bandwidth that seems always to be just around the corner and for which we are always told to wait). But many of the demands here are, of course, social not technological. Reciprocity, as we have described it, is similar to what Lave and Wenger refer to as legitimate peripheral participation.[38] Intriguingly, new communications technologies have gone a long way to provide peripherality. This allows us to lurk on the side of interactions in which we are not taking part and of communities of which we are not members.[39] Better technologies will also support increasingly fuller participation. None the less, it remains for social groups, not technologies, to determine legitimacy.

The rewards of reciprocity, we believe, are high. But it also has demands. It limits the control that can be exerted through communication. And it also limits the scope of participation. Full reciprocity is only possible among relatively small groups. Reach, by contrast, sometimes seems infinite. Ignoring reciprocity only makes technologically mediated participation more difficult. But technology that can recognize and to some extent parse how relations *within* communities (where the need for reciprocity is high) differ from those *between*, may actually help to extend reach between communities without disrupting reciprocity within. We suspect that coming to understand the challenges of the *between* relation should be a significant issue for new design.

One important issue here involves the way the local informality found within communities is distinct from a certain level of explicitness and formality demanded between. In the past, digital technology has focused heavily on the explicit, ignoring how, on the one hand, much that is implicit simply cannot be rendered explicit and, on the other, when what can be is rendered explicit that transformation can profoundly affect the social relations in play.

For instance, in many situations, asking for explicit permission changes social dynamics quite dramatically – and receiving a direct rejection can change them even further. Consequently, people negotiate many permissions tacitly. A great deal of trust grows up around the ability to work without explicit permissions. Contrast this with what are now called 'trusted systems'. These are technological systems that in fact eliminate the need for social trust. They simply prevent people from behaving in ways other than those explicitly negotiated ahead of time. Everything must be agreed (and paid for, usually) *ex ante*. For high security demands, such technologies will be increasingly important – people are glad they can trust bank machines. But if new technologies ask people to negotiate their social interrelations like their banking relations, they will leave little room for the informal and the tacit. By contrast, technology that can respond to the implicit in human relations may both help foster trust and remove a great deal of the burden of using technology.

One goal for bringing these divided issues – formal/informal; explicit/implicit; organization/ecology; technological/social

– together may be through thinking not of replacing the social, material world with a technological, virtual one, but to consider bringing the two together. In this way, the virtual should extend and transcend the limits of the social while at the same time honouring its salient features of division and boundedness. Vague though this prescription may seem, it holds for us intimations of what we mean by pursuing both reach and reciprocity in organizing knowledge.

Notes
1. Polanyi, M. (1966) *The Tacit Dimension: The Terry Lectures*, Doubleday.
2. Von Hippel, E. (1994) 'Sticky Information' and the locus of problem solving: implications for innovation. *Management Science*, **40** (4), 429–439.
3. Spender, J-C and Grant, R. M. (1996) Knowledge and the firm: overview. *Strategic Management Journal*, **17** (1), 5–9.
4. Nonaka, I. and Takeuchi, H. (1995) *The Knowledge-Creating Company: How Japanes Companies Create the Dynamics of Innovation*, Oxford University Press; Nonaka, I. and Konno, N. (1997) The Concept of 'Ba': Emerging Ontological Foundation of Knowledge Creation. Paper presented at the Berkeley Knowledge Forum, Haas School of Business, 29 September, Berkeley, CA.
5. Polanyi, M. (1958) *Personal Knowledge: Towards a Post-Critical Philosophy*, University of Chicago Press.
6. Ryle, G. (1949) *The Concept of Mind*, Hutchinson.
7. Cook, S. and Brown, J. S. (1998) Bridging epistemologies: the generative dance between organizational knowledge and organizational knowing. *Organizational Science*, Forthcoming.
8. Lave, J. and Wenger, E. (1993) *Situated Learning: Legitimate Peripheral Participation*, Cambridge University Press.
9. Nonaka, I. and Takeuchi, H. (1995) *The Knowledge-Creating Company: How Japanese Companies Create the Dynamics of Innovation*, Oxford University Press.
10. Von Hippel, E. (1994) 'Sticky Information' and the locus of problem solving: implications for innovation. *Management Science*, **40** (4), 429–439.

11. Daft, R. L. and Weick, K. (1984) Toward a model of organizations as interpretation systems. *Academy of Management Review.* **9** (2), 284–295.

12. Orr, J. (1987) *Talking About Machines*: *Social Aspects of Expertise.* Report for the Intelligent Systems Laboratory, Xerox Palo Alto Research Center, Palo Alto, CA; Orr, J. (1997) *Talking About Machines: An Ethnography of a Modern Job*, ILR Press; Brown, J. S. and Duguid, P. (1991) Organizational learning and communities of practice: towards a unified view of learning, working and innovation. *Organization Science*, **2** (1), 40–58.

13. Bell, D. G., Bobrow, D. G., Raiman, O. and Shirley, M. (1998) Dynamic documents and situated processes: building on local knowledge in field service. In T. Wakayama, S. Kannapan, C. Meng Khoong, S. Navathe and J. Yates (eds.), *Information and Process in Enterprise*: *Rethinking Documents*, Kluwer Academic Publishers. In press.

14. Lave, J. and Wenger, E. (1993) *Situated Learning: Legitimate Peripheral Participation*, Cambridge University Press.

15. Von Hippel, E. (1994) 'Sticky Information' and the locus of problem solving: implications for innovation. *Management Science*, **40** (4), 429–439.

16. Garud, R. and Rappa, M. A. (1994) A socio-cognitive model of technology evolution: the case of cochlear implants, *Organization Science*, **5** (3), 344–362.

17. Florida, R. and Kenney, M. (1988) Venture capital and high technology entrepreneurship. *Journal of Business Venturing*, **3** (4), 301–319.

18. Walker, G., Kogut, B. and Shan, W. (1997) Social capital, structural holes and the formation of an industry network. *Organization Science*, **8** (2), 109–125.

19. Granovetter, M. (1985) Economic action and social structure: the problem of embeddedness. *American Journal of Sociology*, **91** (3), 481–510.

20. Kelly, K. (1994) *Out of Control: The New Biology of Machines, Social Systems and the Economic World*, Addison-Wesley.

21. Eisener-Gillett, S. and Kapor, M. (1997) The self-governing

Internet: coordination by design. In B. Kahin and J. Keller (eds), *Coordination of the Internet*, MIT Press.

22. Innis, H. (1991) *The Bias of Communication*, University of Toronto Press; Beniger, J. (1986) *The Control Revolution: Technological and Economic Origins of the Information Society*, Harvard University Press.

23. Fukuyama, F. (1996) *Social Networks and Digital Networks*.

24. Arrow, K. (1974) *The Limits of Organization*, W. W. Norton.

25. Hayek, F. (1988) *The Fatal Conceit: The Errors of Socialism*, University of Chicago Press.

26. Clark, A. (1997) *Being There: Putting Brain, Body and World Together Again*, MIT Press.

27. Dawkins, R. (1986) *The Blind Watchmaker*, Norton; Turkle, S. (1996) *Life on the Screen: Identity in the Age of the Internet*, Simon & Schuster; Clark, A. (1997) *Being There: Putting Brain, Body and World Together Again*, MIT Press.

28. Buckley, P. and Chapman, M. (1996) Economics and social anthropology: reconciling differences, *Human Relations*.

29. Giddens, A. (1990) *The Consequences of Modernity: The Raymond Fred West Memorial Lectures*, Stanford University Press.

30. Veblen, T. (1967) [1899] *The Theory of the Leisure Class: An Economic Study of Institutions*, Funk and Wagnalls; Veblen, T. (1904) *The Theory of Business Enterprise*, C. Scribner's Sons; North, D. (1981) *Structure and Change in Economic History*, North & Co; North, D. (1990) *Institutions, Institutional Change and Economic Performance*, Cambridge University Press; North, D. (1992) *Transaction Costs, Institutions and Economic Performance*, Institute of Contemporary Studies.

31. Spender, J-C and Grant, R. M. (1996) Knowledge and the firm: overview. *Strategic Management Journal*, **17** (1), 5–9.

32. Williams, R. (1961) *The Long Revolution*, Chatto and Windus.

33. North, D. (1981) *Structure and Change in Economic History*, Norton & Co.

34. Chandler, A. (1977) *The Visible Hand: The Managerial Revolution in American Business*, Harvard University Press.

35. Brynjolfsson, E. (1993) The productivity paradox of information technology. *Communications of the ACM*, **36** (12), 67–77.

36. Though for a qualified argument see Sichel, D. (1997) *The Computer Revolution: An Economic Perspective*, Brookings Institution Press.

37. Spender, J-C and Grant, R. M. (1996) Knowledge and the firm: overview. *Strategic Management Journal*, **17** (1), 5–9.

38. Lave, J. and Wenger, E. (1993) *Situated Learning: Legitimate Peripheral Participation*, Cambridge University Press.

39. Brown, J. S. and Duguid, P. (1996) *The Social Life of Documents*, Release 1.0.

Chapter 4

The learning organization

Lilly Evans

Why learning organization? New language of organizations

A new term is starting to appear in the management literature more and more – the learning organization. Yes, organizations can learn. This chapter will help you to become familiar both with the importance of this new outlook and its implications for the way we will be working in the future.

Most organizations are the product of the Industrial Era. Since the 1920s the emphasis has been on increasing the ability of managers to run these corporations efficiently. This soon came to mean a growing focus on development of skills, methods and tools for:

- command
- control
- predictability.

These relate directly to the four distinct features of industrial organizations:

- hierarchical structure, where pyramids, levels and boxes represent employee positions
- bureaucratic nature, governed by rules and procedures
- financial success measures, both internally and externally.

However, the world is now rapidly moving into the Knowledge-based Era. First change from the industrial organization is the recognition of the value of people in the organization. You often hear slogans such as, 'People are our most important asset'. Next, a visionary company is distinguished by its outstanding organizational architecture, as Collins and Porras show in their recent bestseller *Built to Last*.[1] In most cases, we see the changes in the corporate structures towards more flexible forms, teams and networks.

Finally, the measures of success that matter now are the ones that continuously improve their 'habits for survival in a turbulent business environment', as explained by Arie de Geus, former Head of Planning at Royal Dutch/Shell in his book *The Living Company*.[2]

Clearly, the old management theory and practices above cannot deliver all this. So, what is needed? *The learning organization.*

An example of a learning organization: Applied Energy Services

There are many well-known examples that you can find in the most popular books on the subject.[3] So, let us pick one from a mature industry: the utilities – Applied Energy Services (AES).

Applied Energy Services was started by two people in 1982 as an enterprise its founders would be proud of – they cared more about the kind of company they would build than its bottom line.[4] Today that same company is the multinational AES Corporation, an independent power producer, with revenues of over $500 million (circa £300 million) in 1994, stock market value of over $1.5 billion (over £900 million) and return to shareholders better than most high-technology companies.[5]

Their commitment to values matches the Body Shop. Executives from AES feel a moral obligation to satisfy all stakeholders, to shape all strategy and make all decisions with an eye on employee fulfilment, community welfare, customer satisfaction, fairness to suppliers and a clean environment.

Co-founder and current chief executive officer (CEO) Dennis Bakke says, 'The most socially responsible thing we can do is to do a really good job of fulfilling our business mission, which is to provide reliable, safe, low-cost electricity around the world'. Their shared values are: integrity, fairness, fun and social responsibility.

Where does learning come into this? Applied Energy Services acquired the 50 per cent stake in the two Northern Ireland power plants being privatized in 1992. In charge of the financing for this deal were two control room operators. Says chief finance officer (CFO) Bill Sharp, 'Sure, it took time for people to get up to speed. But, they were challenged, and that's the point. Whenever you reinvent the wheel, you expend the knowledge in the corporation'.

So, AES is committed to giving all its people as much decision-making responsibility as they can handle. Frequent and intensive cross-training, role rotation and finance education for all are the rule. 'The risks are that there will be mistakes and that they'll be significant,' says CFO Sharp. But both he and Bakke maintain that traditional structures fail, too.

Concern expressed by co-founder and current Chairman Roger Sant that the carbon dioxide emitted by AES plants contributed to global warming has been resolved through planting enough trees in Central America to offset fully all carbon that their coal-plants put into the air over their forty-year life span.

Both, Bakke and Sant have spent some time working for the US government, which gives them deep aversion for written policies, procedures, job descriptions, organizational charts and all else that goes with the bureaucracy. Instead, the value is put on fairness and integrity. The company stresses also two other values, ownership and ambiguity, implying that if you see a problem, it is yours – you take the initiative to solve it, irrespective of your particular place or job in the organization. This kind of freedom means fun. But it also means that placing blame, however reasonable, is not acceptable. Tolerance of ambiguity is another characteristic AES wants from its people. It is not everyone's cup of tea.

So where are the controls and boundaries? They show up in measurements, peer pressure, open information, accounting and auditing. For instance, the measures are visible to all and reported daily to everyone in the plant. They include: safety, environment (gas emissions relative to US Environmental Protection Agency [EPA] recommendations and their trends), availability, heat rate and income (reported as cost per kilowatt/hour and the plant income statement). Applied Energy

Services workers exercise powerful control, management gover-nance comes through simple peer pressure. After all, who better to know what is going on at the shop floor but the insiders.

Applied Energy Services managers manage their values with the same care they show to the plant performance. All people know that training, hiring, measurement and storytelling collab-orate to keep the culture vibrant. The values are also upheld through appraisal process. Old-fashioned storytelling plays a sig-nificant part in sharing values at AES. Master storytellers are the keepers of the culture, in this case this role is taken by two of the most senior people, Bakke and Bob Hemphill, who use some of the most important events in the short corporate history as role-plays for the orientation of new employees and their spouses. The stories get re-enacted with zest. In this way, AES makes its points about integrity, fairness, trust, fun in almost impossible situa-tions, ambiguity, ownership and just raw perseverance that has built the company from nothing into the true learning organiza-tion. At AES they do not just tell stories, they live them.

With competitors like these, how is your company doing? As the industries and commerce change radically, the nature and complexity of problems and information cannot be managed in the traditional sense. This introduces a new language, tools, and behaviours for managers, as we have seen in the case of AES.

Basic terms and their meaning

The theoretical and philosophical underpinnings for operations like AES come from a deep understanding of the twentieth-century sciences of relativity, quantum physics, chaos, complex-ity and self-organization. The idea is simple (this definition is derived from Peter Senge of MIT): 'A learning organization is one in which people at all levels, individually and collectively, are continually increasing their capacity to produce results they really care about.'[6]

Why should organizations care? Because, the level of perfor-mance and improvement needed today requires learning, lots of learning. And, as Professor Chris Argyris of Harvard University says: 'Learning occurs when the discovery or insight is followed by action.'[7] He goes on to distinguish two kinds of learning (by individuals, within groups and in organizations):

- single loop learning, which occurs when mismatch between intention and what actually happens is corrected by altering behaviour or actions
- double loop learning, when the underlying values are changed and then new action follows from them.

An alternative definition is that by D. Garvin of Harvard Business School: 'A learning organization is an organization skilled at creating, acquiring, and transferring knowledge, and at modifying its behaviour to reflect new knowledge and insight.'[8] He goes on to distinguish three types of learning in organizations:

- learning before doing, as with the Manufacturing Game[9]
- learning while doing, as in the case of AES above
- learning after doing, as with learning histories (an approach to encouraging learning and reflection in organizations developed by George Roth and Art Kleiner at the Center for Organizational Learning, MIT).

Any new approach that claims to provide a major new benefit should have a solid methodology and be proven in the real world. Only in this way can a company develop new organizational capabilities or enhance its capabilities in reliable and reproducible ways. The organizational learning discipline deals with these issues through combining three bodies of theory and practices:

- dynamic systems
- action learning science
- emerging dialogue theory and practice.

Main tools and techniques

An inquiry into how one's own thinking contributes to both our understanding and interpretation of data, and to the actions performed to improve the situation, requires a new approach and a new set of skills. This is where the five disciplines of learning organization – namely personal mastery, mental models, shared vision, team learning and systems thinking – become important (as originally identified by Peter Senge in the classic of the field,

(*The Fifth Discipline*).[10] The dynamic or systems thinking provides both the philosophical and practical base. Systems thinking methodologies have been developed over past forty years, but are still relatively new in management practice. The main systems thinking observations are:

1. Cause and effect are often separated in time and space.
2. Obvious interventions do not always produce obvious results.
3. Long time delays and systemic effects of actions can make it almost impossible to judge effectiveness of those actions.
4. Managerial practice fields are the most appropriate settings where teams who need to take action together can learn together.

So, there is a growing body of evidence that one learns far more by attempting to change a system than by observing it stable in its standard operating procedures. Similarly, dynamic systems experience shows that almost never do all the necessary facts become available at the same time. Hence, the importance of learning before doing and playing the game (like the Manufacturing Game) through a sufficient number of operational cycles that allow for the interactions of differing time constants to occur on a number of occasions. In addition, the consequences can also be organizationally distant from where the processes and definitions of best-planned maintenance are being used. Further, dynamic systems theory provides through the models the capabilities to look into situations where setting the right boundaries is critical.

For example, simply playing the Manufacturing Game[11] helps people make the transition from a reactive mode, where the maintenance problems seem to happen to them, to a proactive mode, in which they recognize they are responsible for their own problems. The game does not have any losers (in other words it is about sustainability), in that it does not stop until all teams are making profit. The game provides a unique setting for organizational learning, without the dangers of making serious mistakes. Through the guidance of experienced facilitators, it embodies the practice of dialogue and applies the action theory methods. And facilitators are mostly former maintenance people.

Summary

The education in basic contemporary thinking – in many fields –
can provide more openings for action than we can imagine and
at little cost. In most industries, in utilities, in health care, in
banking and insurance, and in most areas of government, there
is no clear path to success, no clear path to follow. Yet, stories like
those in AES give clear guidance and provide vivid examples to
follow. All we need to embrace are practices that emerge from
three new distinctions of the learning organization:

- ability to be poised at the edge of chaos
- capability to deal with complexity
- competence in generative conversations.

Notes

1. Collins, J. C. and Porras, J. I. (1994) *Built to Last:
   Successful Habits of Visionary Companies*. Harper Collins.
2. de Geus, A. (1997) *The Living Company*. Harvard Business
   School Press.
3. See in particular: Garvin, D. (1993) Building a learning
   organisation. *Harvard Business Review*, July–August; Senge,
   P. M. et al. (1994) *The Fifth Discipline Fieldbook: Strategies
   and Tools for Building a Learning Organization*, Doubleday
   Currency; Thurbin, P. J. (1994) *Implementing the Learning
   Organization: the 17-Day Learning Programme*. Pitman;
   Waterman, R. H. Jr (1994) *The Frontiers of Excellence:
   Learning from Companies that Put People First*. Nicholas
   Brearley.
4. Much of the culture related material comes from Waterman,
   The Frontiers of Excellence.
5. Financial information and quotes from executives are from
   Birchard, B. (1995) Power to the people: fun and gains at
   AES Corp. *CFO Magazine* (The Economist Group), March,
   pp. 38–43.
6. This definition is derived from Senge et al., *The Fifth
   Discipline Fieldbook.*
7. Argyris, C. (1996) In Moingeon, B. and Edmondson, A.
   (eds). *Organisational Learning and Competitive Advantage*.
   Sage Publications.

8. Garvin, Building a learning organisation.

9. See Evans, L., Ledet, W. and Monus, P. (1995) Preventive maintenance: what is it and why it matters. *Russian Oil and Gas Journal 'Neftegaz'*, **2**, April, pp. 55–63; Senge et al., *The Fifth Discipline Fieldbook*.

10. Senge, P. M. (1990) *The Fifth Discipline: the Art and Practice of the Learning Organisation*. Doubleday Currency.

11. See Evans et al., Preventative maintenance.

Chapter 5

The extranet solution

OneSoft Corporation

Introduction

The extranet represents the bridge between the public Internet and the private corporate intranet. The extranet connects multiple and diverse organizations on-line behind virtual firewalls, where those who share in trusted circles can network in order to achieve commerce-oriented objectives. The extranet defines and supports this extended business enterprise including partners, suppliers, distributors, contractors and others that operate outside the physical walls of an organization, but are none the less critical to the success of business operations. With the Internet providing for public outreach or communication, and the intranet serving internal business interests, the extranet serves the business-critical domain between these extremes where the majority of business activity occurs.

Extranet solutions are designed to emphasize and foster the customer relationship. As successful businesses know, the cost of obtaining a new customer far outweighs the cost of maintaining a current one. With commerce-enabled extranets, companies are now able to establish and maintain one-to-one relationships with each of their customers, members, staff or others at very low cost through the Web, offering a customized and individualized experience that can be dynamically generated or modified, based upon a user's privileges, preferences or usage patterns. Information entered by the user (registration form, on-line surveys, etc.) can be compiled with statistics and other information that is captured automatically by the system (searches performed, products purchased, time spent in each site area, etc.) to

provide the company a complete picture for each and every
visitor of the system. This comprehensive user profile offers
unprecedented opportunity to present relevant information,
advertising, product and service offerings and other content to a
qualified, targeted interactive user community on a one-to-one
basis.

What is the extranet?

The extranet concept is quite simple: *Extranets are permeable,
yet secure commerce-enabled networks which electronically link
distributed organizations or individuals over the Internet in a
public, semi-public or private forum.* These emerging networks
establish 'virtual firewalls' to extend the benefits of a company's
intranet and enable collaborative business applications across
multiple organizations. Secure, collaborative and interactive
work spaces serve to connect companies and their customers,
suppliers, and other stakeholders, and produce efficiencies in
such representative business models as electronic commerce, collaborative publishing and supply-chain management.

Most costly slowdowns occur not within a particular
company, but instead are accumulated throughout the distributed
communication and management constructs that define a given
business process. Extranets are extremely powerful in that they
can mirror, support and streamline these business processes across
distributed companies, creating market efficiencies for both internal and external influences. Extranets can control access to information, applications and other capabilities on-the-fly, allowing
participating organizations to determine and enforce who has
access to what information throughout the on-line business cycle.

Extranets can provide the most logical and immediate benefits for businesses within their 'natural markets'. Natural
markets consist of groups of partners and alliances that participate in common business scenarios such as buyer and seller,
product-to-market, consultant or contractor arrangements, customer service/responsiveness, sales and lead generation, and
other established business relationships. Within these natural
markets, extranets can achieve breakthrough efficiencies including collapsed cost structures, economies of scale and other
returns on investment for organizations involved with or con-

tributing to this process.

Prior to the existence of extranets, software solutions that were implemented across different organizations were extremely expensive to build and consisted primarily of customized proprietary programming. These closed systems environments made it difficult, if not impossible to link the entire product supply chain – manufacturers, suppliers, dealers, off-site contractors and customers – especially if each organization followed a different networking and development plan. Web-based extranets are inherently flexible, scaleable, portable and extensible to achieve integration across distributed, cross-platform or heterogeneous system environments, and greatly reduce traditional barriers to cross-organizational networking.

Key characteristics and underpinnings of an extranet

Internetworking of unrelated, distributed organizations poses unique challenges for an extranet to be successful. Regardless of the type of business or number of organizations involved, there are key characteristics and underpinnings that most system integrators would agree must be present within an effective multiorganizational extranet presence.

Extranets require a Web-centric network and business model

The integration and coordination of a diverse and distributed group of business entities and individuals, each with potentially dissimilar networking and computing environments, require the commitment to an open systems platform that supports universal standard protocols for information exchange. The WorldWide Web provides the ideal platform to fulfil these requirements. The Web can support the wide range of data types for distributed information transfer, and offers a flexible development environment for site and application assembly, transaction management and software deployment activities.

Extranets must be goal-oriented

Extranets are most effective if they support a common goal, objective or process that benefits all of the involved organizations. Business objectives such as cutting inventory acquisition times from weeks to days, guaranteeing customer response time within an hour, or even having the ability to customize a product while still on the assembly line are all possible using an extranet networking environment. Working toward a specific goal not only helps determine the success of the extranet, but helps to justify universal buy-in for all of the participating organizations. With a well-focused objective, extranets can be developed to serve the business interests of commercial, governmental or non-profit organizations.

Extranets are future oriented and legacy sensitive

Successful extranets are designed to produce immediate benefit for the participating organizations and simultaneously prepare for future enhancements to the on-line system environment. It is not necessary for a company to discard its existing infrastructure in favour of a totally new direction. Extranets can breathe new life into existing business processes by integrating legacy systems, enhancing communication systems and improving employee productivity through the utilization of Web server and browser technology. Effective extranets also provide the extensibility to integrate 'best of breed' technologies to position the system for future enhancement and integration with advanced applications. Extranets can become a meaningful and practical tool to translate a corporation's vision into reality.

Extranets require powerful software applications

An extranet supported by powerful, commercial grade software applications will serve its enterprise community effectively and efficiently. Applications are the keys to an extranet's success and should be scaleable to meet the growing and changing demands of the user community.

Extranets require coordination and commitment

Effectively coordinating and managing a system across multiple organizations is a complex endeavour and should not be understated or overlooked. Management must commit to and adopt standards, methodologies and practices throughout their organization to support the utilization of the extranet environment.

Fortunately, advanced extranet solutions are specifically designed to make it easy to deploy, manage and maintain extranets that serve virtual distributed enterprise.

Sample extranet scenarios

Sales and customer service

Before the advent of Internet-based technologies, companies traditionally relied on paper transactions, face-to-face meetings, phone calls and other repetitive communications to conduct sales and customer support activities. These extremely laborious and cost-intensive activities have long been considered compulsory drains on company resources due primarily to the individualized processes associated with each customer or account. For those organizations that manage a direct sales effort or deal with value-added resellers (VARs), independent software vendors (ISVs), system integrators (SIs) or other third-party marketing vehicles, however, the challenge exists to harness the power of the Internet to put the right information in the hands of the people who need it in a cost-efficient manner.

Extranets permit companies to preserve the integrity and distinctiveness of these one-to-one relationships, while reducing the time and effort involved in managing the sales or customer service process. Extranets can offer improvements to the selling function by making employees more productive, supporting the customer throughout the sales process, and assisting the acclimation and 'ramp up' of new sales representatives or third-party marketers.

Fundamentally, extranets can provide a single, unified tool that offers immediate access to information, materials and data needed to support the sales process from prospecting through closing a deal to account management. Information on a customer or competitor (including financial information, recent news articles and press releases), is instantly available through any Web-enabled computer and is protected by a robust extranet security architecture. Customer presentations, proposals and contracts, marketing literature and boilerplates, templates, internal forms and product brochures can all be made accessible through the Web or available for download depending upon a user's access rights and privileges.

Clears bottlenecks

However, more than a static data repository, sales or VAR representatives can automatically initiate a work flow or procedure, eliminating the hurdles of needing to know who to call or awaiting for approvals or confirmations. Integration with e-mail gateways and pager systems give the ability to send 'alert' messages to appropriate personnel across multiple departments or organizations, greatly reducing the disconnects that frustrate customers and compromise business deals. Task management and groupwork tools within an extranet presence can instantly display where bottlenecks exist so that appropriate action can be taken. Additionally, fully or semi-automated communications ensure that customers, managers, system integrators or other personnel are kept informed at each stage of the sales/implementation process.

Faster staff induction

Perhaps one of the most notable impacts that extranets can provide for a given sales initiative, is in the lessening of the 'learning curve' for new sales reps or others integral to the customer acquisition process. For a new representative, each day lost to training, system updates or other downtime is a day of not reaching quota. For dynamic and especially high-growth firms, tapping new hires or partners into the knowledge and information network that exists within every business is crucial for reaching peak effectiveness and profitability. Extranets can dramatically ease the burden of acclimation and learning for new employees, affiliates or strategic partners.

Electronic commerce

Electronic commerce has interesting implications when combined with an effective extranet-based sales initiative. An entire customer experience (or selected parts) can be managed including qualification, sale, delivery and ongoing support – all securely and effectively through the WorldWide Web. This integrated sales process is currently being used by such companies as Virtual Vinyards, (www.virtualvin.com) a company that sells wines through the Web, and the IIS organization (www.iso14000.org) a subscription-oriented site that sells access to ISO 14000 information and services. Firms can greatly reduce the labour cost required in qualifying, closing and processing a sale, and simultaneously capture customer information for future support services.

Customer support

Customer support in all its forms (help desk, e-mail, voice mail, etc.) can be greatly facilitated with an extranet solution. For example, at relatively low cost, each customer can be provided with their own private and personal work space that can be automatically updated with information such as on-line newsletters, tips for product effectiveness, promotional campaigns, customer surveys, and other client-oriented content. This information can be distributed electronically to a broad customer base or can be tailored by individual or customer group (i.e. different information delivered based on product type/model, customer preferences or customer histories).

Feedback mechanisms to report problems or questions to a customer support representative can be automatically forwarded to a corresponding Web-based conference, e-mail or pager, and these requests can then be managed through the extranet to a point of resolution. For example, if a customer request requires a phone call or on-site visit, the request can be effectively queued and automatically forwarded to the appropriate staff member for assignment and follow up.

Other benefits offered by an extranet to enhance a firm's customer support function include integration of back office operations such as call/issue logging, reporting and analysis to evaluate employee effectiveness and to guide future product development efforts. Integration with billing and help desk systems can also be achieved to bring increased contribution and accountability to the customer support life cycle.

Product to market

The costs that can be incurred across the entire supply chain – from order management and the sourcing of raw materials through installation of finished products at customer site – can account for a major portion of a product-oriented company's balance sheet. Couple this with a business environment that consists of fierce competition and low profit margins and you have a market situation that can greatly benefit from the advantages of an effective extranet.

One advantage of extranet systems is that they are neither industry nor product dependent. Extranets can effectively track performance measures to address critical areas of operations. Results can then be used to drive change and cost-reduction initiatives. Extranets can serve to manage an organization's metrics to optimize productivity and quality assurance initiatives. Regardless whether you are producing high-technology software or lug nuts, extranets can map to and support virtually any business model or process for bringing products to market.

Specifically, the Web potentially offers certain classes of providers participation in a market in which distribution costs or cost-of-sales shrink to zero. This is most likely for firms in publishing, information services or digital product categories, although companies dealing in harder goods may benefit from disintermediation or even the eventual elimination of costly intermediaries.

Moreover, suppliers, distributors, wholesalers and retailers can access and contact each other directly, potentially eliminating some of the marketing cost and constraints imposed by such interactions in the terrestrial world. This may also have the effect of streamlining the channel and making the process more efficient mainly due to reduced overhead costs through such outcomes as uniformity, automation and integration of management processes.

Extranets give visibility and insight into potential slowdowns or inefficiencies that can adversely affect overall productivity. With advanced workflow management tools, a costly backlog or delay can be immediately recognized and dealt with before compounding into a larger problem. If a problem cannot be easily resolved, affected personnel across multiple organizations can be immediately notified of the situation and appropriate measures can be taken.

Extranets allow for the effective management of multiple vendors, contractors and other contributors to the production process. Not only can this translate into capturing and serving a potentially larger market share but it also provides more options

for selecting the most dependable and strategically aligned partners for future business development.

Contractor/distributed partner

Today, more than ever, a distributed team-based approach is
gaining favour as the preferred method of doing business. In
many instances, projects are staffed with 'virtual teams' of managers, consultants, administrative assistants and others drawn
from offices and practices all over the world. These teams can
come together for an assignment based on their expertise and
may never work together again. So the ability to get up to speed
quickly on each other's specific areas of expertise is key.

Geographic distance, lack of personal knowledge of individual contributors and the diverse agendas that factor into the mix
make locating knowledge and information – let alone leveraging
it – a cross-organizational challenge. Extranets are ideally suited
to institutionalize the time-effective sharing of information and
skills among employees and teams to a mutually beneficial end.

Representative projects where the management of distributed teams is especially useful are proposal writing, subcontrac-
tor relationships, document-driven revision and exchange, group
committees or task forces, multinational collaboratives and other
activities that require contribution or input from a geographically
dispersed community.

In some instances, especially within larger organizations, the
objectives involve interdepartmental cooperation, with representatives from marketing, product development, R&D, production,
distribution, accounting and other divisions joining together to
produce a given result or deliverable. Frequently, however, the
project also involves input from other organizations, with their
various departments and influences all contributing to the good
of the project. Effectively managing all of these entities, with
secured access to relevant information, naturally lends itself to
the open, scaleable, and extensible system environment of a Web-
based extranet.

Advantages and benefits of an extranet

An extranet offers impressive advantages and benefits to a distributed group of organizations with common goals or objectives.

These advantages can be justified based upon cost, time and other resource efficiencies that can be recognized across the various organizations.

Specific advantages that an extranet can provide if developed with a flexible, scaleable, open and secure architecture are as follows:.

Ease of set-up, use and maintenance

Extranets should be simple to set up, use and maintain. The time it takes to develop a complete and functioning extranet with a robust Web-standard software solution amounts to days or weeks, rather than months or years with proprietary network solutions. Modifications can also be implemented with little or no interruption to the extranet's activities.

Scaleability

Extranets require the flexibility to grow to include additional users or organizations, or to expand to a new hardware server array without compromising the system's usability or integrity. Solutions written using non-industry standard format or proprietary architectures can significantly restrict an extranet's ability to scale to include new users, applications, servers or other components.

Versatility

An extranet should serve fundamental business activities such as document exchange, collaborative discussion groups, on-line submission forms, database queries, etc., yet have the ability to be customized to satisfy a particular business purpose. For example, companies transferring text or document files have different requirements than those that transfer movie, video clip other multimedia files to be viewed on-line. Some organizations may wish to sell directly on-line through the extranet and others may wish to only automate the back office operations. Regardless of the business objective, extranets require versatility to accommodate a dynamic company's changing mission, goals and objectives.

Security

Security is perhaps the single most important characteristic possessed by an extranet that serves multiorganizational interests. Ensuring that all participant and contributor content is protected within a secure and accountable framework provides the basis for system usability and dependability. Although no system is ever 100 per cent secure, recent advancements in security technology provide extranets security that exceeds industry standards and protects on-line information and intellectual property.

Cost and return on investment (ROI)

Costs associated with building, launching and maintaining an extranet presence are remarkably low, and can be easily justified with immediate efficiencies and cost savings for the organization.

Results

The simplest answer to what benefits an extranet offers is they're fast, they're easy to use, and they work. The mix of low buy-in and maintenance cost, simplicity, and ubiquitous interface commands a second look at what extranets can do for today's complex business environments.

Chapter 6

Electronic commerce: the coming of the perfect market – and how to escape it

David Flint

Economists define a perfect market as one in which all the participants have complete information about the state of the market. Real markets, of course, are always imperfect. Buyers are unaware of possible suppliers. Suppliers are unaware of possible buyers. And everyone is ignorant of most of the deals being done.

Although economists disparage them, imperfect markets are the salvation of many businesses. A huge number of companies would go under if their customers knew of the alternatives and could take advantage of them.

There is, of course, a long-term trend towards more perfect markets, expressed in regional free-trade treaties and the General Agreement on Tariffs and Trade (GATT). Today, Internet-knowledgeable companies are giving the trend to perfect markets the biggest kick forward it has ever had.

Welcome to the brave new world of electronic commerce!

It is not the Internet that provides the energy behind this kick any more than motorways create traffic. But just as motorways release traffic that would otherwise have stayed at home (or gone by train), so the Internet permits kinds of trade and shopping that were previously impractical. The real drivers are quite basic:

- Buyers want choice, convenience and low prices.
- Sellers want access to new markets, lower sales and support costs.
- Some sellers want to build relationships with customers.

The Internet helps them to meet these needs. Electronic commerce (e-commerce) is set not merely to move into the mainstream but to *become* the mainstream.

Extending markets

E-commerce based on the Internet extends the reach of sellers and buyers. It provides both with more information and makes markets more international.

Sellers reach further

The Internet is the key enabler for e-commerce because it is:

- widely adopted
- international
- fast growing, despite being immature.

The Internet is widely adopted

According to industry analysts there are over 50 million Internet users, and the number is growing rapidly. (Actually these numbers, like most of those alleged to apply to the Internet, are speculative; but almost anyone will agree that there are certainly a lot of Internet users.)

This general population already provides an attractive market because Internet users are said to:

- have higher-than-average disposable incomes
- be reasonably homogeneous
- be more than average short of time.

The problem is that relatively few people are, as yet, prepared to *shop* on the Internet. However, the sales of some items, such as computers, books and music are already well established; while the sales of other products are expected to follow on as the market grows. Already, a major European motor manufacturer estimates that 40 per cent of its target market will have PCs with modems within the next twelve months.

The business market is starting to look attractive too. In North America, and increasingly in Europe, a high proportion of major enterprises already uses the Internet. For businesses that wish to reach out to their partners electronically the Internet is now the obvious choice. Consider Boeing. Over fifteen years it had managed to get only sixty of its suppliers on to its proprietary electronic data interchange (EDI) system. When it introduced an Internet-based system it recruited 350 suppliers in just three weeks!

The Internet is international

Using the Internet, sellers can easily reach potential customers outside their own countries. This is most significant for small and medium-sized businesses and for start-ups, who have traditionally not been able to reach into international markets.

For example, Hole Farm of Haworth, which overlooks the village where the Brontë sisters wrote their books, offers bed and breakfast and self-catering accommodation for tourists in a handful of bedrooms and cottages. This is not a high-technology business. Last year, though, the proprietor paid £50 for a Web page and immediately began to receive bookings from North America. The page 'paid for itself within days'. Other small specialized businesses have found similar results.

Larger companies also benefit from the ability to attract business from territories in which they have no staff on the ground. For example, Dell Computer takes orders worth $2 million a day over the Internet. With its direct sales model, Dell may be ideally organized to exploit the Internet – but it is far from alone. Many other large international companies are accepting sales orders through the Internet.

Yet, even though the Internet is inherently international, it is not always so in practice:

- Some laws and regulations prevent vendors from offering services outside their home territories.
- Some laws prevent people from buying from overseas or from buying particular goods from certain sources.
- Sometimes local culture and standards impede the development of international trade.

While the government hand cannot be avoided, some cultural differences are becoming less imposing. English has become the *lingua franca* of business in many sectors, and the Internet, dominated by the USA, can only increase this. Also, businesses are becoming increasingly adept at recognizing cultural differences. In fact, in many sectors a mixture of *de facto* standards and ingenuity makes 'world products' increasingly common.

The Internet is immature, but fast growing
The immaturity of the Internet shows in the things it lacks – for instance performance standards, user authentication, enough addresses and clarity about intellectual property. Growth is a matter of record. According to John Curran, Chief Technical Officer of GTE Internetworking (formerly BBN), Internet traffic is doubling every four months – an annual growth rate of 700 per cent. (This is highly disconcerting for those who have to fund the growth; especially since no one has the least idea how long it will continue.)

Precisely because it is immature and very fast growing, the Internet is extremely attractive to entrepreneurs. Since no one has yet established a secure leadership position in Internet commerce, a new entrant can hope to gain that position for itself. This is an extremely important concern for late Internet adopters; *they are at risk of losing market leadership to these e-commerce entrepreneurs*.

Market leadership
Leadership in e-commerce is more than leadership in one sector or channel – it is leadership in the future of commerce in every channel.

In the last forty years IT has become a crucial part of every sizeable business, and of many small ones. Yet, most IT systems have operated only within a single organization. Only in supply-chain management has IT routinely supported interbusiness operations – and even here its penetration is small in most sectors. The arrival of e-commerce signals that IT is leaving the corporate nest to address the central functions of business: *buying, selling and customer service.*

This change is both inevitable and profound. It indicates that the future of commerce includes having IT become a part of every channel and every business relationship. In doing so, it will affect both channels and relationships in unforeseen ways. In fact today, because of the rapid rate of technological change, these effects are not merely unforeseen – but unforeseeable. This uncertainty about future channels and relationships should make every business consider seriously the emergence of e-commerce. This means coming to terms with the leading edge of e-commerce – the Internet, today.

Buyers reach further

What is sauce for the selling goose is sauce for the buying gander. While sellers will use the Internet to reach more buyers, buyers will use the Internet to reach more sellers in order to find the best buy. Buyers can use a buying network or an agent or take part in an on-line auction. For example:

- General Electric's (GE's) Trading Process Network (TPN) is an example of a buying network. Using an Internet client, purchasing officers specify their needs and select possible suppliers. The TPN then notifies suppliers and manages the bidding process. Orders worth $1 billion a year with 1,400 suppliers are placed using TPN. As a result, GE (now more likely to buy from outside the US) reports a halving of the procurement time and cost savings of up to 20 per cent due to increased competition. This year, GE expects savings of $200 million to result from its use of TPN.
- The World Merchandise Exchange (Womex) is an on-line service supporting general traders around the world. Womex's database provides traders with details of thousands of products – including many from small companies that do not advertise in international trade magazines. Early users report

that Womex not only gives them access to more suppliers but also reduces the hassle of dealing with overseas suppliers. Retrieval from Womex databases replaces faxes requesting information, and e-mail replaces strained telephone conversations in broken English.

● Netbot Inc. of Seattle offers Jango, a 'shopping robot', a PC program that enables the user to specify a product that he or she wants to buy. Then Jango retrieves quotes from all the Websites that sell products of that kind. The user then decides which one to order from.

All these products and services increase the reach of buyers and their ability to get what they want at the lowest price. Future offerings will support comparisons of quality and service as well.

More available information

In an electronic market your every move is visible to every other player.

Just as e-commerce makes it easy for buyers to get information about products, it also makes it easy for sellers to get information about their competitors. Thus in the cut-throat US domestic air travel market, the main players monitor each others' prices and deals and respond to price changes with changes and deals of their own within hours.

But measuring competition includes more than monitoring price data. How good is the product? How reliable is the supplier? How good is the after-sales service? This is much harder information to find, but the Internet helps here too:

● Edmund's, a US publisher of vehicle guides, operates a Website which provides comprehensive information on new and used vehicles.

● Discussion forums, newsgroups and other interactive communities provide a place where curious potential customers can obtain advice from existing users, and curious vendors can lurk to learn more about their customers.

At present, these facilities are only incompletely available – but they are bound to spread as vendors recognize their attractiveness and hence their power to bring users to their Websites.

Suppliers enter 'commodity corner'

Customers will demand equal services and pricing across the physical and electronic channels.

For both buyers and sellers, in almost every case, e-commerce results in lower costs for those who practise it. The result of this is that many suppliers will be pushed into a commodity market in which they must compete principally on price. Most businesses hate this.

And yet, this will be exacerbated when customers who use both physical and electronic channels start to demand the same low prices for *both* channels. When the higher cost of physical channels make it impossible for some suppliers to match these prices and stay profitable – they will be facing some nasty dilemmas – and pricing is just one of them.

Customers will also want the same level of off-line service as they get from the on-line world. The on-line buyer will be used to twenty-four hours a day, seven days a week service and a service that is increasingly customized to his or her needs. Unless off-line shops recruit more and better staff and invest in the type of IT systems increasingly being used by on-line vendors, they will fail to meet customers' expectations – at a time when margins are under growing pressure.

Escape from 'commodity corner'

Faced with this pressure to become commodity suppliers, businesses must increase their efficiency significantly.

Since the Internet supports a world market, companies will have to compete with the best suppliers in the world, not just in their home territories. Inevitably many will seek to cut their costs by more outsourcing and downsizing.

The alternative is to differentiate and find a way to maintain higher prices. There are three fundamental ways for a business to differentiate itself from the competition:

- product/service leadership
- superior brand management
- customer intimacy.

While the first two are familiar and their pros and cons well understood, the third is uniquely important to electronic commerce.

Product/service leadership gives customers a real reason to buy from you – the superiority of your product or service. But, although patents offer protection in some fields, product innovations can usually be copied and service innovations can always be copied. Product/service leadership therefore requires continual innovation, a process that is impossible for some organizations.

Branding gives customers a way to recognize predictable quality and value. It saves the customer's time and provides a focus for loyalty. Some businesses have created brands that are desired for the status they represent and therefore command substantial premiums. But these premiums can be obtained only by a limited number of firms as there is only space for a limited number of top brands. For every Disney, Rolls-Royce or Givenchy there are many 'worthy' brands commanding small premiums.

Customer intimacy is the process of getting so close to customers that they won't want to do business with anyone else. Customer intimacy has been practised unconsciously by shopkeepers for centuries and consciously by consultancies for decades. But it has not been seen as an option for companies serving a mass market, many of which have difficulty knowing how many customers they have – let alone their preferences.

Information technology changes this. Customer databases can hold information about thousands, even millions, of customers. Apart from the obvious identification and communication information, a customer-information database can hold:

- Personal attributes: sizes for clothing, hats and shoes; and how large a garden does the customer have?
- Purchasing preferences: what goods and services does a customer buy; what goods and services does he or she own – and when will they need replacement?

- Communication preferences: does the customer prefer telephone calls or letters; when on the telephone does he or she like to chat or be terse?
- Tastes and morals: what colours does he or she like; what companies or industries does he or she favour or detest?

The database can, of course, hold a great deal more. The problem is that, although all this information is obviously relevant to the customer's purchasing, it is harder to see how it can be applied. In fact, there is too much information for it to be applied by a human being – only when a computer is part of the transaction can more than a trivial part of this information be used.

Which brings us back to e-commerce. Electronic channels make it easier to use and to collect this type of information. By knowing customers' preferences, e-commerce systems can present them with the options they are most likely to choose. Leading vendors are already racing to master this trick.

In the US book trade, for instance, Amazon.com outflanked all the shop-based booksellers with its Internet shopping facility. In 1997, Barnes and Noble, the leading US bookseller, countered by creating its own on-line bookshop – BarnesAndNoble.com – run by a new business unit. BarnesAndNoble.com will gather book preferences from its users and exploit a technique called collaborative filtering to generate book recommendations for those users. Amazon.com then responded by announcing its own use of collaborative filtering (from a different software supplier). Each hopes that once a user has taken the time to explain his or her preferences to one on-line shop he or she will be unwilling to do so again for another. Each will therefore benefit from customer lock-in. And each will be right – providing that customers do not find a way of capturing their own preference data. In fact, preference data is likely to become portable, reducing the competitive advantage of this approach, but perhaps not soon.

But whether or not it creates lock-in, *customer intimacy raises the bar to new competitors.*

Intimate agents
Suppose, though, that preference information does not become

portable but that customers are unwilling to share it with suppliers. Two factors favour this scenario:

- Customers may see the collection of personal information as an invasion of privacy.
- Customers will resent the loss of choice.

Given this, and recognizing their potential power in the commercial situation, customers will seek ways to use that power. Large organizations have always used their purchasing power to get low prices and favourable terms. But in recent years they have begun to do so more systematically – spreading the benefits to indirect purchases. Individuals and small businesses, though, have rarely been able to take advantage of the power they have in aggregate.

Computers and networks will help customers to link up in order to exercise their aggregate power. Customers may do this through buying consortia – which already exist in some sectors. They will also operate through new intermediaries. Unlike most of today's intermediaries – financial advisers and brokers, for instance – they will represent buyers, not sellers, and will be paid by them. They will know enough about their principals to represent them and to negotiate on their behalf.

Although many organizations have begun to collect customer data, this new role – which we call the 'intimate agent' – is not an easy option. To be credible the agent must give up any hope of selling any non-agency services to the customer – and must show that he or she always puts the customer first. Most suppliers will prefer to stick with the provision of their established products and services – but will often find that they have to deal with intimate agents, who will be among the toughest possible negotiators.

The need to choose

The advance of electronic commerce will release new commercial pressures and demand new strategic choices. Businesses that fail to get involved now, may have their choices limited to playing 'catch-up' as the market continues to evolve around them. But, you do not *have* to do it. Survival is not mandatory.

Chapter 7

Electronic consumerism

Deloitte and Touche

Executive summary

Electronic retailing has been reincarnated in the form of computer-based shopping. In contrast to earlier forms of electronic retailing, such as kiosks and TV home shopping, this reincarnation of computer-interactive based electronic retailing (CIBER), will leap-frog the catalogue as the second largest retail channel behind store-based retailing.

Imagine the following scenario for a target customer – a mother, working part-time, while raising two small children.

She starts her day by 'quick booting' the computer (almost as fast as turning on a TV), while the kids are eating breakfast. She hears a beep as the computer reminds her that today is grocery day and that her youngest child's birthday is only two weeks away. She engages her preferred on-line grocery store and reviews her preferred list of weekly replenishables. She makes changes to this list on an exception basis, then adds some spontaneous buys (cross-marketed to her as she shops the virtual store). She then toggles over to a suggested list of gift items for her child's birthday, pulled together for her by her on-line personal shopping agent. She selects several items from different stores and pays for them on-line. She then shuts down the computer and resumes the balance of her daily routine. That night, after the groceries and gifts have been delivered to her home, she puts away the groceries and wraps the gifts before heading off to bed.

This scenario is quickly becoming viable because of:

- *The emerging power of the street-smart consumer* Consumers have become incredibly demanding of the marketplace. They have high expectations for better quality, cheaper prices, better information and better service. They are able to enforce these demands due to the explosion of information that is available to them today. Electronic retailing, as described in the scenario above, offers consumers a better alternative to meet these high expectations.

● *The emergence of key enabling technology* The emergence of several important enabling technologies will allow consumer computing to move beyond the hands of the intellectual élite and into the hands of masses. Combined, these converging technology trends result in easier to use, more affordable computers, stuffed with better, standardized, and increasingly richer content.

Street-smart consumers, further empowered by advancements in technology, are an increasingly scary proposition for retailers. Simply, these consumers are in control of the consumer supply chain today. In fact, the industry has shifted from an era of *caveat emptor* (i.e. let the buyer beware) to an era of *caveat vendor* (i.e. let the seller (retailer) beware). The reincarnation of electronic retailing stands poised to exploit this shift.

Electronic retailing has been reincarnated

Electronic retailing first showed up in the 1980s with kiosks, TV home shopping and infomercials. While innovative and interesting, these formats have not emerged as legitimate contenders to replace catalogues as the second largest retail channel for consumer products. However, the mid-1990s version of electronic retailing, including computer-based shopping and interactive TV shopping, has recaptured the attention of both the retail industry and the media. While the interactive TV experiments have not nearly met the industry's expectations for building consumer demand and creating significant business, the jury is still out on the impact of what we call CIBER.

Although CIBER will never replace the store as the primary retail channel for consumer products, it certainly has the potential to be at least as significant as the catalogue business. A pair of trends are at work today that will drive CIBER to become much more important to retail executives.

CIBER arises from two larger trends

In 1454, Johann Gutenberg perfected the use of movable type. At the time, most people could not foresee the eventual impact that this invention would have on religion and society. But because movable type enabled the broad distribution of the Bible to the common people, the religious elite lost control over the distribution of religious information, and therefore lost control over their constituencies' knowledge base. This loss of control led directly to the Ninety-Five Theses of Martin Luther and the start of the Reformation. In 1996, most retailers seem to be taking a similar view of this reincarnation of electronic retailing. See Figure 7.1.

From a big picture point of view, today's revival is arising from the combination of two trends:

1. The emergence of an all-powerful, highly informed, street-smart, consumer.
2. The emergence of a number of enabling technologies to feed and accelerate trend 1.

Trend 1: the street-smart consumer

Today, the street-smart consumer, not the retailer or the supplier, is driving the competitive activities of the consumer marketplace. Like a young child, today's consumer is learning and building knowledge at an ever increasing rate (see Figure 7.2). As a result, the consumer is placing demands on retailers, direct marketers and service companies.

Consumer groups are beginning to band together to exercise their combined purchasing power in the marketplace. For example, parents are combining their purchases for groceries and restaurants through receipt exchange programmes. In exchange for a discount, funnelled to local school operating budgets, these parents agree to shop at specific establishments.

Trend 2: emerging technologies

The power of this shrewd consumer is being further magnified by the recent emergence of several technologies:

Era	Events/triggers	Big picture	Significant effect
1400s	Perfection of movable type by Gutenberg	Allowed broad distribution of the Bible and other religious documents	Took control of religious information from the religious élite to the broader masses, leading to the Reformation (Martin Luther)
1700s	Invention of the locomotive and creation of the railroad system	Created an economic, fast method to transport people over great distances	Enabled the mass migration of the US East coast population Westward and opening of minerals and oil resources
1800s	Invention of the cotton gin	Allowed cotton to be mass harvested, cleaned and converted to cloth	Created significant wealth for the Southern states and conflict over the use of slaves to fuel this wealth; led directly to the American Civil War
1950s	Building of the US Defense Highway system, beginning in 1954 with a two mile stretch in New Jersey	Easy, fast, personal transportation between cities and from city to suburbs	Enabled flight of middle class from urban to suburban living; jobs followed. Resulted in suburban shopping malls and decline of cities
1990s	Interactive-based shopping, combined with rapid advancements in technology and high-speed interconnectivity	Instant access to vast comparisons and alternatives. Unleash and magnify the emerging power of the consumer, by empowering more choices and unprecedented competition	Will gradually dismantle the existing value propositions of various players in the supply chain, while providing significant opportunity to others to contact consumers directly

Figure 7.1 Brief history of information distribution and consumer choice

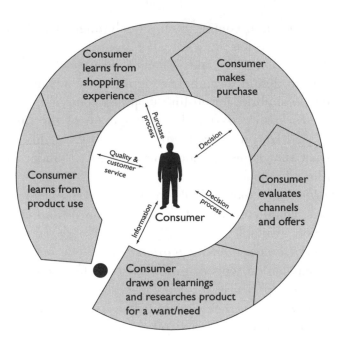

Figure 7.2 The street-smart consumer learning process

1. *User-friendly, affordable access for consumers* Personal
   computer innovation is shifting from an emphasis on computing performance to an emphasis on ease of use and afford-
   ability. For example:
   (a) *$500 computers* The technology community has set stan-
       dards and will be bringing to market 'network computers'
       or NCs. These NCs, designed to interact with the Internet,
       will have streamlined software and storage capabilities,
       but will be rich with memory. They are targeted to retail
       for $500 or less.
   (b) *Reintroduced, less powerful PCs* PC manufacturers are
       reintroducing lower power machines, such as 486-based
       PCs, to provide a more narrow range of capabilities and
       to target specific price points (>$1,000).
   (c) *Used PCs* The used PC market is rejuvenated, with
       average price points for Pentium machines of $750.
   (d) *Simply interactive PC* Software companies are working on
       'quick boot' operating systems, that will enable a PC to be
       started up almost as fast as a television.
2. *Compelling and standardized content* – The actual user

experience is becoming more closely aligned with consumer wants and needs.

3. *Digitalization*   The conversion of video, books, software and music to digital formats has significantly advanced the creative possibilities for on-line shopping content.

4. *The WorldWide Web*   The Web section of the Internet has provided consumers with an easy-to-use, readily accessible format that is being widely adopted as a standard for most on-line development.

5. *On-line store tools*   Tools for rapid development of on-line stores, complete with transaction standards and capabilities, are now available.

6. *On-line services and navigation tools*   The on-line services and navigation tools continue to strive for more simple and effective experiences for end consumers.

7. *Electronic commerce*   Computers everywhere are linking and communicating with each other via more open networking capabilities. At the same time, the platform for daily business transactions is moving beyond the four walls of most companies and onto the Internet. As a result, consumers' reach and access to markets and information are growing exponentially.

The emergence of these enabling technologies is setting up a profound impact on the consumer goods marketplace, by unleashing and magnifying the already burgeoning power of consumers. With easy to use, affordable interfaces, and broad access to the entire globe, consumers already are able to:

● gain direct access to a multitude of merchandise sources, including retailers, manufacturers, distributors and other third parties anywhere

● obtain extensive detailed knowledge about merchandise prior to making a purchase

● bypass traditional channels via the emerging on-line choices for shopping

● raise the standards (physical and virtual) for better quality, lower prices and improved levels of service.

Combining the technologies described above with the emerging power of the consumer is like outfitting Michael Jordan with booster rockets and is the larger issue for retail executives to consider. We labelled this effect *electronic consumerism* which is already significantly affecting industries beyond retailing (see Figure 7.3).

Industry	Changes	Example
Banking	Branches replaced by electronic ATMs	Citicorp's, Wells Fargo's on-line banking
Health care	Advanced customer service call centres	Health maintainance organizations
Manufacturing	Produce and distribute direct to consumers	Levi's custom jeans
Public sector	Adopting private sector type consumer direct mail programme	US Dept of Motor Vehicles licence and registration
Travel	Eliminate low-value ticketing process	United E-Ticket
Investments	On-line trading	Charles Schwab

Figure 7.3   Electronic consumerism

The era of the consumer

It is this electronic consumerism that has allowed electronic retailing to successfully re-emerge in the form of CIBER (see Figure 7.4). Therefore, this revival of electronic retailing is fundamentally about the empowered consumer, and not about the related technologies.

What do we mean by the following:

- *Electronic commerce* is about *transactions*. It focuses on the electronic facilitation of specific, predefined transaction sets, aimed at a known destination.
- *CIBER* is a subset of electronic consumerism, focused for now on the retail industry.
- *Electronic consumerism* is about *interactions*. It focuses on the

use of technology to greatly enhance consumer interactions with businesses across all industries such as banking, travel, insurance, health care and telecommunications.

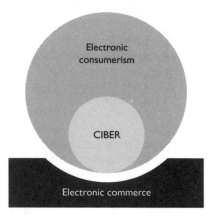

Figure 7.4 Emergence of CIBER

Once a company makes a commitment to CIBER, it will find that computer-based electronic retailing consists of three interrelated and continuous process loops (see Figure 7.5):

- marketing and merchandising
- consumer order and fulfilment
- supply.

All three of these loops are necessary to operate as a fully functional alternative retail channel. Ironically, a majority of the

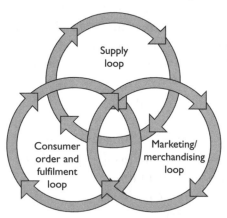

Figure 7.5 CIBER presents significant tactical issues

activities related to electronic retailing are traditional retail/catalogue type activities (e.g. order fulfilment – pick, pack, ship).

Those retailers who choose to attack will need to navigate the operational and information technology issues related to these loops.

Operational considerations

Each of the three loops of electronic retailing presents potential operational issues for electronic retailing.

Merchandising and marketing loop

The full merchandise offerings of most retailers will not translate directly into the on-line shopping world. In fact, some products and/or shopping situations may lend themselves to on-line shopping, while others may not (see Figure 7.6).

Retailers should evaluate the fit of their current offering against a three-tiered filter:

1. *Product fit* How well does this category of merchandise fit the on-line world (physical characteristics, demand

	Fit well	*Uncertain fit*	*Poor fit*
Shopping situations	Repeat purchases of known items Any purchase of commodity goods	Gift purchasing Complex product early in decision cycle	First time purchases Purchase requiring coordination of multiple products
Products	Digitizable products e.g. software, music, books Wide assortment products	Fashion apparel Product infrequently purchased, but known	Custom apparel Large, fragile or otherwise difficult to ship One of a kind

Figure 7.6   Merchandising and marketing loop

variability, cost/value, perishability, etc.)?

2. *Supply chain leverage* To what degree does the company's retail nameplate identity exceed the strength of its suppliers' brand identity with the end consumer for this category of merchandise? For example, if Dillard's carries Levi jeans, which company (Dillard's or Levi's) has the greater power to influence the purchases of the end consumer?

3. *Consumer preferences* How do current or targeted consumers prefer to purchase this category of merchandise? (Although digitizable products such as software, music and video can be purchased on-line, some consumers may still prefer to buy them in a store.)

Consumer order and fulfilment loop

To effectively execute this loop, a retailer will need capabilities similar to those of catalogue or direct mail operations. A typical direct-to-consumer operation is geared to handle a relatively large number of small orders, delivered to the end consumer. Unfortunately, a typical retail operation is geared to handle a smaller number of larger orders, delivered to its retail stores.

As a result, most traditional retailers do not have the capabilities to support the business generated by the on-line store and will be forced to develop operational strategies and tactics for providing these capabilities. Retailers have several solution alternatives for providing the operational processes required for supporting the on-line store as portrayed in Figure 7.7.

The matrix in Figure 7.7 represents a dynamic world in which companies may shift from one approach to another approach as their order volume increases or decreases. In addition, hybrid combinations will vary depending upon desire for control, and upon current in-house operations and information systems capabilities.

Supply loop

The procurement and physical flow of merchandise will need to be carefully synchronized with the ongoing changes to the virtual, on-line store environment. The supply-side loop will need the ability to handle the complexity associated with meeting the

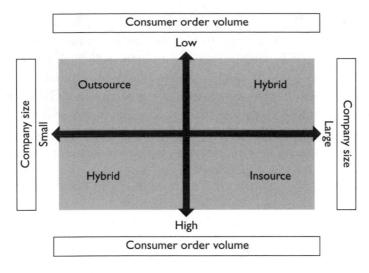

Figure 7.7 Operations alternatives matrix

demand and inventory mix requirements of multiple channels. The requirements will likely require different lead times, quality assurance (QA) processes, inventory locations, vendor certifications, and perhaps different suppliers, across these multiple channels.

Information technology considerations

To meet the information technology requirements demanded by CIBER, current retail information systems (IS) capabilities will need to change dramatically. Therefore, a flexible, reliable computing platform, increased network capacity and new business applications supporting the three operational loops are requisites for the technology architecture of tomorrow's electronic retailer. In addition, information systems departments must quickly develop the capabilities to select, design and install these systems, ensuring they are integrated with current technologies and processes.

Much like the alternatives for providing the required operational capabilities, the IT capabilities will likely be provided by a blend of internal and external resources.

The retailers who will be successful in electronic retailing will be those that systematically address the issues described above.

What next?

Beyond the immediate strategic and implementation issues surrounding CIBER, electronic consumerism will have a more profound effect. It is already changing the historic linear consumer
supply chain. In the same way that re-engineering has changed
most executives' view of their businesses from departmental view
to process view, electronic consumerism will change their view of
consumer delivery away from the supply chain to a new concept.
We labelled this new concept as the *consumer wheel* (see
Figure 7.8).

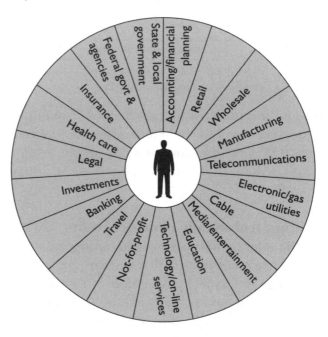

Figure 7.8   Consumer wheel

What do we mean by the consumer wheel? Because of
CIBER, companies across many industries will have increasingly
direct access to the end consumer (just look at Amazon Books at
Amazon.com). Customers will increasingly view retailers as just
another intermediary. Therefore, the linear supply chain, with
the retailer as the final gateway to the consumer will be less and
less appropriate. A wheel, centred around the consumer, is a
much more appropriate representation of this new business paradigm.

In this paradigm, new core competencies are already emerging. In the past, competencies, such as merchandising, manufacturing and marketing defined a company's role in the supply chain. These competencies are no longer as relevant as new competencies in the consumer wheel are emerging:

- *Consumer-focused competencies* Competencies surrounding direct interaction with the end consumer will become extremely important. These competencies are an integrated bundle of service offerings centered on customer contact and relationship. They include consumer database management/ analysis/marketing, promotional planning, consumer order processing, consumer payment processing and collection, and customer service operations.
- *Supply-focused competencies* Competencies on the supply side will feed the consumer-focused competencies. These competencies are an integrated bundle of offerings, including product development, sourcing, forecasting, procurement, order fulfilment, replenishment, transportation, production planning and execution, and financing.
- *Consumer agent competencies* Competencies surrounding the value-added brokering of goods and services on behalf of the end consumer. Consumer agents are already negotiating purchase discounts and are providing value-added services (e.g. saving time) on behalf of large consumer special interest groups. Another example will be the inversion of the traditional real estate transaction, wherein a buyer's broker armed with extensive computerized information about the market, will match wants with supply, charging a fixed fee to the buyer and bringing the value of the seller's broker under serious pressure.
- *Infrastructure and support competencies* Other competencies required to support those above are emerging. Previously focused on outsourced services for information technology, these competencies are growing in scope into other disciplines such as distribution and logistics, accounting and financial reporting, and human resources. These competencies will be offered across traditional industry boundaries.

These competencies are best represented as concentric circles around the end consumer (see Figure 7.9).

This consumer wheel construct suggests a dramatic shift from competing between industry segments to competing from industry to industry. In the late 1980s, department stores lost share to discount stores and warehouse clubs. Increasingly, retailers and their suppliers will become direct competitors for the end consumer. Retailing in all segments will remain as <u>the</u> primary channel of distribution for the large majority of consumer products. However CIBER will hasten the demise of the weakest as the overall retail channel slowly shrinks while electronic consumerism grows.

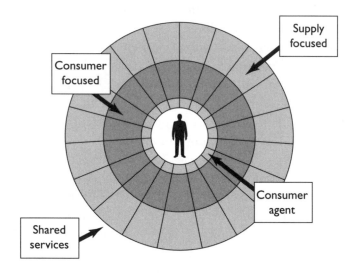

Figure 7.9   New competencies in the consumer wheel

Gutenberg never foresaw the impact that his contribution to movable type would have. The downstream effect was much greater than the simple change in the way that Bibles were duplicated. CIBER will slowly, but steadily, drive the formation of the consumer wheel from the prior supply chain paradigm. This time retail executives have the opportunity to look forward and assess the big picture impact of CIBER on their individual businesses. Seize this opportunity! Now is the time to rise to the challenge of this new, provocative channel.

Winning industries	Losing industries
• Entertainment	• Retail
• Travel	• Education
• Telecommunications	• Banking
• Publishing	• Wholesaling
• Consumer products manufacturing	

Figure 7.10 Winning industries/losing industries

Chapter 8

Competitive advantage through information[1]

Frank Abramson and Graham Telford

Organizations which harness the powerful new benefits of information to established intangibles, such as service quality, should enjoy an enhanced and sustainable competitive advantage.

Marketing personnel are continuously searching for the holy grail, the sustainable competitive advantage, particularly in customer-led service industries, such as financial services, travel and leisure where products are more commoditized than say, those in fast-moving consumer goods (FMCG). But do they give themselves even a starting chance in tackling this issue?

During the 1970s competitive advantage was sought through tangibles such as product differentiation, location, delivery channel and even pricing. As the decade progressed and the early 1980s arrived, it became apparent the ease with which these so-called differentiators were rapidly copied, thus neutralizing any advantage. This led many major organizations and grail seekers in the late 1980s to pursue the development of intangibles as possible competitive differentiators, such as quality, service, image and brand values.

We would describe these tangibles and intangibles as representing the old world order and even to be a player on the playing field today they should be more aptly described as 'givens' or 'hygiene factors'. They are certainly not strong enough to lead to sustainable competitive advantage for most multichannelled distributors (e.g. banks, building societies, travel agents, etc.) particularly when compounded by decreasing staff numbers. However, it is conceded that one or two centralized direct distributors, such as Direct Line Insurance, First Direct or Saga Holidays, may enjoy success through the tangible/intangible route and they may continue to sustain a level of competitive advantage for some time. Significant funds have been, and continue to be, expended on brand image and value advertising as well as on service quality programmes with the intention of delivering 'better service than our competitors'. How believable, attainable or practical is this?

Again, with the possible exception of one or two newly established direct to consumer businesses (some benefiting from a halo effect) there are few signs of any of the major banks, building societies or even insurers breaking through the barrier, let alone turning these intangibles into competitive advantage from the consumer's perspective. Certainly, some money has to be spent to get on to the playing field and achieve acceptable intangible standards. But, how can a multichannelled distributor guarantee a continuous 'better than others' sustainable quality service and value standard, throughout all its delivery channels including branches, automatic teller machines (ATMs), agents, representatives, phone, mail, etc.? Perhaps this is why there are so few good examples of best practice to follow.

Rather than continue, lemming-like, to pursue this expensive, if not tortuous and virtually impossible route to the Holy Grail, we would like to suggest another, possibly more rewarding but no more costly path to sustainable competitive advantage, namely through information. This, we refer to as the new world order, with information being enabled through technology (see Figure 8.1).

Old world order: **Tangibles** and **Intangibles**
New world order: **Information** (via technology)

Figure 8.1   Sustainable competitive advantage

Let us develop this paradigm, first in theory then later in practice. Back in 1985, Michael Porter said: 'The recent, rapid technological change in information systems is having a profound impact on competition and competitive advantage because of the pervasive role of information in the value chain'. Here, the emphasis was on technology, but some six years later, in 1991, Rashi Glazer put the boot on the other foot with the following observation: 'Increases in the speed and amount of processing are functions of technology but the emergence of new ways of packaging information suggests the importance of considering information itself, above and beyond the technology'. Glazer was switching the emphasis to information. John Reed, Chairman of Citicorp/Citibank, put it very succinctly, if somewhat tongue-in-cheek, when he remarked: 'Information about money is becoming more important than money itself'.

Since the late 1980s, but particularly so in the 1990s, with the advent of more cost-efficient technology (through parallel processing and relational databases, complemented with open systems), the ability to obtain, store, manage, update and use information has increased to such an extent that it can now be harnessed by those businesses who genuinely want to be customer led, creating a real dialogue with their customers and ultimately achieving a genuine sustainable competitive edge. Those financial institutions that are emerging as likely long term winners have changed or are changing processes, culture, systems and organization structures; there is no gain without pain!

This new world order has come about in practice through a techno-marketing evolution as illustrated in Figure 8.2. Marketing strategies tended to be very product-led during the 1970s (for a few financial players today they still are!), but by the late 1980s many of the emerging winners (but not necessarily the biggest, or even perceived industry leaders) had developed and successfully implemented segmentation strategies. Now in the 1990s the emerging winners are concentrating on building relationships with these segments through motivation and retention-based strategies and are seeking to develop further refinements which will enable them to appeal to identifiable niches and ultimately direct to individual customers. This approach is information dependent and, as intimated earlier, none of it could have

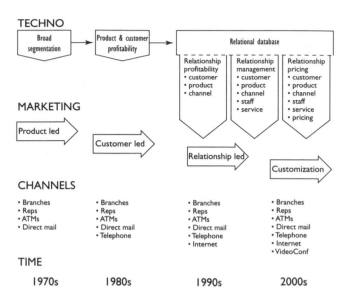

Figure 8.2   Techno-marketing evolution

happened without the enabling technology, particularly in
helping to refine segmentation, but also in understanding and
implementing relationship profitability (i.e. product and customer profitability), relationship management (bringing staff
and customer service into the equation) and, most recently, the
emerging issue of relationship pricing.

To create this new world order based on information, we
have considered those components necessary in its development.
Here we have taken a pragmatic approach based on our experience to date as outlined in Figure 8.3.

Capacity and capability
to understand the
Information Cycles

Creating **Relationship Information**

Overcoming **Barriers to Entry**

Figure 8.3   Essential components to develop information as the competitive advantage

First, and briefly, one needs the capability and capacity (and we do not just mean bytes) to understand the information cycles (Figure 8.4). While it may not matter which of the information cycles one adopts, it is essential to understand the role each step in the process plays. The simple definitions are given below but can be adjusted as necessary; some players may even wish to combine steps within the cycle:

- Identify: deciding what piece(s) of information is/are needed (ranked against criteria).
- Acquire: getting the right information from right source.
- Gather: putting information together (storing).
- Manage: interpreting the information.
- Use: providing solutions for the customer.
- Update: ensuring information is as up-to-date as possible before using it; including both transaction and contact data.

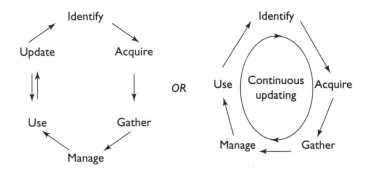

Figure 8.4 Information cycles

Secondly, there is the need and ability to know what are the right questions to ask (here for example, the design of customer applications forms needs a total rethink by many organizations); furthermore, eliciting the right responses and information, and being able to manage and use them.

The American Express (Amex) Card application form, like most in the financial services sector, used to ask up-front detailed financial, employment and personal/family questions. Amex found this put off some potential cardholders, so they redesigned the form making it simpler and customer-friendly while still covering data required for credit checking. Once the customer was on board, Amex welcomed him or her by phone or mail and then followed up by collecting useful supplementary information. Recruitment was made easier and Amex still obtained the data they needed to develop their card usage and marketing programmes. Only with the right information can one go back to customers with a tailored solution or product which meets their needs. This two-way exchange process, on whatever scale (segment, niche or individual) is what we refer to as relationship information (see Figure 8.5). Relationship information facilitates a relevant, continuous and individualized dialogue between a service provider and its customer. In other words the organization can understand the customer's expectations and requirements and hence meet his or her needs more accurately.

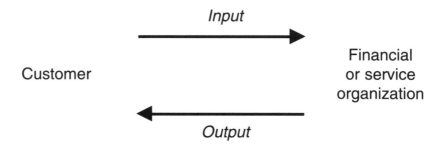

Figure 8.5   Relationship information

One particular recent example of relationship information being effectively exploited is where tailored information is being made available to customers of TSB Bank who have four or more product relationships. The personal financial statement (currently being sent to 3,000 customers) provides up-to-date information on their current accounts, credit cards, mortgages, savings and investments, loans and insurance policies. Citibank provides similar information in its newly launched personal banking package. These were not born out of techno-masochism, but rather to meet customer expectations and requirements.

But there are barriers to entry (see Figure 8.6).

While expense is often claimed to be the reason why a relationship information strategy cannot be considered, let alone adopted, it is becoming less of a genuine issue with falling hardware costs, open systems, and when taken in context with other

```
┌─────────────────────────────────┐
│                                 │
│            Costs                │
│                                 │
│            Skills               │
│                                 │
│     Organization structure      │
│                                 │
│     Legal and social issues     │
│                                 │
└─────────────────────────────────┘
```

Figure 8.6 Overcoming barriers to entry

budgets and the overall need for information at all levels; that is not only for customer, but also management, financial and reporting information within an organization. Perhaps what is more of a genuine problem at present is identifying the sponsor or owner of the information database, an issue which can only be resolved within an organization's overall structure. While many businesses split such responsibility, or give it to finance, marketing and/or IT departments, others are setting up new functions with the creation of posts such as Director of Information and Chief Knowledge Officer. Depth of access to the data is then dependent on the level or role within the organization.

Identifying, selecting and training the right people with the appropriate skills, not only for customer interface (relationship management) but also for the development and manipulation of the database itself for marketing or reporting purposes, still appears to elude many organizations. However, undoubtedly the biggest issue and key barrier to entry with such a customer-led approach is that of *organizational structure*. Financial institutions in particular can no longer afford to organize exclusively along traditional functional lines, rather they have to reorganize with the customer interface as their focus and all processing and administrative functions, such as technology, acting as support for this customer relationship. Marketing should become an ethos of an entire organization, not simply a function or a department. One or two of the more dynamic service companies are experimenting with 'segment' rather than 'product' managers in their marketing area; a first step to recognizing fully the need for customer interface focus. A very simple operational structure for part of a bank, finance house or insurance company could soon resemble that in Figure 8.7.

Such an issue as *organizational change* might best be described as 'organizational schizophrenia' – what is best for the organization versus what is best for the customer – a disorder that needs to be addressed urgently by most financial and many other service companies. Further, how often have we seen a major business announce detailed organizational changes to be followed by the development of a new strategy, an approach which can be described as 'Ready, Fire, Aim!'. Surely it should be strategy first followed by the creation of an organization structure to deliver that strategy.

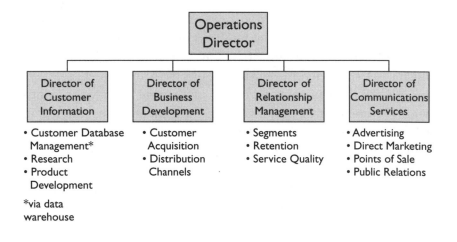

Figure 8.7 Organizational structure

But perhaps the most interesting innovation in organizational change in the financial services market is the recruitment and appointment of CEOs and other senior managers from outside the financial services sector. Not unsurprisingly, it is these organizations who are making real changes in culture, processes, etc. and identifying themselves as emerging winners. Finally, for financial services companies there are some legal and social issues that have to be accommodated and overcome, including Financial Services Acts, Data Protection Acts, European Union (EU) Directives, consumerism and most especially, the overall image of such institutions. However, while we have concentrated mainly on the financial services industry, there is evidence to show the principles are applicable to other service sectors including retailing, travel, leisure and the professions. Those organizations that have, or are, addressing these components overall are not only seeing, but beginning to reap the rewards and benefits represented by this new world order for a sustained competitive advantage.

Thus, if one chooses to follow such a direction, we see information becoming the business driver with the need for organizations to restructure accordingly; that is, a gradual erosion of functional barriers as the interface with the customer (through dialogue) becomes the focus and hence the critical success factor. It is at this point of contact through the unique exchange of information by way of dialogue that the sustained competitive advantage can be achieved. Every transaction or contact provides the opportunity for relationship information to be obtained, given or stored.

The way in which relationship information is identified, acquired, gathered, managed, used and updated provides a business with unique benefits ensuring that competitive advantage can be sustained and maintained. It is a position which cannot easily be replicated due to the architecture and standardization adopted being unique to an organization. Importantly, such information can be obtained and directed at segments, niches or even customized to the individual.

Those organizations which manage to harness the powerful new benefits of information to established intangibles such as service quality, will conceivably enjoy the fruits of enhanced sustainable competitive advantage, or rather, competitive advantage with added value!

Note

1. This chapter has been published previously in the *EFMA Newsletter*, No. 138 (November 1996).

Chapter 9

Automating the virtual sales force[1]

Tom Siebel and Michael Malone

The informed sales force

If the fundamental task of the corporation is to sell, then the customer is the ultimate arbiter of the company's success. Given that, it follows that every action the company takes, and every decision it makes, must be in support of its relationship with that customer. Most of all, the individual sales representative, as the company's advocate in that relationship, must be at the very least the focal point of all of the company's energies. Technology helps not by stripping these salespeople of their power or stealing away time that could be spent with customers, but by increasing that time and enhancing each contact. This is *virtual selling.*

But companies are vast and complicated structures, full of cross-currents and sidepools of information and expertise. The only way to harness such an entity is to give it a common direction. And that is possible through a common, suitably distant and demanding, goal. The best such goal is a perfect correspondence between the needs of sales and the operations of the rest of the company. This is *total sales quality.*

When an alignment occurs between the events at the customer/salesperson contact and the operation of the company itself, the salesperson is empowered with the total knowledge and talent of the organization. The company is now operating at its best. The salesperson repays the company's efforts by becoming its best and most knowledgeable representative. And when this is true of every member of the company's sales staff, the enterprise has reached its peak efficiency. This is an *informed sales force.*

A sales scenario

It is 7 a.m. on a warm July morning. The kids are in the den watching the last bit of TV before they leave for summer school. Andy's wife, in her suit, is in the kitchen, making bag lunches before she leaves for the office. The dog is pacing by the front door, waiting to be let out.

Andy, still in his bathrobe and carrying a mug of coffee, tucks the newspaper and his notebook computer under his arm and shuffles out to the back patio. 'Gonna be a beautiful day', he decides.

Sitting down at the patio table, Andy takes a slug of coffee and then turns on the computer. He types in his password, and then, as the machine uses its wireless modem to call in, Andy turns to look at the newspaper. He is hardly through the headlines, when his software agent – a blue square on the screen bearing the logo 'Andrew Moeller's Assistant' – announces, 'Good morning. We've received some items during the night. Do you wish to see them?'

Beats the tripe in the newspaper. Andy taps the return key. Up on the screen comes his company's daily newspaper, complete with stories, videos, classified ads, even an active bulletin board. Andy checks the latest news – he whistles at the announcement of Bob Trotter's sale to Volvo ('Maybe I ought to transfer to the Stockholm office,' Andy says to himself), checks the stock price and saves a technical article for later reference – then moves on.

'Do you wish to see your schedule for the day?' asks the agent. Andy taps the key. Up comes the day's schedule, blocked out by the quarter hour.

First up, at 10 a.m., is Protectron Corp. Andy smiles at the memory. Protectron. Carl West, director of procurement, the toughest buyer in town. Protectron is the hottest company in electronic home controllers – from an apartment to $2 billion in six years – so you couldn't ignore it. But dealing with West was like walking into a tree shredder. The man prided himself on his encyclopaedic knowledge and his merciless interrogation skills. Some veteran salesmen and saleswomen had walked into West's office and staggered out an hour later – after a barrage of questions and charges about benchmarks, service contracts, options, availabilities, delivery dates, and pricing – with their egos shattered and their contracts torn in two.

Andy remembered that his knees had actually knocked on that first visit to Protectron. The guys back at the office had a bet going whether he'd even emerge from West's office alive. Andy remembered Larry Stills pointing at the new computer in Andy's hand – this was right after the new TSQ system had been installed – and laughing, saying, 'Buddy, that thing may be small, but it's too big to have to eat.'

West even looked like a firebreather: brush cut (and not the hip type), white short-sleeved shirt, square-toed shoes and a tie that must have been twenty years old. He was the kind of guy who could say hello and shake your hand, both in a millisecond, and be back in his chair glaring at you before you even knew what happened.

Andy remembered feeling like a stain on the office chair. 'Well?' asked West in a way that made a question sound like a challenge to a fistfight. 'I don't have much time.'

'This won't take long, Mr West,' Andy had said. 'I want to show you our new 64-bit microcontroller, the 911436. It's to be formally announced next week and ...'

'Read about it in EDN,' said West dismissively. 'Doesn't look like much.'

'It will when you learn more about it,' said Andy. He tossed his laptop on the table (a nice casual touch, he'd used it ever since), popped up the screen and booted up. For an instant he thought about using the slick new multimedia presentation that advertising had sent out the week before, but shrewdly decided to pass. It would kill with most procurement managers; but Carl West wasn't like most procurement managers. Instead, he went straight to the data sheet. It popped up on the screen, with a window in the upper right showing the new chip floating in space, followed by moving images of a number of potential applications.

West glanced at the screen. 'I know all this. Tell me about your DSP.'

Andy slid the cursor to the entry 'Digital Signal Processing' and tapped a key. Up came eight densely packed pages of detailed performance specifications. 'Will this do?' Andy asked, suppressing a smile, 'or would you like the circuit diagram?'

'This'll do,' West muttered. He read for a few minutes. Finally, without looking up, he muttered, 'Can I get a copy of this?'

'Sure,' said Andy, pulling a portable printer out of his briefcase. He reached over and touched the print key on the computer. The printer, not plugged into anything, hummed in his hand, printing out the eight pages in less than a minute. 'Here you go,' said Andy, handing the sheets over.

West's eyes flickered for a moment, then recovered. 'Even if you've got the specs, that doesn't mean they're real. And it doesn't mean you can deliver. I get sales guys coming in here all the time with phony stats and vaporware they can never deliver. It's one thing to print out a data sheet, it's another to build a real product and deliver it on time.'

Don't get angry, Andy had told himself. He forced a smile. 'Mr West, if I didn't believe in my company or its products I wouldn't be here. I am not interested in selling to you once and then disappearing. My goal is to develop a long-term business partnership with Protectron. And that is only going to happen if I give you what you want, when you want it.'

West made a disbelieving smirk; he'd heard all this relationship stuff before. 'Okay, pal,' thought Andy, 'watch this.'

He reached over and typed a command into the computer. It would take twenty seconds to load the file. 'Now, Mr West, if you would be interested, I'd be happy to share with you the results of our beta tests. As you can see (up came the file with perfect timing), the 911436 – by the way we code-named it Dragonfly in-house – has proven itself in a number of applications to meet the specs we've assigned to it.' Up on the screen came one test result after another. 'However, I do note your ... scepticism, and I'm happy to say that one of our beta's was willing to identify himself and talk about the product.'

'Yeah?' said West, leaning forward. 'Who?'

Up came a windowed movie of Samuel Eastman, director of product development at Medi-Sys Corp., the medical equipment giant. Eastman looked like an old football player, which only added to his eloquence. As he extolled the performance of the Dragonfly in a number of testbed applications, other windows popped up showing the empirical results of the Medi-Sys tests. They validated, even exceeded, all of Andy's claims.

Now West was interested. He read the data with great intensity – so great that West barely noticed Andy getting up from his chair, walking around to stand beside him and begin tapping keys on a small side window.

That's what Andy had hoped would happen. He wanted to make the next part appear seamless.

A memo had come down from corporate a week before requiring at least one senior manager in manufacturing be on call at all times to receive communications from the field. As he heard the computer's on-board modem click on and softly begin dialling, he silently prayed that manufacturing hadn't ignored the dictum from above – those fab guys were notorious for ignoring even desperate pleas from the field.

The line connected. 'Thank God.' Andy turned to look at West, and found him watching the new little window. 'Now Mr West,' said Andy, not giving him time to speak, 'you asked about availability.' He quickly typed in name and greetings. Pleasepleaseplease, he said to himself, let it be somebody important.

On the screen came the reply, 'This is Raymond Norling. I'm currently at Fab Facility 4 in Phoenix.' Bingo! The vice-president (VP) himself! Andy had to restrain himself from throwing a fist in the air. 'Mr Norling, I'm here with Carl West of Protectron. He has some questions about the Dragonfly. May he speak directly with you?'

'Yes,' came back Norling's typed words and he listed the phone number of the nearest videophone. Andy hung up and typed in the number. Out of the corner of his eye, he caught West staring at him respectfully. Outside of a few little start-ups where everybody was an executive, West had probably never talked to a manufacturing VP in his life – especially not one of a Fortune 500 company. Neither had Andy, but he wasn't going to tell.

Andy moved closer to West and adjusted the little camera on the top of the computer. As he did, a new window popped up in the middle of the screen. There was Raymond Norling, in suit and tie, looking just like he did in the annual report. 'Hello,' he said in a sober baritone.

'Mr. Norling, I'd like to introduce you to Mr West.'

'A pleasure to meet you, Mr West. I've long been an admirer of Protectron, and, after what Andy's told me about you, I've looked forward to meeting you.'

Andy! Like we're old buddies. Andy almost laughed. What's Norling doing running factories? He's a born salesman.

'Now, Mr West,' the face on the screen continued, 'how can I help you?'

There was a surprising new note of respectfulness in West's voice. 'Well, sir, we're looking seriously at your new controller. But we want to make sure that you'll be able to deliver it when we need it and in the quantities we desire.'

The two men watched Norling glance down for a moment, and heard the tapping of keys. Norling glanced up again. 'Here, Mr West, I'm sending you (a new window filled with statistics appeared on the screen) my current data on production figures and delivery estimates. You now know everything I do – and I think you'll see that we can meet just about any order you give us.'

'Yes, well, er, thank you, Mr Norling,' said West, 'I won't take up any more of your time. I certainly appreciate you doing this.'

'Oh, it's my pleasure, Mr West,' said Norling, without a trace of irony. 'And, as I'm sure Andy will tell you, we are more than prepared to send over a team to help you design the 911436 into your new product for the maximum performance and efficiency. I look forward to talking with you again.'

As Andy turned off the videophone, he secretly rolled his eyes: who would have ever thought it? Before the meeting was over, Andy used the computer one more time: to draw up a sample contract.

A $15 million sale. A design win in the hottest new consumer product on the market. And a ten-day trip to Europe for two. As twenty-four e-mails later confirmed, Andy was the toast of the company. He, of course, gave due credit to Ray Norling and the designers in the IS department and marketing.

The close

Every element in Andy's story is possible right now. Recently history has shown that technology only succeeds when it begins and ends with the people (like Andy) who will *use it*. Virtual selling succeeds where sales automation fails because, in the end, it is more *human*. And that essential humanity lies in the philosophy of total sales quality.

When we properly begin with *people and perfection*, we create the same goal that Sales Force Automation has claimed all along. *Only this time, we actually get there.*

Note

1. This chapter is an edited version of a chapter published previously in Siebel, T. and Malone, M., *Virtual Selling: Going Beyond the Automated Sales Force to Achieve Total Sales Quality* (1996). Reprinted by permission of the authors and The Free Press, a Division of Simon & Schuster (www. simonsays.com). © Thomas M. Siebel, 1996.

Chapter 10

The elusive strategic alliance

Lawrence G. Friedman

The 'strategic alliance' is one of the most difficult and elusive concepts in the business lexicon. What exactly is an alliance, anyway? Is it sort of like a normal business relationship but with a lot of trust, or is there something qualitatively different about alliances? There is also the question of whether you need one – of whether there is some key business objective that requires an alliance to be achieved. The biggest issue, of course, is how to make this new breed of business relationship successful in the marketplace. These difficult and oft-unresolved questions go a long way toward explaining some of the occasional cynicism out there about alliances. As one VP of sales put it: 'My prime directive to my reps is: get out there and close deals. Alliances are just a distraction from the task at hand.' That is not an uncommon view, particularly among sales line executives.

In the last few years some healthy scepticism has, in fact, grown up around alliances. The early enthusiasts touted alliances as a fundamental paradigm shift in business relationships. The message was perhaps a naïve one: 'discard your old, worn-out selling relationships and get into partnerships!' Books appeared claiming that selling was dead, replaced by a never-quite-defined concept called 'partnering'. What the early enthusiasts did not account for is that many selling relationships are fine just as they are, the basic sales relationship having worked reasonably well for, say, 8,000 years. In contrast to successful, tested sales models, many of the early experiments in alliances turned out to be expensive, while delivering meagre results and having a failure rate, according to the infamous McKinsey statistic, of over 50 per cent within six months.

Certainly the research which Neil Rackham and this author conducted for the book *Getting Partnering Right* corroborated that finding.[1] By the time the book was ready to go to the publisher, about a quarter of the alliances we had had researched had been dissolved by the participants, in some cases with the 'partners' barely talking to each other. Like others who had experimented with or observed alliances, we were suitably brought down to earth about alliances as a business strategy.

Today's scepticism about alliances, though, is a good sign. It means that alliances have begun to migrate out of the enthusiast phase and into the cold, demanding world of marketing economics: what are the returns on investment? How will these things cut costs and improve profitability? How soon will they deliver revenue growth and increased market share? No business concept can last long without answering these questions.

There is a growing body of evidence that alliances, when managed and structured well, do deliver the goods. This is occurring across a broad range of industries, even in some unlikely places. Public Service Electric & Gas, for example, a utility company based in New Jersey, and their wire cable supplier Okonite have reduced inventory costs by over $100 million through an active, far-reaching partnership. In another industry, distribution logistics, Motorola and UPS's process-redesign partnership has led to a 65 per cent reduction in shipping time and the ability of Motorola to assemble, test and ship products from a factory in Asia to anywhere in the world – within seven days of the order.

Of course these anecdotes do not even begin to scratch the surface of what has been accomplished in certain industries, like high technology, where companies using alliances as a core marketing strategy frequently are able to reduce their cost of sales by 20 to 30 per cent while simultaneously reaching into dispersed, global markets for sources of new revenue growth. Ponder for a moment where companies like Microsoft, Oracle, Cisco, Hewlett-Packard and Sun Microsystems – each of whom relies on huge networks of thousands of business partners – would be today without their partners to sell, service and support their products around the globe. These companies probably would not exist, at least not in a form we would recognize. The phenomenal growth of the high-technology industry has undeniably been fuelled and perhaps been made possible by the business partner 'channel'.

Today, alliances are becoming ever more productive and successful due to improving technologies of collaboration. For example, a large client of ours uses proprietary intranets to provide twenty-four hours a day, seven days a week support, reorder capability and low-end transaction processing for its key accounts, thus leaving more time for both their sales teams and customers' purchasing teams to focus on larger, more complex transactions. Lotus Development uses a Notes database for its thousands of business partners to share leads, communicate with Lotus and form partnerships with each other to identify, sell to and service accounts. There are hundreds of varieties of clever uses of technology to support collaborative relationships. Technology has done more than any other factor to transform 'partnering' from a buzzword to a tangible, productive form of business relationship.

The challenge for many companies experimenting with collaboration technology is to recognize that the technology is simply a means to an end – an enabler of organizational collaboration – and not the end in itself. The end goal of an alliance is business results – results like increased market share and revenue growth. These kinds of results require people, and specifically, people making thoughtful, sound judgements about how to extract the maximum value out of an alliance opportunity. No computer can do that yet. In the alliance game, techno-wizardry is still not a substitute for a clear business purpose and an ability to execute soundly and successfully against that purpose.

What is an alliance?

One company placed an advertisement in *Business Week* and in the background was a variety of stock photos of some business executive types shaking hands and, presumably, making deals. In the foreground was a simple message: '*We Want to Partner With You.*'

How is it that this company knows it wants to partner with someone they've never met and know nothing about? Perhaps you run a business that, in a partnership with them, would collapse, leaving thousands of people unemployed and a pile of worthless stock certificates on the floor. Perhaps you are a convicted criminal who has actually killed several of his business partners! The truth is even if you are entirely on the up and up, the odds of your business being a natural fit with theirs is rather low. So what gives? The simple answer is that, putting the words aside, this company is not really trying to communicate that they want to develop a partnership. In fact their advertisement would be much more accurate and honest if it just said the following: *'We Want To Sell You Stuff, Hopefully Over A Long Period Of Time.'*

Of course, few would ever say something like that quite so directly, so many fall back on the rarefied, bland lexicon of partnering, where everyone is a partner and people work collaboratively to create win-win situations in synergistic relationships. Herein lies the challenge of the alliance, or partnering, concept. Is it a 'thing' – a tangible, measurable entity with rules, systems and goals – or is it a catch-all slogan that describes everything from the Intel-HP Merced alliance to the wishful thinking of vendors and their public relations (PR) departments?

Thus it is useful to have a workable definition of an alliance. What is it you are trying to build with your partner and how will you know when you get there? The simplest, and yet perhaps most effective, definition of an alliance is as follows: An alliance is a business relationship between organizations in which key business processes (such as product development, marketing or sales) are tightly integrated, and in some cases merged, to achieve measurable and specific business results.

This definition contains two important truths. First, organizations that partner are partnering to the extent that tight integration and mutual accommodation have taken place in how they do business. Two companies just buying and selling from each other are not in an alliance, regardless of how good the overall relationship is. Think about alliances that are widely acknowledged as value-creating. What is it that they always have in common? The answer is that something – and usually something important – has been changed inside each organization to extract the potential value of the partnership. That change could involve the streamlining of selling and purchasing processes at the inter-faces between the organizations, a redesign of how they go to market, or perhaps shared facilities and jointly managed teams. There are hundreds, if not thousands, of varieties. Whatever variety is chosen, strong alliances are about mutual change and adaptation to create 'surplus value' above and beyond that which can be achieved in a normal selling relationship.

Second, alliances are meaningful only in so far as they pursue and achieve specific, measurable business results. Two organizations may sponsor a conference together or contribute their employees' time together at a local charity. However useful or noble, these do not typically constitute an alliance. Organizations are in an alliance only when they are working together to achieve specific business results: increased profitability, new product roll-outs, increased market share, etc. Companies are getting better and more sophisticated about this. A few years ago many 'alliances' consisted of firms looking for cheap new lead streams. Most could not begin to communicate what, if anything, they were actually trying to accomplish with their partners. Today, on the other hand, it is not at all unusual for serious alliance practitioners to meet monthly or even weekly with their partners to track progress against specific revenue, market share and R&D targets. Particularly for smaller companies, who want to forge alliances but typically do not have an experienced alliance executive to manage the effort, an excellent test is whether the partnership can identify specific business targets or is mainly looking at 'working together'. In fact a good metric for an alliance is whether alliance metrics exist.

So, assuming two companies have something that reasonably approximates an alliance – tight integration and specific, measurable performance targets – what does it take to make the alliance a success in the marketplace? This question was the focus of the book entitled *Getting Partnering Right*. Here is what resulted from the book's analysis of 135 successful alliances.

The critical success factors of alliances

The phrase 'critical success factors' is a dangerous one; it often implies that there is some bullet-pointed list of things to do that will translate directly into success. Anyone who has worked through an alliance knows it is not that simple. There is no magic bullet, no singular action to take, that in and of itself is going to yield a healthy alliance. With that said, there is great commonality between successful alliances in terms of their core underlying principles, the things they make sure they get right and the things in which they invest. At its simplest, the most successful alliances seem to have healthy doses of what we called *impact, intimacy,* and *vision*; floundering alliances tend to be missing one or more of the three. A view of this is shown in Figure 10.1.

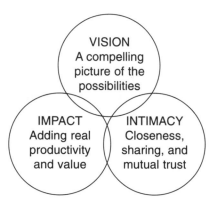

Figure 10.1   Critical success factors of alliances

1. *Impact*   A term to describe a partnership's capacity to deliver tangible results. Successful partnerships reduce costs, increase revenues, improve profitability, increase market share or go after a similar type of tangible business objective. Every successful partnership has one or more of these goals as its *raison d'être.*
2. *Intimacy*   The ability of partners to function together seamlessly to accomplish a business objective. Implicit in the idea of intimacy is that two or more organizations make structural, procedural and behavioural changes to create a climate of seamless cooperation.
3. *Vision*   A clear, compelling business case for the partnership. In a marketing partnership (such as those usually found between technology firms), the strength of the joint value proposition can be the single determinant of whether customers 'buy it' and make the partnership successful.

Alliances that are durable and give the partners competitive advantage tend to have all three: tangible business benefits for the partners, sufficient organizational integration and collaboration to enable the business impact, and a clear compelling reason to partner in the first place.

Nursing the baby partnership

At some point, every alliance needs to migrate from the 'cool idea' phase to an institutionalized entity with a real support infrastructure. Though alliances vary in type and style, most successful ones have in common a core infrastructure of management, organizational and investment support. Usually all five of the following must be in place for an alliance to progress from a good idea to something which produces business results:

1. Agreed, documented business targets, such as joint sales goals or cost-reduction goals.
2. A business plan or operating model that clearly specifies how the business targets are going to be achieved.
3. People assigned and empowered to manage and grow the partnership.
4. Terms and conditions specifying what is expected from each party and what the conditions are for continued partnership.
5. Sufficient funds to support the key activities of the partnership (such as joint marketing, sales or product development initiatives).

Over the last few years, many organizations, and particularly technology firms with huge partner networks, have begun pruning their alliances. This is largely a reaction to the limited business benefit that most alliances achieve, and the belief that a few solid, high-performing alliances would be easier to manage and grow than hundreds of non-performing partnerships. This makes good sense, and is a trend likely to continue over the next decade. Most companies would be far better off with a smaller number of high-performing, durable, profitable alliances. In the end, the alliances that will last will be those that deliver real results, that continue to improve organizational closeness – particularly through the use of technology – and that have a clear and compelling understanding of why they are partnering in the first place.

Note

1. Rackham, N., Friedman, L. G. and Ruff, R. (1996) *Getting Partnering Right*. McGraw-Hill.

Chapter 11

Why virtual teams?[1]

Jessica Lipnack and Jeffrey Stamps

The virtue of virtual

It was not until the 1990s that the word 'virtual' made it into the headlines on a regular basis. As a word, virtual has the same Latin root as virtue, an intimately personal quality of goodness and power. Its archaic meaning is 'effective because of certain inherent virtues or powers', an apt expression for successful virtual teams.

More recent use brings newer meanings:

- Virtual as in 'not in actual fact' but 'in essence', 'almost like'.
- Virtual as in 'virtual reality'.

The 'almost like' part of the definition, as in 'they act virtually like a team', is on target. 'Virtual' is used in the same way in the terms 'virtual corporation', 'virtual organization' and 'virtual office'. A virtual team conjures up a different picture from the one of people in the same organization working together in the same place.

When we use the term 'virtual', we do *not* mean it as another dictionary definition puts it: something that is 'not real' but 'appears to exist', something 'that appears real to the senses', but is not in fact. It is a bit like the old TV commercial about a brand of audiotape: 'Is it live or is it Memorex? With Memorex, you can hardly tell.'

With a virtual team, can you tell? It feels like a team and acts like a team, but is it a live team? Answer: *Virtual teams are live, not Memorex. They are most definitely teams, not electronic representations of the real thing.*

The newest meaning of 'virtual' attests to forces that are fast moving teams into an altogether different realm of existence – virtual reality – or more precisely, digital reality. Electronic media together with computers enable the creation of spaces that are real to the groups that inhabit them yet are not the same as physical places. The eruption of the WorldWide Web in the last decade of the millennium has allowed virtual teams to create private electronic homes. These interactive intranets – protected members-only islands within the Internet – signal a sharp increase in the human capability to function in teams.

Virtual teams are going digital, using the Internet and intranets.

And the definition is ...

So what exactly is a virtual team? A virtual team, like every team, is a group of people who interact through interdependent tasks guided by common purpose. Unlike conventional teams, a virtual team works across space, time and organizational boundaries with links strengthened by webs of communication technologies.

The image of face-to-face interactions among people from the same organization typifies our older models of teamwork. What sets virtual teams apart is that they routinely cross *boundaries*. What makes virtual teams historically new is the awesome array of interactive technologies at their disposal. Virtual teams now use myriad electronic technologies to cope with the opportunities and challenges of cross-boundary work.

Regular meetings, encounters in the hallway, getting together for lunch, dropping into one another's offices – these are our standard methods for getting things done. They lag behind everyday reality. People rarely see one another when they are in different places, spread out around the world, or even housed in different parts of the same city. Motorola, for example, has some twenty locations just in the Northwest Chicago area, each of which has multiple buildings. In the most extreme cases, some teams never meet face-to-face but work together on-line. Such is the case with the 1,200 employees of Buckman Laboratories in Memphis, Tennessee, who form and disband numerous situation-specific virtual teams on a daily basis – even though they are spread all around the globe.

A major reason that many of today's teams are ineffective is that they overlook the implications of the obvious. People do not make accommodation for how different it really is when they and their colleagues no longer work face to face. Teams fail when they do not adjust to this new reality.

Close is really close

What first comes to mind when you think of a team? A group of people working side by side, in close proximity to one another – a basketball or a rugby team, perhaps.

How close do you have to be to get the advantage of being in the same place? That is, what is the 'radius of collaborative collocation'? The startling data that MIT Professor Tom Allen has been compiling for the past several decades show that the radius is very small: based on proximity, people are not likely to collaborate very often if they are more than 50 feet/15 metres apart. The probability of people communicating or collaborating more than once a week drops off dramatically if they are more than the width of a basketball court apart. To get the benefit of working in the same place, people need to be quite close together.

To put this in perspective, think of the people you regularly work with. Are they all within 50 feet of you? Or are some of your co-workers a bit more spread out, down the hall, on another floor, in another building, or perhaps in another city or country? Increasingly, the people we work with routinely are no longer within shouting distance. Any team of more than about ten to fifteen people is by sheer physical mass probably more than 50 feet apart (see Figure 11.1).

From a team perspective, the important distances are the personal ones. How close people like to be for interpersonal inter-actions varies by culture. How far away do people have to be before they need to worry about compensating for distance?

The farther apart people are physically, the more time zones they have to cross to communicate. Thus, time becomes a problem when people who are not in the same place need some of their activities to be in sync. The window for routine synchro-nous work shrinks as more time zones are crossed, closing to effectively zero when people are on opposite sides of the globe. People who work together in the same place also can have time problems. Salespeople or consultants, for example, rarely occupy their offices at the same time. Even apparently collocated teams often cross time boundaries and need to think virtually.

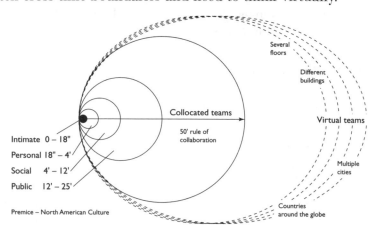

Figure 11.1 Collocated virtual distance

Virtual team principles

Work in a world in which the sun never sets is very complex. There are few maps in this new world of work and lots of complaints. People are trying to feel their way, uncertain that they are making the right decisions.

Most of us never received any training for living and working in a fluid, instantaneous, 'global village'. Thus, we need new models for teams that also incorporate the timeless features of working together.

Three words capture the essence of successful virtual teams:

- people
- purpose
- links.

People populate small groups and teams of every kind at every level – from the executive suite to the subcommittees of the local school's parent association. *Purpose* holds all groups together, but for teams, the task – the work that expresses the shared goals – is the purpose. *Links* are the channels, interactions and relationships that weave the living fabric of a team unfolding over time. The greatest difference between in-the-same-place teams and virtual ones lies in the nature and variety of their links.

The people/purpose/links (Figure 11.2) model unfolds into nine virtual team principles, which provide a framework for practical, adaptable approaches to the creation and management of virtual teams.

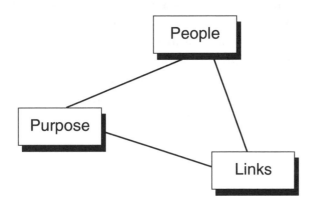

Figure 11.2   Virtual team model

Three slants on people

- Independent members   *Parts*
- Shared leadership   *Parts-as-wholes*
- Integrated levels   *Wholes.*

Virtual teams comprise *independent members*, people with a modicum of autonomy and self-reliance. Although leadership tends to be informal, invariably the diversity of technical and management expertise required in cross-boundary work means that most members take a leadership role at some point in the process. In virtual teams, *shared leadership* is the norm. Finally, the team is a human system arising from people parts. It has at least two levels of organization – the level of the members and the level of the group as a whole. Teams also grow out of and are embedded in organizations; they are parts of larger systems. To be successful, virtual teams must *integrate levels* both internally (subgroups and members) and externally (peers and super-groups).

The point of purpose
- Cooperative goals   *Do*
- Interdependent tasks   *Doing*
- Concrete results   *Done.*

Purpose, which defines why a particular group works together, expresses some minimal level of interdependence among the people involved. Virtual teams are far more dependent upon having a clear purpose than face-to-face teams. Because they operate outside the bounds of traditional organizational life without bureaucratic rules and regulations to guide them, they must rely on their common purpose to stay in tune.

Cooperative goals are what purpose looks like at the beginning of any successful teaming process. This is why so many books about teams begin by focusing on goals. A set of *interdependent tasks*, the signature feature of teams, connects desires at the beginning with outcomes at the end. When a team completes its process, it expresses its purpose as *concrete results*, the measurable outputs of joint effort. These three elements – cooperative goals, interdependent tasks, and concrete results – enable virtual teams to stay focused and be productive.

The web of links
- Multiple media   *Channels*
- Boundary-crossing interactions   *Communicating*
- Trusting relationships   *Patterns*

What gives *virtual* teams such distinction is their links. Relatively suddenly, multiple, constantly enhanced modes of communication are widely available, providing access to vast amounts of information and unprecedented possibilities for interaction. We choose the term 'links' for this defining feature of virtual teams because it bridges three key aspects of communication.

First, people need the actual physical connections – wires, phones, computers, and the like – that provide the potential for communication and are the prerequisite for interaction. *Multiple media* are moving virtual teams from the extraordinary to the ordinary as the technology wave of the Information Age change reaches the mainstream.

Connections make *boundary-crossing interactions* possible. The back-and-forth communication between people – the activities and behaviours – constitute the actual process of work. It is here – at the boundaries of interaction – that virtual teams are truly different. In virtual teams, people's interactions across boundaries require behaviours that are fundamentally new.

Through interactions near and far, people develop trusting relationships, the invisible bonds (and baffles) of life. People's patterns of behaviour mark the outlines of their relationships that persist and feed back into subsequent interactions. As important as positive relationships and high trust are in all teams, they are even more important in virtual ones. The lack of daily face-to-face time, offering opportunities to quickly clear things up, can heighten misunderstandings. For many distributed teams, trust has to substitute for hierarchical and bureaucratic controls. Virtual teams with high trust offer this valuable social asset back to their sponsoring organizations for use in future opportunities to cooperate. It is far better to cross boundaries than to smash them.

Note
1. This chapter has been published previously in *Virtual Teams* (Wiley, 1997).

Chapter 12

Virtual teaming and virtual organizations: twenty-five principles of proven practice

David J. Skyrme

Introduction: why has interest grown?

Why has the interest in virtual organizations grown significantly over the last year or so? I believe there are three main reasons:

1. The inexorable growth of the Internet – it enables virtual organizations to function efficiently. I know from my own experience. I am a member of several virtual teams and organizations, which could not operate at all if it were not for the Internet. We communicate daily by e-mail, use a private Website for developing documents and transfer spreadsheets and presentation files across continents at the click of a mouse.
2. Companies need flexibility and access to the best talent, wherever it is. They enter into strategic alliances and need access to experts. If they can be effective through working virtually while avoiding the cost of relocation, they will. They will create multifunction, multilocation teams to assemble their best talent worldwide. Project teams will come and go, as needs dictate.
3. Talented individuals are more discerning. They can increasingly dictate where and how they will work. If they want to

surf (in the ocean, not on the net!) six months a year in California, and work the rest, they will. If they like the lifestyle in Southern France or Tuscany and can still offer a good service, that is the lifestyle they will adopt.

Hence a combination of technology advances (such as better networking, groupware and video-conferencing) and social trends (more individual choices and more flexible labour markets) make the growth of virtual teams, either within a single organization, between organizations, or between dispersed individuals more of a norm. In the words of a title of a *Financial Times* article 'The rise of the virtual corporation: the question is not if, but how'.[1]

The working hypotheses

Making virtual teams work is about empowering, communicating, enthusing and listening. Like a lot of management: 'common sense but not common practice'. It is these kinds of 'common sense' principles that need to be used in a virtual team or organization environment, even though a team may have less permanence and not be collocated (this covers both types of virtual team – virtual in space or time or both). I developed the principles while creating a self-managed team when I worked at Digital Equipment Corporation in the late 1980s – and they have stood the test of time. However, before I detail my twenty-five principles, the reader must first consider the elements of my working hypothesis:

1. Organizations today need a balance of the highly innovative and the tightly coordinated. The former needs a networked approach, the latter a structured approach (some bureaucracy). Many established organizations have too much of the latter and too little of the former.
2. More and more work will be knowledge work – processing information, not physical product. Where it is done is less important than how it is done, and how it is delivered to the client.
3. Knowledge does not exist in isolated compartments. Its capacity to grow is enhanced if expertise can be tapped from as wide an 'expert' base as possible – people with different per-

spectives, experiences, age, gender, knowledge and cultural traits. In other words, people worldwide provide the best base for enriching knowledge and creating worthwhile innovation.

4. Tasks and the interrelationships between various tasks are becoming more complex. Variety in the environment is increasing (partly aided by technology and communications). There is more choice. Simplistic solutions no longer suffice for many business and societal problems.
5. The role of managers is changing from a 'director' to a 'facilitator', 'coach', 'mentor', 'adviser' and, indeed, a peer in the exchange of knowledge and experience.

The twenty-five principles

Prerequisites (individual attitudes and behaviour)

1. Every individual must have a sense of self-value and must value every other team member for their contribution – these should become explicit and expressed as the team's 'core competencies'. Individuals should learn from each other, from the results of their own actions, and from collective experience.
2. There must be a high level of trust – this may take time to build up. The starting point is to trust every other person until they abuse this trust.
3. Individuals must be mutually supportive; commitments made should be met and when circumstances prevent this, other team members must be informed as soon as possible.
4. Reciprocity must reign – give as much as you get, in terms of support, transfer of information and knowledge. Lack of reciprocity leads to unbalanced relationships and ultimately to hierarchy, withdrawal or team collapse.
5. Individual feelings must be recognized and expressed. Sharing these is a good way to start and end team meetings.

Teams and teaming (composition)

6. Teams are the organization units that create focus and allow work to proceed. Work in a team or on your own if you want to continue to develop your knowledge and success.
7. The most productive teams for knowledge work are small

multidisciplinary groups, e.g. five to eight people with a variety of backgrounds and personality traits.

8. Teams of large numbers are not productive for knowledge work – they are assemblies, gatherings, committees which may be used to pass information (often ineffectively), motivate (or demotivate) or provide a sense of importance. Their most valuable use is creating and maintaining a sense of belonging, cohesion and reinforcing values – and, of course, networking opportunities (but many people who organize meetings, conferences and such gatherings do not provide enough 'white space' for this to happen effectively).

9. Every knowledge worker should belong to at least two separate teams. This helps the organization achieve cross-functional cooperation and it helps the individuals gain a broader perspective.

10. An individual can have one of several roles in the team. These roles can change and be exchanged (for example during holiday periods, to balance workloads or to broaden individual experience). Distinguish the role from the person.

Team norms and relationships (mission, purpose and culture)

11. Every team must have a purpose if it is to act as a team and not as a collection of individuals. Its must have its own vision, mission and goals which reinforce those of a higher level.

12. Every team should develop a strong set of cultural norms and values. Hence regular team meetings should take place. A set of working principles should be developed (print them on a laminated card).

13. Each team should identify other teams carrying out related or dependent activities. It should draw a network diagram with:

    (a) itself (and its mission) at the centre
    (b) an inner ring of teams (nodes) where interdependencies are high (formal relationships)
    (c) an outer ring of collaborative teams (mostly information-sharing).

Where possible major activity sequencing and interdependencies should be shown (who provides what to whom).

14. Individual members of teams should be encouraged to maintain their personal networks, even beyond the identifiable needs of the current project or team. Professional and external networks are particularly important.

15. Some 'slack' should be built into the network. A certain amount of duplication/overlap should not be viewed as bad. This slackness permits a higher quality of output, plus a resilience to cope with the unexpected.

Communications

16. Just as in electronic networks a set of protocols needs to be defined and agreed. These may be implicit (common standards set by cultural values or 'like minded people'). Often it needs to be made explicit what the various signals mean, e.g. trial balloon, idea, request for action, demand, vote, decision, etc. Poor communication is probably the worst obstacle to effectiveness in any organization.

17. Frequent communication throughout the network (including outer ring) must be encouraged. This is particularly valuable for half-baked ideas and tentative positions. A small group developing its own 'final communique' docs not foster the network spirit.

18. Also in electronic communication 'NODE NOT RESPONDING' is an important signal. If something has not registered, or some work is falling behind, then a signal *should* ripple round the network so that the repercussions can be analysed.

19. Formal relationships (e.g. inner ring) are best cemented by having agreed written processes (hand-offs) and/or common members on both teams. Critical linkages need higher trust and openness rather than higher formality. In a sequenced set of tasks this can be provided by cascading teams (i.e. shared members).

20. Recognize the unpredictability and fuzziness of the process for making decisions. Who makes decisions will often be ambiguous. An action taken might imply a decision taken. In general, decisions should be made when and where they

need to be made, by whoever is appropriate. Be guided by the mission, values and principles. Types of decision which are fundamental should be agreed up front, and simple formal processes developed for these. Otherwise formality should be kept to a minimum.

Technology and working over a distance

Enabling technology is the most effective means of enhancing the quality of network communication. Electronic mail, distribution lists, groupware products such as Lotus Notes and video-conferencing all contribute, but they must be used effectively. Here are some principles to apply in virtual team communications. They apply mostly to the lowest common denominator – e-mail – since that is how many virtual teams start and is still the daily bread-and-butter of most.

21. In your e-mails, select the TO and CC addresses appropriately. Use explicit titles – in particular avoid simple replies which generate Re: Re: titles when the subject matter has moved on. Be explicit in what action you want the reader to take – is it for information or action, or is it a request for help? Similar principles apply to threads in a computer conference – use appropriate titles.

22. Use one e-mail per topic, especially when multiple recipients with different roles and interests are involved. This allows each to be filed and actioned separately. Keep e-mails short – give some opening context, repeat portions of incoming mail selectively and close with requested actions (if any).

23. If a face-to-face conversation is important, capture the essence in a follow-up e-mail. It also acts as a point of reference for the parties involved. It may throw up different interpretations of the same meeting, and highlight ambiguities that need to be resolved. It also acts as part of the 'team' memory.

24. Build on knowledge that exists or has been expressed. Recognize the contributions of others. Ideally appoint a knowledge editor who takes the best from transitory infor-

mation and compile it into a more structured document or Web page.

25. Above all – be human and informal. E-mails and discussion lists are conversations, and if you are not face to face, you need to insert a level of informality and 'smileys' or emoticons where appropriate.

Additional comments

Flexibility

Flexiblity is key. Recognize that team players change, tasks change. Hence any protocol, formal process should be simple and concise and adapted when needed. A few statements of principle are much better than binders of process manual.

Success and failure

There is no *a priori* evidence with today's travel and electronic network that a geographically dispersed network is any less effective than one based at a single location. On the contrary, there is some evidence that people put more effort into making remote linkages and communication work, because there is less opportunity to meet face to face. In my experience the biggest causes of failure are:

- not having a compelling shared vision
- not clearly identifying network participants and their respective roles
- having team missions and goals incompatible with each individual's aspirations
- having dominant nodes (i.e. a competitive or pressure relationship rather than a truly collaborative one)
- not communicating sufficiently and clearly enough.

The principles I have outlined above are those that I have tried to apply in my professional work. Is it easy? Is twenty-five too many? The short answer is 'No' and 'No'. Developing collaborative work behaviours needs considerable effort and skills (which can be learnt). Twenty-five is a very low number compared to the overall number of techniques and behaviours we use in our daily lives. Think of them as five groups of five, and tackle one at a time in each group.

If you apply these or similar principles, and your virtual team members do likewise, you will all achieve collectively what none of you individually could have achieved. Collaborative working over a distance can be incredibly effective, but it does require some agreed basic principles to be effective. These are ones that have worked for me. Specific situations and contexts may call for adjustments, but if your virtual team has not yet got its own set, why not start with these?

Note
1. *Financial Times*, 4 June 1997.

Chapter 13

Transactional communities as organic market systems

Andrea Saveri

Not only do on-line communities foster the exchange of thoughts and feelings, they facilitate the exchange of actual goods and services – and not just on the myriad of on-line shopping networks. In fact, before the proliferation of on-line shopping, there existed a moneyless system of trade and barter that both derived from the unique traits of on-line communities and held those communities together.

Community-based exchange follows the rules, guidelines and values of community – in other words, the community governs the transactions, not vice versa. Commercial experiments with on-line transactions such as electronic malls, sales through home pages, and even customer service Web pages are not governed by the conventions of on-line community trust, loyalty, reciprocity, shared value and individual connection to the whole – that exist in community-based transactional spaces. Indeed, much of what passes for electronic commerce on the Internet undermines the very notion of community, except for some classified ad groups on the Usenet and in smaller communities and local bulletin boards, such as the WELL. Attempts to introduce inappropriate commercial activity into newsgroups or other on-line conversations lead to community sanctions. Commerce and exchange do have a place on the Internet but *at the right time, in the right setting, and under specific guidelines.*

Behind the growth of commercial business on the Internet flows a thriving undercurrent of commerce of a different kind – trading. The Internet facilitates exchange as easily as an old town square or the Roman marketplace and does so without the elaborate electronic security necessary for commercial exchange involving money. Whether trading for Star Wars memorabilia, scuba diving gear, antiques or recipes, the open nature of the Internet makes it easy to find people, contact them, and arrange for a fair and suitable exchange. It is a self-mediated arrangement governed by the codes of behaviour of the telecommunity.

Trading forums

Perhaps the best example of true transactional communities are tape trading forums such as the [Grateful] Dead Trading Forum, the Phish Trading Forum, and the Allman Brothers Band Tape Trading Post. Other examples include electronic bulletin board forums for the exchange of information about services, such as the AutoMechanics BBS, which discusses and evaluates auto repair services in the Boston area.

As with the Western frontier, to which it is sometimes compared, the behaviour codes of the on-line world are fairly well regimented. The community defines its own means for establishing value, rates of exchange, concepts of fairness and sense of worth. The main notions driving these exchanges are sharing, communication and the growth of intellectual capital. The main goal is not to make a profit, but to share valuable resources among the greatest number of people. Unfortunately, also like the Western frontier before them, these cyberspace trading posts are threatened by the incursion of 'Big Capital' in search of profits. The jury is still out about how the profit motive will affect the more egalitarian transaction communities on the Internet. Trading tapes of live performances (with the permission and even assistance of the bands themselves) has fostered many new distribution systems-tape trading forums for exchanging information, tape trees and pyramids, and support networks that match newbies to more experienced traders.

The Grateful Dead Trading Forum

In its thirty years of touring, the Grateful Dead never played the same concert twice, improvising on hundreds of combinations of songs and sounds. To preserve these unique events, Grateful Dead fans have long traded and collected live recordings of concerts as important artefacts.

The goals of tape trading are:

- *Acquisition* Members join in to expand their music collections. Common interest in the music forms the community and perpetuates its vitality.
- *Interaction* Setting up tape trades is one of the easiest ways to meet other people on-line and move to one-to-one conversations from a crowded bulletin board. The subject is predetermined so that, though a conversation may stray off topic, the basic exchange of e-mails for arranging a trade is fairly standard. Such exchanges are simple, yet they entail a sharing that feeds into the whole and enhances the transaction with the values of the community.

The Internet as frontier

The metaphor [of the frontier] has been widely used vis-à-vis the Net not only because people, working sometimes alone but always within a social fabric of interconnections, have created and settled new electronic spaces, but also because on their heels have come the lords of capital using all means possible to take over, incorporate and valorize these spaces. The subordination of the net to commercial and industrial profit has become the name of the game … But just as pioneers on the Western frontier resisted the enclosure of their lands or the takeover of their small businesses by corporate interest, so too the pioneers of cyberspace resist commercialization of the Net. Like other free spirits (e.g. some musicians and artists), the pioneers of cyberspace can create new spaces for their own (very special) purposes (pleasure, politics, etc.) as part of a process of self-valorization that at least initially threatens or transcends existing norms of capitalist society.[1]

Setting guidelines for behaviour

The culture of the Grateful Dead is strong on this point: live recordings of shows should not be bought or sold, but rather shared. An intricate web of protocol has sprung up to facilitate the flow of this non-monetary trade. For example, asking for extra cassette tapes along with those you agree to dub for someone is tantamount to asking for money and thus generally frowned on.

To achieve this level of equity, members create highly detailed protocols. One individual who offers to dub tapes for others has explicitly detailed instructions to incorporate a simple and fair structure into all exchanges, so that neither party is dissatisfied or exploited:

Do not include a return mailer. These do NOT, as a rule, handle analog tapes well. I have seen too many damaged blanks come into the studio here from people over the past year. I supply the return mailing supplies, which include envelopes, bubble wrap, etc. This is what most of the additional $.25 I ask for goes to. And, except for the outside mailing envelope or box, all the shipping materials can be reused by you folks.[2]

One way to make sure that such information is broadly understood is to use both the Web and Usenet to distribute behaviour guidelines, an approach the band Phish has successfully mastered. The band's Website will introduce the newbie to any and all possible questions or concerns, beginning with its basic philosophy and continuing to technical specifics concerning stereo equipment and 'netiquette', including a separate manual with instructions for starting down the trading path: 'So you wanna jump right in and get tapes, but wait, that's not a good idea. The first thing you need to do, if you have not already, is go to the Phish archive (ftp archive.phish.net) and get the FAQ (Frequently Asked Questions).'[3]

Standards of exchange

Disseminating extensive guidelines furthers the functioning of the whole system and maintains the quality of the traded goods (in this case, tapes). Increasing the general awareness of the quality cultivates the shared value and resources of the group by improving individual collections. If a large group of people is to continually exchange materials, trust and commitment to standards must be maintained. Accepted standards have emerged to help maintain quality:

1. Common consensus exists regarding quality control measures, including the type of blank tape used, source and generation of recording, and other technical choices.
2. Because there is no way to meet and listen to the music before trading, a self-graded system is in place to determine the sound quality of the tape.
3. Each individual maintains a current list of tapes that is honest, accurate and organized, thereby maintaining a fair environment. In this sense attention to detail is collectively enforced.

Offers to nurture newbies

For those who would like more active help in learning how to trade, there is a grassroots system of support. A newbie can be 'adopted' i.e., paired up with someone who already has tapes and is willing to dub for anyone who wants to send blanks, by putting their name on a list. The administrators of these arrangements maintain guidelines for smooth functioning. They are also clear about eligibility so that there is no exploiting the self-designed system.

Helping each other is the most overt means of giving back to the community. Since no two members have the same tape lists, everyone has something to gain by sharing. The more people obtain music, the better the chance that they may one day help someone else in the community.

Violations and sanctions

As in all human systems, misunderstandings occur. If a transaction seems to be unfair, say a partner has not returned tapes, one usually sends several e-mails before taking further measures. If that does not work, eventually, one might post the trader's name to the newsgroup to incite a response, and sometimes disputes are taken up and resolved by the whole.

Other times violations are only misunderstandings of commonly accepted protocol and are quickly remedied. For example, one trader approached members of the rec.bluenote.blues group with an offer to trade, using polite language and offering first to exchange tape lists to see if a fair exchange could be made. A newsgroup member stepped in to correct what he thought was inappropriate to this particular group, 'Rick, these are nice people here, leave them alone! (Don't worry folks, we're dragging him back to rec.music.gdead where he belongs)', thereby suggesting that trading should be kept to the groups where it is a common activity.

This type of trading works because a community agrees to make it work; essentially, the trade and the protocols growing up around the trade are the glue that keeps the community together. Specific benefits include the following:

- The tape-trading activities fuel the networks within the greater community by developing points of conversation that are fed back to the larger group. As people get new tapes, they are inspired to post, which evolves into debates and discussions.
- Trading lowers barriers to open and easy conversation – the ease with which someone may be contacted spontaneously with a comment or question determines how frequently people meet one another and form links on-line. Like the fur trappers of the old West, whose trade routes made the way for pioneers and settlers, tape traders establish communication links that can be used for other kinds of communication.
- One-offs from the whole strengthen the network – e-mail communication spawned from the larger whole creates closer ties. The interaction increases intimacy and builds on traders' reputations.

Conclusion

Viewed through the lens of community, electronic commerce takes on very different characteristics from industry-sponsored electronic shopping and financial transactions. Community-based trading and exchange derives its own set of values within the community. They are not imposed externally. As Cleaver points out, the community goes through a process of self-valorization. Imagine on-line communities of exchange and geographic-based communities, such as neighbourhood or town-based networks, that are superimposed – one on top of the other. In many ways the trust of the community and the efficiency of the network in coordinating exchange could support a very effective system of local barter that could bypass the traditional market system for many products and services. For geographically remote towns or regions, this may be quite attractive to residents, who would not have to worry about giving out credit card or PIN numbers on-line to complete a transaction.

The important lesson for businesses is to not underestimate the power of community-based trust and loyalty in matters of exchange. Using their presence on the Web, for example, companies may want to try to build relationships, provide information in response to customer inquiries, and interact with customers rather than simply broadcast product features and prices. Particularly for selling cycles with long lead times, the Internet or Web may be a low-cost but continual flow of interactions that help initiate relationships with potential customers.

Notes

1. Harry Cleaver (1995) *The 'Space' of Cyberspace: Body Politics, Frontiers and Enclosures*, University of Texas Austin. (http://www.lawyernet.com/members/JIMFESQ/wca/1996/22/SPACEOFCYBERSPACE.html).
2. Phish Newbie Manual (http://www.rit.edu/pmh4514/newbie_manual.html).
3. Phish Newbie Manual (http://www.rit.edu/pmh4514/newbie_manual.html).

Part Two

Web-Weaving in Practice

Following the structure of Part One, Part Two shows how the theory of the web-weaving *inside, outside* and *in-between* organizations has been put into practice.

Chapters 14, 15, 16 and 17 focus *inside* the organization with case studies of intranets, changing corporate culture, knowledge-sharing and creating virtual learning environments. Here you will find out how IPC Magazines and the British Library enhanced their communications with an intranet; why Parsons Brinckerhoff focused on creating strong teams before introducing the information technology; and what City University Business School in London learned about the benefits and challenges of creating a virtual learning environment in a non-distance learning faculty.

Chapters 18, 19 and 20 illustrate the benefits of combining internal and external communications. Boeing was one of the early pioneers in this area and experts say Boeing's approach to intranet management could become the norm for IT departments at the world's largest corporations. Another explorer in this field is British Petroleum (BP) which has pioneered virtual teams both *inside* and *outside* the organization, and used the technology to support an alliance with its partners such as Halliburton Brown and Root, who have written about the experience from their side of the fence.

Chapters 21 and 22 focus on *outside* the company. In these chapters we see technology used to strengthen and enhance relationships with trading partners and customers through an extranet at Oracle and through electronic commerce at Cisco Systems. Chapter 23 focuses on the customer's perspective. This selection of real life vignettes serves as a reminder of what happens when the organizational focus is on internal systems and they forget about the customers, whose experiences are sometimes in crying need for improvement.

Chapter 24 is an example of how technology can enable exceptional alliances *between* organizations. The Global Office Network describes the process of how a group of serviced office providers in different continents evolved naturally from communicating by paper and fax to a CompuServe community and then on to a web server which connects members from nineteen countries over fifty-eight locations.

Finally, in Chapters 25, 26 and 27 we have examples of individuals making connections and leading edge networking. Team syntegrity shows how a very structured method was used to integrate the contributions of thirty people from all around the world collaborating to author a publication in tribute to the 'Father of Cybernetics', Stafford Beer, who originally created the process. BrainPool and Trading Post are two fast-growing communities which offer interesting and progressive people a safe place to meet each other and explore avenues for collaboration and learning. They facilitate the exchange of ideas and offer a support system of peers – something sorely needed by inquiring individuals in these times of great turmoil.

Chapter 14

Assembling a simple intranet at IPC magazines

James Roberts

Why IPC magazines chose an intranet

With seventy different publications in the group, IPC Magazines effectively has seventy minicompanies in one, each with its own staff, business practices and information resources. The company wanted to unite these pockets of knowledge and share information across the entire business. IPC Magazines felt that an intranet reflected the company's culture, whereas management information systems did not. The goal of the intranet implementation was to deliver information, not technology.

Jeremy Hughes, IT Strategic Planning Manager at IPC, said, 'It was the vast amount of e-mails being sent around the offices that first made me realize the company needed a new means of communication. The e-mail system had started to get overloaded so we thought the intranet would be a new channel of communication.

Why they chose British Telecom

With those reasons in mind, IPC was keen to experiment with British Telecom's (BT) Intranet Complete package. British Telecom claims the package offers a complete intranet solution and will build, design, support and maintain the site. This 'no hassle' promise attracted IPC who wanted to outsource the maintenance and technical aspects.

Hughes says: 'With a mix of PCs and Macs in the offices the technicalities were a potential nightmare and needed a lot of

143

people to resolve them. We don't have the internal resources or the technical skills to do that so we used BT to implement the intranet so we could relax.'

Although IPC's IT department put together the proposal for the intranet and managed the development and initial contents, the aim is to leave the daily running of it to each department. He added: 'We're building an infrastructure where departments will update their own areas – we will provide design standards and capability and make it simple to use.'

The role of IT: keep it simple, get it started

Unsurprisingly, the impetus for the intranet project – called Infonet – at IPC came from within IT: the Innovations Unit within IT undertook the research into the proposed intranet, contacted British Telecom about an external solution, and ultimately brought a presentation before the company board. As with a high percentage of corporate intranets, IT was not only behind the creation of the project, but heavily involved in every aspect of its development – not just the technical side of things, but the design specifications, content provision and the other look and feel issues to which IT has traditionally been impervious/blissfully unaware. In other words, IPC seemed to be heading for yet another technically accomplished, but very user-unfriendly intranet: a tool of ruthless efficiency and precious few fans.

Although IT can help to get an intranet project up and running they cannot be expected to drive it – nor can they be expected to define its business applications. The intranet 'white elephant' scenario – a site that is inflexible and unloved – can only be avoided if those sections of the business which will ultimately appear on the company intranet become enthusiastically involved in its conception.

As soon as the necessary approval had been given, IT began to work alongside the internal Creative Solutions team and Siemens Nixdorf, the networking partner (as well as BT). There was a wide spectrum of experience and opinion here to draw upon. By evolving a less blinkered approach at an early stage the intranet project became a more democratic venture, soliciting feedback from every level of the company.

Starting simple

IPC put in place a rudimentary site using existing material, then expanded outwards. Departments such as HR already had large repositories of electronic information (Word documents, etc.) which could be transferred on-line with a minimum of fuss. Similarly, marketing information already existed in abundance and was easily imported on to the site. The early watchword was 'simplicity' – and therefore economy.

Design

Design was kept relatively straightforward, while still aiming to reflect IPC's rich heritage as Europe's largest consumer magazine publisher. Every screen is based around a standard frame; different areas of the business are represented on-line in a colour-coded way; the site is driven by a small number of immediately recognizable icons for easy navigation.

Because the site design was completely undertaken by an internal creative department, which already had comprehensive experience of IPC's corporate branding, there was no danger that the intranet would feel alien to its users. It would definitely have the imprint of IPC written all over it.

'The aim is to make Infonet easy and attractive to use with employees encouraged to choose to pull pages up on screen in favour of ploughing through pages of company policy books', says Hughes. The format of the Intranet is based on a simple design throughout, with the aim of being 'recognizable' and 'consistent'. Hughes says, 'New users will be able to learn how to use it within five minutes'.

Content

Similarly, content was determined by a cross-section of end users, not IT. Responsibility for the relevance and timeliness of information fell to the content managers within each localized intranet community. The adherence to companywide standards of content was also determined at the ground level; in turn, this helped to develop greater user buy-in and therefore a more parochial, less authoritarian intranet.

So far 650 pages of content have been produced, covering everything from magazine circulation figures and advertising information to general information, such as who is the company's chiropodist.

The roll-out

IPC Magazines has a local area network of approximately 2,000 desktops (both PC and Mac) But the Infonet, was not rolled out in one big bang.

In keeping with the 'small is beautiful' ethic it began with pilots in two sites and only sixty users – just enough to get an adequate level of feedback. The quality of this feedback was significant. It led to taking sections of the IPC intranet back to the drawing board for a redesign. Just as importantly, the board was consulted four times since the project began and received regular project briefing documents. It is this rapport between developers, designers and end users that determines how well an intranet project will ultimately be received.

A complete roll-out to all 2,000 users commenced in October 1997. Infonet will contain information on all aspects of the company's business, from the latest ABC (Audit Bureau of Circulation) figures for *Country Life* to health and safety policy. Every magazine and business area in the company will be represented on Infonet.

Budget and benefits

IPC is optimistic it will see return within a year. Hughes says the dedicated budget set aside for the project was not only stuck to – they even managed to finish under it. He adds: 'The cost benefits are built application by application depending on the department or magazine. It's like setting up a network, you can't think about the cost savings initially – but they will come.'

IPC expects to make most of its savings by halting the production of printed matter. A substantial part of the intranet content will be information from the human resources and other central departments and Hughes says, 'They expect to review just how much this saves the company after the first year'.

'The intranet will also provide a reference point for all staff which will be especially useful for those magazines or areas of the business which are very different and separate from one another' says Hughes. 'Also many of our publications overlap, so to have a general reference store of corporate and competitor information on the intranet will afford ease of access and avoid duplication of research. This will all save time and effort.'

Some of the other benefits from the IPC intranet include:

- providing 'enabling information' to every person within the company
- promoting a more open culture and enable increased remote working in the future
- offering IPC's advertising sales force instant access to the latest information on all IPC titles
- reducing production of paper-based manuals and reports.

Improving communication

IPC considers their intranet primarily an investment made to improve communication. The new intranet provides a better way of delivering information than e-mail. It also helps those who are producing the communication materials to have a 'better experience' of this production process than the inflexible and time-consuming effort of producing printed brochures and manuals.

Sharing departmental information

The intranet is both an enabler and a conduit of information. Each department or magazine within the company will post their own information on to the Intranet as and when they are ready to. Jeremy Hughes says, 'We expect that once a few very good sites are established and recognized this will encourage other staff to follow suit'.

Other possibilities

Looking to the future the possibilities for sharing information between editorial and business staff and learning about one another's activities are endless. Company and magazine design standards and in-house advertisements could eventually be held on the site, editorial content and management information could be stored and easily reused, and individual members of staff can be brought together through use of personal pages and records.

Conclusion

The success of an intranet depends more upon its conception than its implementation. IPC saw an intranet as a means of enhancing their existing administrative/technical infrastructure, rather than supplanting it. With full buy-in from the board, key business areas and interested staff their simple intranet has become a valuable tool, and not just an end in itself.

Note

1. This chapter has been published previously in *Intranet Communicator*, October 1997.

Chapter 15

Making an intranet by the book at the British Library

Peter Judge

As businesses become more driven by information and knowledge, they can take a leaf out of the librarian's book. Information handling has been the core business of the library for – well, for millennia. Despite the number of dusty books they handle, libraries have always been focused on knowledge rather than the physical publications that hold it. Nowhere is this more obvious than at the national archive, the British Library.

To some people the Internet looks like a great big library, and as more information comes on-line, one could be excused for wondering why we need 'real' libraries. The answer lies in the finding, indexing and presenting of information, as well as storing the primary records it came from. Internet technologies have become crucial for such an organization. They offer the chance to increase access, while reducing the demand on fragile or valuable physical records by putting them on-line. At the same time, it lets the users get more directly to catalogues and other material, and gives them better and more powerful searches.

In other words, the library's intranet has to do the same tasks as anyone else's – only more so.

Looking out and looking in

The world famous British Library (BL) has clearly seen this point. It runs the highly regarded public Website, Portico, which bring the library's material ever closer to a distributed group of end users. At the same time, and independently, the library has not neglected its own staff's information needs so it has spent the last two years developing an intranet.

The goal of the library's intranet project is to provide an on-line information service for managers, spanning across all the dozen so-called directorates which make up its structure. So far over 700 people have been introduced to the BL's intranet, out of about 1,500 PC users in the organization. In total, the library has 2,500 staff and four-fifths of these use desktop computers, according to Caroline Halcrow, systems analyst at BL. The plan is to extend intranet usage to all employees, but this involves getting PCs at the right price points and specifications to meet varied requirements.

The system

The set-up is consciously budget oriented. Halcrow observes that this factor – linked with the relatively low set-up costs of the core intranet technology – means the intranet promises to be a cost-effective project which builds on and enhances the existing infra-structure.

The British Library's intranet is an internally hosted network which spans two main sites, including all the library's London locations and the Document Supply Centre at Boston Spa. Each main site has a separate firewall. In fact, the goal is to supply a set of centralized services – based on the file servers – within the intranet fabric, which then become available to all authorized users.

Intranet supports office move

When the BL moves to its new central location at St Pancras in London, it sees the intranet as integral to providing support for the relocation and settling in of staff to this building. Since the St Pancras project has cost over £500 million and has taken longer than projected to complete, this support for relocation is vital as the operational phase is about to begin.

Plans to spread

Initially the intranet was set up by the IS department, although sponsorship and adoption was quickly picked up by the Planning and Resources (P&R) directorate. An initiative to spread intranet usage across all the directorates will start in the early part of 1998, according to Halcrow. This could time well with the opening of the St Pancras library. The P&R intranet went live in March this year and has been used as the infrastructural model for each directorate to follow.

Content

Almost all the content on the BL intranet is sourced internally, being mainly archival in nature. Halcrow sees the possibility of adding some external feeds, maybe including an IT reporting or market intelligence firm. A number of links to external Websites have also been included. At present, the intranet carries the BL telephone directory, project management documentation and information regarding the management board meetings. The staff handbook has been rendered in the Acrobat PDF format, containing all the employment terms and conditions.

Security and culture

Given the sensitive nature of the minutes from management meetings which are posted on to the intranet, the IS management within BL is clearly satisfied with the security of its intranet. As well as firewalls to the external world, access to confidential material is protected with passwords. Overall the BL will be experiencing a cultural change moving from paper-based output to all material eventually being published on-line. While staff notices and so forth are still printed, when the intranet has reached all BL staff the aim is to discontinue this practice altogether.

What is next?

There are no plans to develop the BL intranet with added extranet capabilities. Halcrow explains that the BL already has extensive links with European and other international libraries. Several significant ongoing projects on this front include the OPAC Network in Europe – geared towards providing public access to resources from libraries – an Internet information server for European libraries called Gabriel and CoBRA, a project with EU support to find ways of connecting all Europe's national libraries.

The benefits

There are a number of benefits the BL expects to gain from the intranet. Putting information on-line will save substantial amounts in terms of document reproduction and distribution. As mentioned earlier, the information resources on the BL largely comprise archive material. This is due to the vast amount of static information, to which BL staff need regular access. Providing this via a Web-based network, available through a commonly deployed browser, will assist greatly in the dissemination of such information. Training processes can also be given a boost through the intranet, with courses and materials to be made available for self-tuition.

The culture issue

Halcrow has identified a few challenges as the intranet has developed. An example of this is the predisposition among managers for e-mail usage, at the expense of using the newsgroups which have been set up. This is a by-product of the spontaneous development of Web usage among the user base. From the point of view of encouraging intranet usage – which Halcrow reports is on the increase generally – one challenge remains, to be patient and mature when demonstrating to managers what benefits can be derived from the network.

Chapter 16

Fostering information flow at Parsons Brinckerhoff

John Chow

The emphasis of this article is that corporate culture is a key component of ensuring that technical knowledge and information flow within an organization. The strength and commitment of a corporate culture is at least as important as the communications technologies implemented for knowledge-sharing.

If the corporate culture encourages and fosters the exchange of information among its people, then information will flow through whatever communications media are available, by phone, fax, videoconference, e-mail, groupware, intranet and Internet. However, if a culture of knowledge-sharing has not taken hold among the people working in the organization, then even the most technologically easy or advanced communications medium may not foster the flow of information.

This article demonstrates how one international engineering company, Parsons Brinckerhoff (PB), implemented a knowledge-sharing network and continues to foster a corporate culture that rewards the sharing of technical information. While a significant commitment of time, effort and money is usually required for an organization to develop its technical skills, the investment in developing culture at PB has been rewarding to its clients, the firm and the employees themselves.

This chapter then suggests four key components of a corporate culture that your organization could implement to better solve problems.

Assumptions

Efficient horizontal flow of information makes a stronger organization

A common theme in this book is that the efficient flow of information within an organization can create a stronger and more powerful operation. Smooth communication of information and know-how is essential, especially if the organization is contained in more than one location. It is likely that you are in an organization which could improve productivity by creating a corporate culture that encourages the sharing of technical information.

Traditionally, information has flowed vertically, along the same lines as the vertical hierarchical structure of an organization. Commands come down the chain of command from upper levels to lower levels. For example, suppose a worker such as an engineer needed assistance on a task from someone more experienced in the same skill or discipline, but did not know anyone with the appropriate knowledge. The worker traditionally had to communicate that need for assistance or information through the vertical organization. The request for information or skills generally had to flow up the chain of command, and then back down to find the parties with the knowledge. Then the response (i.e. the knowledge itself) had to flow back up and down the vertical chain to the engineer requesting it.

Corporate culture can encourage knowledge-sharing

A key component in causing knowledge to flow is creating a corporate culture which rewards people who share information. One way is to create knowledge-sharing networks. One important item to note is that, while a 'network' may connote computer technology, this network is first and foremost a network of people. When the people in the organization have a culture and desire to share information, it will happen more readily.

If your corporate culture can foster more direct communication horizontally within a discipline, then you create better links and knowledge can flow faster from people who have it to those who need it. The individuals who are empowered to share information will likewise gain knowledge and confidence. For the long-term health of the organization, it is critical that professional staff transfer their knowledge and skills to their colleagues.

Communications technology is a vehicle for knowledge-sharing

Once the corporate culture is in place and the people have formed their networks, they will communicate using whatever technology is available. There is no question that more advanced communications technology allows for more effective networking. Within a firm, the technology can evolve from local area networks (LANs) to wide area networks (WANs); from e-mail to groupware; from separate unconnected databases to powerful search engines working on a corporate database. Each technological advance makes it qualitatively easier to share information.

Introduction of knowledge-sharing networks

In 1995, in order to ensure that knowledge-sharing was reaching all levels of the organization, the technology transfer committees were transformed into networks call 'practice area networks' (PANs). Each PAN is a network of people working in the same discipline or practice area. Forty PANs were established in PB's key practice areas, which are primarily different fields of engineering for infrastructure planning, design and construction. The new networks or PANs were open to all staff at all levels. Because everybody has a different set of skills, expertise and experience, each person can join up to four PANs of their choosing. Each employee's PAN enrolment choices are stored and maintained on a corporate database along with their personnel data.

The mission of each network or PAN is to foster the horizontal flow of knowledge among the people in the PAN, and improve the professional training and mentoring available to the staff. A PAN ties together all professional staff who are either full-time or occasional practitioners within a specific discipline. Practice area networks provide significant and continual opportunities for individuals to interact and share similar training and skills, project experiences and professional interests.

Each PAN is given a budget and is led by a coordinating committee. The committee, headed by a coordinator, organizes the PAN's activities, such as:

- communication among PAN members
- newsletters and other mailings
- mentoring
- compilation of skills and projects
- review of technical software
- review of research and development needs
- dissemination of lessons learned.

Benefits from networks

After just two years, PB's PAN programme has fostered a heightened level of technical knowledge-sharing within the firm, and appears to be unique in the engineering industry. The PANs play a role in supporting the firm's vision statement: 'PB will become the preferred provider of infrastructure services – worldwide.' Networks are particularly helpful in a firm like PB, whose offices and staff are dispersed at many locations in different time zones all over the world. Practice area networks are well established among the US staff, and interest is growing strongly outside the USA, especially in offices in Europe and Asia.

One of the most effective ways that PANs take advantage of communications technology is to help professionals answer specific questions on their projects, similar to an Internet bulletin board. When an engineer faces a technical problem or question that he or she cannot solve with assistance from people he or she normally asks, he or she sends a brief e-mail synopsis of the question to the coordinator of the appropriate networks. For example: 'PB's Virginia office has been short-listed on an airport project, with the interview scheduled next week. The client has specifically requested information and PB experience in two specialized areas: airport access via water (ferry) and helicopter service. Please reply by Friday if possible.'

The coordinator forwards the message to some or all the members of the PAN. The PAN members know to respond directly to the original questioner with answers or suggestions. Useful responses come back within hours (sometimes even minutes), with additional responses trickling in over the next few days.

In another example, a PB office in California needed a junior-level travel forecaster with experience in a certain software package and level of experience to complete a project, because the previous staff person was leaving the firm. The Travel Forecasting PAN had previously conducted a survey of PAN members' skills, which listed a PB office location as having individuals with the appropriate experience in MINUTP software. E-mail to the New Jersey office led to the right person, who soon left for a two-week assignment in California to finish the modelling project.

According to the Travel Forecasting PAN coordinator, 'the PAN ... surely expedited the process – it took maybe fifteen minutes to arrange all this instead of probably several hours of phone calls and dead-ends. The system works'.

The system works because the questions are targeted to people who are likely to know – members of the appropriate PANs. People willingly respond because they recognize that they will be making similar requests themselves in the future, and because there is a corporate culture that encourages the exchange of information.

A corporate culture for knowledge-sharing

To be more responsive to the needs of our projects and clients, PB also employs other complementary programmes for learning, maintaining and transferring state-of-the-art skills and techniques, which are implemented cooperatively by several corporate departments. The programmes encourage employees to grow technically, professionally and personally, and are championed at the highest levels of management, Some key programmes include:

- a one-to-one mentoring programme to provide counselling on career opportunities
- a programme to prioritize and deliver training of technical (engineering) topics to the networks who need it and to help staff keep their skills at the state-of-the-practice
- 'professional recognition' programme, awarding 'Professional Associate' titles to key staff with specialized expertise

- annual technical exchange seminars (two-day retreats with lectures, workshops and opportunities to network) for groups of Professional Associates
- designation of 'Technical Director' titles to the select world-class experts in their disciplines
- a Project Management Development programme, providing training and certifications for project managers and project administrators
- development of in-house manuals of standards and guides for various engineering disciplines such as *PB Project Management Manual*, *PB Quality Manual*, *Electrical Engineering Manual*
- a research and development programme, with opportunities for company-paid funding to professionals to pursue research ideas with applicability to PB's project work
- the William Barclay Parsons Fellowship programme, named after the firm's founder, with funding for one outstanding research fellow each year
- a general technical newsletter (*PB Network*) and separate technical newsletters from each of the PANs, containing articles written, compiled and edited by engineers
- a total quality management programme, which has been instrumental in the ISO 9001 quality certification of many PB offices.

Use of communications technology

With a strong corporate culture fostering knowledge-sharing, the professionals in the firm are taking advantage of the available communications tools. Most of the PAN communication today takes place over the phone, hard-copy newsletters and e-mail. Video-conferencing facilities are also available in-house at approximately twenty offices, and staff at other locations can participate at public video-conferencing rooms. Each new communications technology can be superimposed on the strong interpersonal infrastructure of the people network.

Microsoft Mail is the firm's standard for e-mail, with roughly 90 per cent of the global staff connected to PB's WAN, and most with direct access to the 'Global Address List' in late 1997. Most of the remaining staff send and receive Internet e-mail through third-party service providers. Examples of successful e-mail queries like the ones cited above are abundant.

Groupware in the form of Microsoft Exchange is being rolled out in 1997–98, with roughly one-third of the global staff having access to Exchange in late 1997. The public folders of Microsoft Exchange have been organized to provide another vehicle for PANs to share information. There is one public folder for PAN, and within that folder is a folder for each PAN, containing folders for technical discussions and for reference documents.

Many documents (including reports, manuals, standards, resumes, descriptions of projects) are located in the Microsoft Exchange public folders. Employees can search for documents containing key words using search engines with Boolean logic capabilities such as Fulcrum Find.

Once a majority of the staff gain access to Microsoft Exchange, it is envisioned that many of the technical discussions and queries that are occurring now by e-mail will take place in PAN discussion folders. The advantages of discussions in groupware folders compared with e-mail are:

- The queries can be read by everyone who opens the folder, not just PAN members who receive the e-mail query.
- All responses can be seen by all who open the folder, and a dialogue can take place among many participants.
- The dialogue and technical information can be preserved in the public folder for review by others with similar questions later.

A PB Website (http://www.pbworld.com) contains basic information about the PANs, as well as corporate publications and other information. Additional Websites are being used to facilitate electronic communication within joint ventures, with clients and with the public, when public participation or notification is required on projects.

The technology will continue to change rapidly and the

organization, including the networks, will be given new tools to share knowledge and information.

Elements of a corporate culture for technology transfer

This section suggests four key elements of a corporate culture for fostering effective technology transfer in your organization. Each element is followed by a specific action you can take in the implementation phase.

1. Identify the technical skills that are important to the mission of your organization

Technology transfer takes time, effort and money. It is therefore important for management to identify at the outset which technical skills warrant the commitment of resources.

2. Enhance and build your technical expertise in those skills

Once areas of technical development are selected, you must evaluate how much expertise your staff has in those areas and then build upon those skills:

- Identify key people, publish their names in a special directory of key resources and distribute it to everyone in the organization.
- Create a career track recognizing technical proficiency.
- Assign a special title to these key staff that indicates their technical skills and levels.
- Among the key staff, designate one person as the technical focal point for each discipline and provide a budget to support their work.
- Encourage key staff to participate directly in other technology transfer activities.

While the key staff may receive more attention in developing their skills, the skills and technical know-how must not reside solely with them.

3. Create networks to encourage the sharing of ideas and techniques among all staff. Use whatever technology is appropriate to facilitate the flow of information

- Establish a coordinating committee to lead the network.
- Have them develop resource materials such as descriptions of project applications, manuals of standard work procedures and lists of specialized software.
- Develop a mentoring programme.
- Publish newsletters describing innovative work, written by technical staff themselves.
- Sponsor in-technical seminars for exchanging ideas.
- Involve the network leaders in decisions about new communications technology. They will be among the most active users.

4. Encourage and reward creativity, quality, and excellence in the work product among all staff

- Establish a research and development fund.
- Establish a fellowship programme for the best proposed applications of new techniques, with funding and recognition for the winners.
- Establish a separate training budget for staff to learn and use state-of-the-art techniques to effectively solve problems.

<u>Conclusion</u>

As PB expands under its five-year strategic plan, an array of programmes will help maintain a strong corporate culture among the many new employees and practice areas of the firm. That culture must foster openness, inclusiveness, teamwork and technical excellence, while encouraging staff to grow technically, professionally and personally.

If a corporate culture for knowledge-sharing has taken hold among the people in the organization, then as a company's communications technology expands and modernizes, the exchange of information will gravitate toward whatever new technologies are effective.

Chapter 17

Virtual learning at City University Business School

Clive Holtham

Introduction

Historically and currently, most use of collaborative technologies in higher education is for distance education. In the case reviewed here, asynchronous technologies are used with full-time students who normally work in face-to-face mode. Our central concern has been the extent to which active use of collaborative technology can significantly enhance learning in the business studies context. To meet this objective we have designed new methods of student work and collaboration using intranet and similar technologies.

Context

The focus here is on students of business, both postgraduate (MBA) and undergraduate (BSc). Conventional learning takes place via lectures, assignments, private study and face-to-face group work. All of these are valuable for different reasons, and are interdependent. Having carried out considerable research in the business use of collaborative technologies,[1] there were two separate reasons for wanting to use them with business students:

1. It involved new practical skills, valued by both the students and their prospective employers.
2. It offered the prospect of more efficient and/or more effective learning.

The primary concern in this review is with the second of these – more efficient and effective learning. Our starting point is therefore that computer-supported learning methods are not intrinsically more effective or more economic than traditional methods. What we have sought to examine therefore, is under what circumstances either or both of these assumptions might be disproved. How can computers actually improve learning?

Cooperative learning

Perhaps as a natural extension of Western democratic thinking, and certainly as a result of the less hierarchical approach to education which has prevailed since the 1960s, there has been a growth of interest in cooperative learning, especially in primary and secondary education. In business schools, group work has for decades been a central feature of the curriculum and style.

Higher education has not always been aware of the research and development work carried out at primary and secondary levels and as a result of its case study traditions runs the risk of using only a subset of the possible approaches to groupwork.

Within an MBA programme in particular there is a further problem, namely that the overall workload, with multiple parallel groups, makes the sheer logistics of organizing face-to-face meetings a non-trivial exercise.

Proposition

The idea that emerged at City University Business School in 1993–94 was to examine the scope for creating a cooperative, computer-based virtual learning environment. This would use either or both of intranet and Lotus Notes technologies. The following stages were envisaged:

1. Student carries out an individual study into a particular topic or organization.
2. The individual work is entered into a form and thence stored on a shared database.
3. Students are divided into teams of ten to twenty. Each team member reads the individual work of their colleagues, and the team then has to carry out an electronic dialogue to develop a team answer.

4. Students are marked wholly individually – for their individual work and for their individual inputs to support meeting team objectives.

The overall size of student group involved varies from 100 to 180, and we have in practice used teams either of about ten members or about twenty members. The approach has been used over three academic years with both MBA postgraduates and undergraduates. In the first exercise, intranet technology was used exclusively by the students, but at the end of the exercise all material was 'reverse-engineered' into Notes, so that a comparison could be made of the two approaches.

This comparison was very favourable to Lotus Notes due to:

- ease of development
- greatly enhanced information management capability, particularly the scope for multiple 'views' of the data.

On the other hand, Notes has a GUI (graphical user interface) which is not familiar to most students, and has more complex system administration demands. In the event, Lotus's development of Domino has meant that Notes can be a Web server, thus effectively eliminating the distinction between the two.

Learning objectives

These have varied from course to course but have essentially involved:

1. The ability to find and select a sensible topic from paper and/or electronic source.
2. Developing skills in analysing cases against frameworks.
3. Abstracting and summarizing cases for third party readers.
4. Applying business related judgements to the cases.
5. Understanding how to work in asynchronous computer supported teams.

It is perhaps easy to overestimate the novelty of this approach because it uses a modern computer support. Items 2 and 4 above lie at the heart of traditional business case study work. We regard item 3 as an essential skill in the electronic era, but is not unique to this exercise. Students still often continue to find the more discursive essay style easier than this component (used only for part of their input) where brevity and summarization skills are at a premium. Item 1 is a generic skill, although in this course students are certainly forced to become familiar with in-depth Web searching, with searching electronic journals particularly the Business Publications Online collection used at the school, and with combining a picture of a company from both paper and electronic sources. This leaves only item 5 as particularly novel, and even then students are at least used to synchronous team-working.

Database-discussion linkage

Where this exercise most differs from traditional methods is in the fact that students are sharing their individual coursework in a standardized format with each other, as well as the course leader. Also, they are grounding their team discussions not, as often happens, in cases written by third parties, but in ones they have written themselves. It is also possible readily to share not only the ten to twenty cases of any individual team, but also the 100–180 of the whole class. Both of these would be difficult using wholly essay-based, paper-based methods. It is of central significance to this type of virtual learning community that individual work is entered into a database with a combination of keyword/checkbox responses, of short text entries, and finally of truncated essay-style responses. The use of a database means that teams of students can view their work in aggregate in a way that would be difficult by conventional methods. They can also use full text and Boolean searches of both team and especially the full-class database. The latter makes the aggregates of 180 students' work a valuable resource, e.g. for subsequent project work.

The use of individually created databases as a shared resource means that the subsequent electronic discussions are rooted in individual study, and this makes for a much richer dialogue. A minority of students became quite proprietorial about 'their' case relative to others. But the majority are more open minded and very willing to compare and contrast. We were struck by the care with which most students read and analysed their colleagues' work. One of the database entries asked the students to rate, on a scale of one to ten, the overall significance of the case to the topic being studied. Some of these assessments led to active discussion and disagreement, but most of the time students placed great value on their colleagues' judgement and this helped in filtering down to a smaller number of most significant ones.

Discussions

Over many years we observed that asynchronous electronic discussion groups that exhibit many of the characteristics of defective face-to-face groups – failure to achieve critical mass of inputs, overdominance by a few participants, unfocused and unclosed discussions. These seem to occur regardless of technology. Usenet, Notes and intranet-based groups can all suffer from the same problems. This made us particularly anxious to develop an approach which was at the very least rich in content – hence the use of databases. The discussion periods are deliberately kept fairly short – one to three weeks – and during these periods groups have to reach some collective conclusions. For example, 'Which three of your cases are most significant to the overall topic?' and 'Identify three barriers to businesses adopting this approach'.

Students are very aware that they are being assessed individually during the discussions. In addition to the thread and sequential views of the discussion, students can view by individual contributions (across all threads) which is the basis that the assessor will use later to evaluate them. Students are advised on minimum and maximum contribution rates. The minimum is about two per working day of the discussion. It is constantly emphasized that it is not the volume of contributions that matters, but the quality – above all how well the contributions help the teams to converge on their final group answers. *No marks are awarded at all for these group answers.* These are effectively a device to ensure focus, convergence and closure of the asynchronous discussion.

We believe that these forms of structuring of both the individual and team input have been critical in developing successful virtual learning communities. There are clear advantages available to us in undertaking this type of exercise. First, compared to a business environment, we can achieve compulsory inputs on both the case study and discussion sides. Second, there is a relatively hierarchical course leader who very explicitly makes clear the exact performance criteria that are expected and who later produces quantitative rewards and penalties in the form of marks. Third, compared to traditional distance learning IT support, most students are accessing the databases and discussions over a local area network. This has major positive implications for processing speed and the ability to include multimedia and students are not concerned with the cost of phone calls. The use of computer terminals is not trouble free, especially due to physical availability of machines, but it does at least ensure all students on the cohort are physically connected to all aspects of electronic media required, not only for collaborative work, but also to the Web and in the library for electronic journals.

It is also interesting to examine the connection between use of the formal computer conferencing system and forms of communication. Students were assessed on their contribution to the electronic discussion, but there was nothing to prevent them supplementing this with other media. The more skilful groups appeared to make a good parallel use of e-mail, and there were certainly some groups that felt it necessary to meet physically. Especially skilful groups ensured that, where relevant, key elements of these parallel communications were repeated in the computer conferencing system.

Conclusion

In reviewing the students' formal output at the end of the exercises, it is clear that for most students the exercise is worthwhile in acquiring important business skills. More importantly, the learning method involved does lead to a broader and deeper level of student insight into the topic than from individual coursework. It is more difficult to compare the asynchronous group working with what could be achieved via face-to-face group working. Very few students had prior experience of any form of computer conferencing, and therefore much of the early electronic discussion was spent in conferencing skill development. On average about 15 per cent of students disliked the medium as a form of group communications, perhaps not surprisingly in a face-to-face institution. As in previous studies of virtual learning, this form of group working enables students to reveal different skills profiles. In general it was favourably received by students for whom English was not a first language; they value the ability to read and to compose answers at their own pace. It still remains the case that some team members contribute more than others or are more effective in securing convergence of team thinking. But they may be different from those who perform the same roles in face-to-face discussion.

Our experiences with this very specific form of virtual learning community suggests, first, that close attention needs to be paid to the design of the individual and group inputs, and to their interrelationships. With the type of interaction used here, it was of great significance that the database was used to collate and represent the individual work. Second, a valuable role for virtual learning has been identified even within a face-to-face educational environment. This partly derives from a functional need for students to develop virtual working skills. More substantially it provides a different form of learning experience and an additional form of group interaction. Its strength, however, lies much more in augmenting traditional face-to-face group methods than in replacing them.

Since this work has not been concerned with wholly asynchronous learning communities, it may not be valid to extrapolate these experiences more generally. It certainly is likely that the highly structured approach to individual work will be more generally applicable. But the lack of media richness (even with advanced multimedia) and the social drivers for physical meeting are likely to continue to favour face-to-face environments. However, we have observed many students who learnt how to use computer conferencing very rapidly. So it could be that this generation may also be more adaptable to largely asynchronous work and learning than current business generations.

Note

1. Holtham, C. (1992) Improving the performance of workgroups through information technology. City University Business School Working Paper.

Chapter 18

Intra- and extra-netting at the Boeing Company

Anthony H. Kim

Introduction

With the Internet firmly entrenched as a vital component of the business landscape the question remains: what are companies really doing to leverage the Internet and all of its various capabilities? Whether it is used as an internal communications tool, a link to business partners and customers, a marketing vehicle or a high-technology sales aid, the potential benefits are numerous.

While most companies already leverage Internet technology (i.e. a corporate Website or 'brochureware') the usage is frequently limited to brand-building and public relations. Boeing, however, has taken the Internet to the next level by incorporating two similar technological adaptations of the Internet, intranets and extranets, which both serve different purposes and are managed independently. With these two implementations, Boeing is 'netting' some significant benefits.

Intranets: the beginning

Late in 1993 at the Seattle headquarters of the Boeing Company, a group of engineers and researchers attempted to make sense of a graphical portal to the Internet known as Mosaic. Though still nascent, the group felt that it had all the tools for an inexpensive network that would allow its employees to easily share information. During the intranet initiative's infancy, Boeing's senior management wanted a business case made for the project. However, the group who headed the initiative, could not easily identify the benefits of the Web. 'How do you put a price on information? It's like trying to find an ROI for the telephone when it first appeared,' said Joe Meadows, one of the founders of the Boeing web and Product Manager for Proxy Services at Boeing's Information Support Services division. Instead, the Boeing 'web-masters' emphasized low cost and high flexibility to upper management. The idea of enabling any user, on any platform, to access and view documents, share information and exchange e-mail caught the attention of senior executives and enabled Boeing to create a 'pull' information system, rather than pushing information out to employees.[1] In essence, Boeing has implemented a corporate intranet because it can enhance corporate communication. The enthusiastic participation of employees at all levels and from different business units is indicative of the system's capabilities and why the intranet is thriving at Boeing.

Intranet benefits are:

- central information source
- data sharing
- training
- exchanging of ideas.

Intranets: applications

Several observers of Boeing's intranet are calling it the standard by which corporate intranets will be measured. The connectivity capabilities are far-reaching and utilized by various groups within Boeing, including CEO Philip Condit. The way the intranet enhances corporate communication, is to provide a network within Boeing's organization to facilitate information exchange on all fronts. With improving internal communication as its theme, Boeing's intranet has evolved into the primary vehicle for accomplishing that goal in a corporate sense. Improving communication by using the intranet can be accomplished in several ways. Communicating within an organization is no longer relegated to face-to-face meetings, internal paper memos or even e-mail. Chat rooms, on-line continuing education and training, video interaction, project updates and initiatives ... these are just some of the ways in which Boeing has been able to exploit the communication advantages of the Internet through its intranet.

The Boeing internal Website has already facilitated two of
last year's biggest deals for the company. Boeing is building its
intranet for ten years on when much of its business will be conducted over the Web. It has followed a plan that calls for decentralized content creation and delegated authority for many policy
and technical issues. While other large corporations have extensive Web installations, none have moved as quickly as Boeing in
making the Web and applications instantly available, according
to vendors and integrators familiar with Boeing's installation.
'Boeing is the biggest (corporate intranet),' says Srivats
Sampath, Netscape Communications' Vice President of Product
Marketing for Servers. 'Boeing is one of the leading companies to
see the benefits of standards-based computing and is ahead of
the pack in truly leveraging that benefit.' The user numbers are
impressive: Boeing has wired more than 50,000 employee workstations to the Web.

The company offers users a choice of Internet browsers and
provides full Web access to a growing legion of information
workers, all with no restriction on use. New users board the
Boeing intranet at a rate of 500 per week. A corporate policy
adopted in September 1995 makes the Boeing intranet the
primary means for information sharing within the enterprise.
The ultimate goal is to provide unrestricted access for up to
200,000 employees. Administration of Web technologies and
policy runs on an estimated $1 million budget; yet it was not
dollars and cents that encouraged Boeing to take a hands-off
approach. 'The Web is not very structured, and we don't want to
overstructure,' says M. Graeber Jordan, Senior Manager of
Electronic Commerce Deployment for Boeing's Information and
Support Services. 'We don't want to stifle it by managing it to
death. We're trying to find the balance between putting the tool
in the hands of a process business unit and providing the right
sort of guidance.'[2]

Wing Responsibility Centre
One major application of the intranet is Boeing's use of it as the
primary communications tool for its Wing Responsibility Centre
(WRC), an organization created roughly one year ago to build
wings, tails and rudders for the company's commercial airline

and defence units. Where it once would have spent millions relocating workers from all over Washington state, WRC management now brings those people together via its intranet. The WRC site features a customized search engine and specifications for all of its parts. Any WRC employee can reach even the most senior manager via the intranet. Chuck Kahler, the executive in charge, sees the Web as the glue for an organization that is expected to net the company billions of dollars over the next ten years.

Dozens of sites on the company's intranet already make content available to employees, including the Web version of its spare-part ordering and inventory system, employee news service and a library. In addition to what is already available via the intranet, Boeing has recently enabled 150,000 employees to access Web-based forms to access human resource records such as health benefits and enrolment data. There is not only a substantial saving in the handling and processing of paperwork and data entry, but streamlining these tasks through the intranet also frees people's time to do more professional-oriented jobs.[3]

'Boeing is using the Web technology to make massive organization changes in culture and communication,' says Dr Eric Schaeffer, President of Human Factors International, Inc., which is the firm that helped develop the WRC interface. 'In the past, MIS systems were used to provide the information or complete functions. On a visionary level, Boeing is using the Web as a way to support organizational change.' *Experts say Boeing's approach to intranet management could become the norm for IT departments at the world's largest corporations.* Says one IT consultant:

They use a distributed management approach, and frankly, that's the only way to do it. The issue is content. If you have IT people managing content, they would do nothing else but manage phone lists, product descriptions and human resources information. The content has got to be delegated to the divisions because that's where the accountability is.

Boeing Centre for Leadership and Learning

Another recent intranet initiative concerns the Boeing Centre for Leadership and Learning. The centre's executives determined that an intranet would be the best way for Boeing's 8,500 senior executives to get information about training and continuing education courses offered through the centre. So with the aid of Boeing webmaster, Rikel Getty, Boeing sought to implement rich course descriptions along with video and clips for its intranet. 'The true value of the intranet,' says Getty, 'is personalized information access.' This idea can be summed up in the group's *de facto* motto: 'Give people just enough information, just in time and just for them.' Getty stresses the intranet is 'not just a paper catalogue on-line'. Because of the integration of video and audio, Boeing executives can click into course lectures on the intranet that they would otherwise have missed.[4] By giving executives an additional tool to communicate with one another, the Boeing corporate message and vision can be shared and solidified.

At Boeing, a chat forum called Open Mind is a popular user application. Senior management places great emphasis on knowledge-sharing, and Open Mind has become a reservoir of corporate 'knowledge assets'. Due to the popularity of Open Mind, Boeing created Boeing Live Chat, which is a daily interactive chat group that takes place during the company's west coast lunch hour. Top executives eagerly dive into such timely topics as 'retraining skilled employees', 'employee–management communication' and 'diversity training'. Boeing officials are hopeful that the centre's achievements with its intranet will spark participation from other sectors of the company. Boeing feels that its intranet is a positive instrument that not only brings its company closer to the 'brass ring', but also will be ultimately an epicentre for change and an example for other organizations to emulate.[5]

In addition to executive training, Boeing has also begun using its intranet for the training of the rest of Boeing's employees. The company's corporate intranet delivers seven 'channels' of training and news. One channel features managers from Boeing divisions around the world presenting their best manufacturing practices/information that would not be shared otherwise. Through the use of RealVideo, an Internet-based video application, across its corporate intranet, employees now have access to a new, live and on-demand medium for training and corporate communication. 'Video and audio technology deliver a simultaneous increase in accessibility and decrease in programme costs that is a rare and valuable combination from an introduction to a new technology,' commented one senior Boeing executive.

'Delivering video over the Internet and corporate intranets may be the killer application for the late 1990s and beyond,' states Larry Gerbrandt, Senior Vice President, Paul Kagen Associates Inc. 'The challenge is to make video as pervasive on the Internet and corporate intranets as text is today, irrespective of the size of the pipes over which they move.' A recent International Data Corporation study concludes that intranet-based training is the fastest growing segment of the training industry. The International Data Corporation predicts that spending on intranet-based spending will increase 525 per cent by the year 2000.

While spending on intranet-based training may increase at Boeing, cost-savings are also being found. The use of video on the Boeing intranet is decreasing the costs associated with duplicating and distributing videotapes to employees. Prior to the adoption of video, Boeing was spending significant time and money duplicating and shipping several hundred videocassettes to employees each week. In addition to cost-savings associated with video-intranet capability, employees benefit from on-demand access to training videos via the intranet. Boeing employees are currently able to choose from a variety of topics such as 'The Stock Market and the Impact on Boeing' and 'Managing for Value'. Employees can also access video of guest speakers talking about key business competencies.[6]

Extranets

The purpose of an extranet at companies such as Boeing is quite simple: Extranets enable companies to give their business partners and customers secure access to critical information formerly available only to employees. The primary benefits of an extranet are reduced transaction costs, freeing employees' time for other higher 'value-add' tasks, and improved process efficiencies and relations with business partners and customers. The reason why Boeing is one of the leaders of this technology is because it has implemented a large-scale extranet initiative in a relatively quick time span and turned it into a success story based on feedback from customers.

Extranet benefits are:
- reduced costs
- free employee time for other tasks
- improved process efficiencies
- improved customer relations.

Introduction: PART page

The Part Analysis and Requirement Tracking (PART) page is an extranet that allows Boeing's commercial customers to place and track spare-parts orders over the Internet. Using the Boeing website, a customer can query Boeing's spare parts IMS database by type of part or by location of that part on the aircraft. After finding the right part, a customer can then order it by locating the closest warehouse stocking the part. The new set-up is designed to enable Boeing's customers to easily locate what they need, which is no small task considering Boeing houses over 2 million different spare parts. The Boeing website includes links to both Federal Express and UPS so that a customer can track a part after it has been shipped. In addition, if the closest Boeing warehouse is too far away, a customer can use the Boeing website to look for alternative parts from one of Boeing's suppliers.[7]

Customer relations

While still in development in early 1996, Boeing invited representatives from three nearby customers to its Seattle headquarters to act as consultants on a beta version of PART page. Those consultants helped refine the interface to make it as responsive and useful as possible. The site was then presented to 300 customers at an October 1996 symposium in Seattle.[8] Boeing's WorldWide Web listing appeared shortly thereafter. This brief history lesson illustrates Boeing's concern for customers' needs with regards to this new tool. Boeing did not assume that what it thought was best. The company focused on understanding the word partnership with its customer.

After determining internal goals, companies, such as Boeing, must then coordinate with their trading partners' business goals. All interests, Boeing felt, had to be aligned before proceeding any further. It was something as simple as having the forethought of taking the time to create something its customers wanted and needed and prioritizing their customers' interests which has helped make Boeing's PART page a success. Since its WWW listing, Boeing has had more than 150,000 enquiries and orders and Boeing officials expect the number of hits to jump to over 500,000 by year end 1997. About 95 per cent of the page's 2,500 daily transactions are enquiries about such things as part availability, lead time for orders, the status of shipments or the interchangeability of one part for another. Only 5 per cent of the hits are for actual orders, but they have amounted to $25 million in revenue since the inception.[9]

'We are very satisfied with the webpage,' says Chris Colom, Manager of Purchasing at Alaska Airlines. 'The use of this technology has eliminated the need for us to phone/fax requirements for quoting, order placement and expediting. This frees up our staff, enabling them to manage other processes.'[10] By itself, he says, Boeing's PART page saves his department about twenty-five person-hours per month, lowers phone bills, and reduces the number of hard copies sent back and forth.[11] Is it any wonder that all of Alaska Airlines' Boeing purchases are handled through the Boeing website?[12]

With this type of customer-intimate model, Boeing will continue to benefit. 'I don't think they can lose with this. For the airlines that are purchasing these spare parts it's going to allow them to get the parts more quickly,' says Blane Erwin, Director of Business Trade and Technology at Forrester Research. Mr Erwin feels that it is unlikely the Boeing extranet will help Boeing win new customers, but it will help them service and retain their existing customers better. 'This is not going to be the single deciding factor for someone like Delta to decide to buy Boeing aircraft,' Mr Erwin says. 'But it deepens the relationship with customers and it significantly lowers the cost and speeds up the delivery of ordering spare parts.'[13]

Reduced costs and enhanced efficiencies

What the PART page allows even the largest of Boeing customers to do is to easily dig through all purchasing, invoicing and receipt data to find exactly what they want. 'By deploying desktop purchasing within the enterprise, we estimate that companies can reduce the cost of creating and processing a purchase order by more than 90 per cent per order,' says Daniel Aegerter, President and CEO of TRADE'ex, an electronic commerce software firm. 'Automating the process also allows buyer productivity to improve, because with procurement they now can concentrate on higher level activities like negotiating vendor contracts and evaluating potential suppliers instead of handling mundane, repetitive tasks.'[14]

'We did not put this facility [PART page] in to make money,' says Tom DiMarco, the Senior Manager in the Airline Logistics Support Division of Boeing's commercial airline group. 'We did it to expedite the process of servicing airplanes and to keep them moving. And every order we don't have to key in is cost savings for us.' Other Boeing officials concurred with DiMarco's sentiment: 'It costs the airlines about $40,000 per minute to have a plane like the 747 on the ground when it's supposed to be flying,' notes Craig Savio, Director of Technical Data Processing at Boeing's Commercial Airline Group.[15] Mr DiMarco cannot put a dollar figure on the cost savings the PART page has yielded, but feels that the investment was minimal relative to its payback. 'The site easily pays for itself in increased efficiency and cost avoidance,' states DiMarco. Because employees spend less time on administrative tasks like keying in orders, they are free to spend more time on real issues. 'We don't have to answer questions like "When is this going to be shipped?" or "When it is shipped, what air bill will it go on?", he explains. 'Instead, we can answer questions like: "How do we address this certain part availability problem? Do we have to generate exotic materials to finish this order?" We can really tackle engineering problems now rather than simple administrative information-exchange problems.'[16]

Of Boeing's 700 customers, approximately seventy use EDI systems to place orders and control inventories. Electronic data interchange enables standardized document forms to be exchanged between two businesses' computer systems. As good as EDI is, the primary drawback is that EDI systems require special hardware and software, and are ultimately too expensive for many companies, including many of Boeing's customers. The 10 per cent of Boeing's customers that have EDI account for 60 per cent of Boeing's spare-parts transactions. What the PART extranet has done, is to enable non-EDI customers with what amounts to a front-end window to Boeing's Spares Ordering Nonstop Inventory Control (SONIC) system. As a result, customers have to make fewer phone calls and send fewer faxes and telexes, and Boeing avoids a great deal of data entry. So far, over 300 of Boeing's 700 customers use the PART system, and have done $40 million's worth of business through the site.[17]

But as electronic commerce moves beyond the traditional value-added network (VAN) sphere by leveraging the Internet, the business benefits include lower costs and more flexible systems. (A VAN is a communications network that provides services beyond normal transmission, such as automatic error detection and correction, protocol conversion and message storing.) Eventually, this will culminate into more efficient relationships with a wider range of suppliers, partners and customers. The Boeing PART page is a perfect example of the benefits of the Internet. Before the system was installed, only the largest twenty to thirty customers were on-line with Boeing's EDI system. The remainder of Boeing's customers had to order parts by fax, telephone and e-mail, using thick, hard-copy catalogues. The process was slow and cumbersome mainly because of the sheer paperwork involved. The voluminous paperwork also meant that more mistakes were made because information had to be rekeyed from a faxed order into the Boeing system. By leveraging the Internet with electronic commerce, Boeing can offer all, or at least the majority, of its customers a better purchasing system, which requires less time, effort and headache. Loyalty and business relations have strengthened and increased as Boeing's extranet manifests its benefits in the form of reduced costs for not only Boeing, but for its partners and customers as well.

Another benefit of the Internet is the cost factor. Traditionally, VAN providers charged for EDI on a per-transmission basis and as a result, corporations tended to batch transactions and send them all together in one big transmission at the end of the day. But with the Internet, all connect charges are fixed. So now Boeing sends transmissions whenever it wants with no premium and subsequent near real-time commerce.[18] By utilizing Internet technology and applying it in the form of an extranet, Boeing is lowering its cost of doing business and improving the related processes by shortening purchasing cycles and increasing the ease of purchasing.

Conclusion

The Boeing Company is an example of a Fortune 500 company which is at the forefront of leveraging technology, and specifically the Internet. While other large players dread and bemoan the evolution of the corporate culture or processes, Boeing welcomes it, learns from it and aims to improve the business for itself and its business partners. Boeing has been proactive in attempting to harness a portion of the seemingly limitless opportunities the Internet has to offer to aid in this evolution. Whether it be the corporate standard for Internet application, or a trailblazer for other companies to learn from and surpass, one thing is for certain: Boeing is accomplishing multiple tasks such as enhancing corporate communication and information sharing, solidifying business relationships and reducing process costs and doing them well, with the same technology that is available to other companies.

Notes

1. Moeller, M. (1996) Boeing network takes flight with pioneering intranet project. *PC Week*, **13**, (7),
2. Frook, J. E. (1997) Boeing intranet takes off. *Communications Week*, 27 January, 1.
3. (1997) Companies look to web for internal answers. *Electronic Commerce News*, **2**, (10).
4. Paul, L. G. (1996) Flying the intranet skies. *PC Week*, **13**, (48), 62.
5. Ibid.
6. (1997) Boeing deploys progressive networks' realvideo across corporate intranet. *PR Newswire*, 6 May.
7. McCarthy, V. and Varney, S. E. (1997) E-commerce: wired for profits. *Datamation*, **42**, (16), 42.
8. Court, R. (1997) Automatic pilot. *InSite*, 40.
9. Mecham, M. (1997) Boeing scores a hit with WWW parts listing. *Aviation Week and Space Technology*, **146**, (26), 60.

10. Teasdale, S. (1997) Netmarketing: case study: Boeing extranet speeds ordering process for spare-parts buyers. *Business Marketing*, 1 July, 31.
11. Court, Automatic pilot.
12. Teasdale, Netmarketing.
13. Ibid.
14. (1997) TRADE'ex debuts procurement application for enterprise-wide MRO 'Desktop Purchasing' at COMDEX. *Business Wire*, 2 June.
15. McCarthy and Vance, E-commerce, p. 42.
16. Court, Automatic pilot, p. 40.
17. Ibid.
18. McCarthy and Vance, E-commerce, p. 42.

Chapter 19

Virtual Teamwork at British Petroleum[1]

Ernst & Young

Introduction

When equipment failure brought operations to a halt on a North Sea mobile drilling ship one day in 1995, the ship's drilling engineers hauled the faulty hardware in front of a tiny video camera connected to one of British Petroleum's Virtual Teamwork stations. Using a satellite link, they dialled up the Aberdeen office of a drilling equipment expert who was able to examine the malfunctioning part visually while talking to the shipboard engineers. He quickly diagnosed the problem and guided them through the necessary repairs. A shutdown that, in the past, would have meant flying an expert out by helicopter or would have sent the ship (leased at a cost of $150,000 a day) back to port and kept it out of commission for several days, lasted only a few hours.

The equipment aboard the ship was one of the stations installed by British Petroleum (BP) in 1995 as part of their Virtual Teamwork pilot programme. The aim of the project was to explore the benefits of using sophisticated technology to link employees and contractors who needed to share work or expertise: to create virtual teams across the barriers of distance and organizational structure.

New federation required creative communication

British Petroleum's Virtual Teamwork (VT) programme was the result of new initiatives following the company's reorganization into forty-two separate business assets. The corporate vision was to become a 'possibility searching company'. Believing that smaller, semi-autonomous businesses could work more efficiently and creatively, Managing Director John Browne oversaw the transformation of the company into what he described as 'a federation of assets', each of which would have the freedom to develop processes and solutions to met its own local needs.

This idea of a federated business structure is similar to the 'multilocal' structure Nonaka and Takeuchi describe in their book, *The Knowledge Creating Company*. Nonaka and Takeuchi remark on 'the importance of transcending the dichotomy between localization and globalization', an apt description of Browne's aim.[2] British Petroleum would, in effect, be able to draw on the variety and creative power of forty-two moderate-sized companies, sharing their particular talents and experiences.

In addition to creating a federated structure, it was also decided to outsource work that was not part of BP Exploration's core activities, to which its expertise could not meaningfully add value. For instance, the generation and processing of seismic data was handed off to several outside companies; but the interpretation of the data generated was kept in the hands of BP staff whose knowledge and experience were needed to evaluate it. This division of labour meant that skilled BP personnel were able to concentrate on the tasks that most clearly required and benefited from their special expertise. It also brought outside companies into the federation, enlarging BP's network of available resources and its stock of knowledge. British Petroleum sees these relationships with outsourcers as learning opportunities, not just commercial alliances.

Because of the newly distributed business structure, good communication tools and practices would be essential to the success of the new federation. British Petroleum's headquarters needed a way to manage the necessary coordination; the business units needed ways to communicate the creative results of their relative independence and to draw on the company's global expertise to solve local problems.

One such communication tool considered was video-conferencing. Browne and others understood its potential for fostering some of the creative synergy they hoped for from a federated organization. They approved funds for an eighteen-month Virtual Teamwork pilot project to test new communication tools and practices and their willingness to commit these funds (and future funds, if the pilot proved successful) was an indication of BP's focus on value generation, not cost-cutting.

The Virtual Teamwork pilot project was launched

A core team independent of IT

Although the pilot project's group work was laid by the then head of IT, it was decided that the project should be run by a core team which was independent of the IT division for several reasons:

1. To offer the benefit of the perspective of a new group. A new group should be less likely to fall into familiar IT patterns which had proven less than effective in rapid development of new applications.
2. To keep the emphasis on business change and corporate behaviour, not technology.
3. To recognize that using virtual teamworking to cross organizational boundaries may be better served by a group drawn from across all of the company.

A core team of five was appointed, most of whom had had experience in more than one business area. From the outset their focus was on connecting people who had complementary expertise with each other, rather than on gathering or publishing information. The core team was to focus on building a network of people, not a storehouse of data. 'Openness to the unexpected' was one of the operating principles of the core team.

Decision on technologies

The core team specified hardware and software for Virtual Teamwork stations or 'clients' which included:

- desktop video-conferencing equipment
- multimedia e-mail
- application sharing
- shared chalkboards
- tools to record videoclips
- groupware
- web browser
- document scanner
- network connections (via ISDN [integrated services digital network] over standard telephone lines and, when necessary, through satellite links).

For the pilot, the team decided to use Virtual Teamwork clients on five separate projects. The five project communities were chosen on the basis of two principles. One was that they have a clear operational goal. The second was that there be enough variety among the projects to test virtual teamworking in different situations and to leave room for unanticipated benefits to develop.

The five projects were the Andrew Project group, completing a new drilling platform onshore for an emerging offshore oilfield; a mature oilfield group; an established network of experts who had already been communicating with each other by e-mail, newsletters, and occasional meetings; a network of geoscientists and engineers formed specifically for the project; and what the team called a public 'business centre network'.

Measurement was not forgotten

Despite the drive for spontaneity, the core team, recognized the importance of measuring the results of virtual teamworking as objectively as possible. They secured an independent consulting firm that specializes in benefits management. This firm was hired to analyse the project, to generate the list of expected benefits at the start and to track the actual results as the pilot progressed.

Change management team coached technology usage

A subgroup of the core team, called the 'change management team', was responsible for finding ways to show participants how to use the technology and also for helping them to understand how it could further their work. The programme developed was called 'coaching' rather than 'training' to emphasize that the process would be a personal interaction: a 'coach' working with 'players', not a trainer presenting information to passive recipients. The coaches and team members communicated with each other using the VT clients, an ongoing real-life demonstration of the system's value as a tool for collaborative work and knowledge exchange. The ultimate aim of the programme, also suggested by the coaching metaphor, was to encourage project team members to discover and exploit unexpected potential in themselves and the system.

Only 20 per cent of the coaches' time was designated for training in how to use the system. The rest was devoted to helping team members link their business objectives to the capabilities of the system and challenging them to consider new ways of working with the VT equipment. The core team was convinced that an extensive coaching programme was essential to the success of the project; so much so that – *they spent approximately half of the pilot's $13 million budget on coaching.*

Project failure attributed to lack of coaching

Because the money allocated to coaching ran out part way through the pilot, one of the projects was set up without coaching. The members of what was called the 'virtual petrotechnical team' were given VT equipment and left essentially alone to develop uses for it. This project was the only one of the five that failed and one of the reasons was the lack of coaching. The problem was not that the virtual petrotechnical team did not know how to make the technology work – what they lacked was an understanding of why they should bother. Complaints from the team – 'I don't see how this fits in with my work'; 'The people I want to talk to are not on the network' – were similar to those voiced by the other teams and addressed by the coaches. In part because there was no one to help the group overcome their scep-

ticism and explore the value of the system, their VT network fell
into decline and eventually silence.

There were other important and instructive factors that contributed to the failure. The petrotechnical network group was the
only one that did not have a clear operational focus: although
they shared interests and had overlapping expertise, they were
not working on a project together. Also, the team members were
mainly interested in exchanging data, so the VT clients' potential
for delivering much richer communication did not particularly
interest them. This demonstrated the value of attentive and continuous coaching.

The coaching programme set a new standard for user service
and support at British Petroleum. Besides providing sufficient
staff and effective technology when and where it is needed,
Virtual Teamwork coaching redefined the meaning of 'support,'
broadening it from technical training and troubleshooting to a
collaborative exploration of work practices. Coaching means not
only how to, but what and why.

Becoming the knowledge management team

When the pilot began, the members of the Core Team were not
thinking explicitly in terms of applying knowledge management
tools. Their emphasis was entirely on using virtual teamwork
technology and coaching to meet the project's business goals such
as:

- increasing the efficiency and effectiveness of decision-making
- reducing costs
- meeting schedules
- encouraging creative problem-solving.

Meanwhile, the core team's overarching goal was: to change the
way people work together, to make learning and knowledge-
sharing intentional and continuous.

These operating principles clearly dovetailed with knowledge management ideas. Chief among them was the recognition
that the knowledge and experience of employees was an essential
corporate asset. Making knowledge available when and where it
is needed and creating opportunities to generate new knowledge

were ways to ensure that the company would reap the benefits of its knowledge assets. In broad terms, the whole purpose of the project was to provide a means to bring together knowledgeable people and let them talk to each other. Hence the emphasis on communication and collaboration, rather than data management or information storage.

The restructuring into federated business units that preceded the virtual teamwork pilot was similarly based on the idea of providing opportunities within the company to cultivate and share new knowledge. As it became clear to the core team members how much their work had in common with knowledge work, they made explicit use of knowledge management ideas to reinforce their long-term aims.

Thus, the core team became known as 'the knowledge management team' and brought in knowledge management concepts to help keep the project focused on the ultimate goal of turning British Petroleum into a new kind of company rather than on incremental improvements in efficiency (see Figure 19.1).

Knowledge management principles	BP Virtual Teamwork programme
● Management support and resources are essential	● Upper management initiated project, authorizing funds and core team
● Knowledge initiatives should begin with a pilot programme	● Five tests allowed for variety and clear, limited goals
● Knowledge originates and resides in people's minds	● Members of knowledge communities were identified, then linked by technology
● Knowledge-sharing requires trust	● Relationships were built through actual and virtual face-to-face meetings
● Knowledge-sharing must be encouraged and rewarded	● Training and upper management support emphasized importance of new behaviours
● Technology enables new knowledge behaviours	● Technology was used for communication and collaboration; training emphasized goals, not hardware and software
● Quantitative and qualitative measurements are needed to evaluate initiative	● Savings and productivity increases were quantified; expanding VT use and participant enthusiasm were qualitative measures

Figure 19.1   British Petroleum's Virtual Teamwork programme's exemplified knowledge management principles

Benefits in practice

Although six months of the eighteen-month pilot were spent on planning and preparation, virtual teamworking practices quickly became an integral part of BP's projects once in place. With the exception of the uncoached Petrotechnical group, the teams began to experience benefits of the system within weeks – in some cases within days – and enthusiasm and use increased rapidly. The Andrew Project is one example of the positive impact of virtual teamworking.

The Andrew Project group

The Andrew Project group had a clearly defined goal. It was formed to complete a new drilling platform onshore for an emerging offshore oilfield. The use of VT technology was one of two innovations on the project. The other was the decision to complete the platform as nearly as possible on shore rather than finish construction at the offshore drilling site. There was no causal link between the innovations, but they combined to create a willingness to explore new ways of doing work.

The job of building the platform was a joint effort by BP and two other companies: Brown and Root, a design and engineering firm based in Houston with an office in Wimbledon; and Trafalgar House, a Teesside construction company. So the Andrew Project was a test – not only of virtual teamworking's usefulness in connecting employees over distance, but of its ability to link separate organizations.

Initially, Trafalgar House expressed doubt about the project most openly. A traditional company with a firmly established idea of how to do their work, they were sceptical of the unfamiliar technology and questioned the value of viewing distant team members on a computer monitor. Guided by coaching, they quickly experienced the benefits of the system and became strong supporters. Rather than spend half their time flying to London and back, they found they could collaborate more effectively using VT equipment.

Virtual teamworking did not eliminate the need for meetings during the Andrew Project They were still required to establish mutual trust and understanding and to hash out important issues that involved large numbers of team members, though they were significantly reduced. Once they had met face-to-face, participants found that video-conferencing maintained a richness of communication and a sense of direct personal contact that phone calls, e-mail, or memos could not match.

One indication of the difference was that commitments made electronically 'face-to-face' using the VT stations were honoured much more consistently than commitments made by phone or mail. Actually seeing the person to whom you promise to deliver a report or a piece of work by a certain date increases the likelihood that you will follow through. Both the need for some actual meetings and the effectiveness of virtual ones confirm the important role of personal contact in establishing trust: a key knowledge management attribute. This effect emphasizes the fact that the virtual teamworking initiative was principally a behavioural project, not a technology initiative.

Andrew team members took advantage of the application-sharing feature of the VT clients to write joint memos in ten or fifteen minutes that would have involved hours or days of sending drafts back and forth by mail. In all, virtual meetings and VT work sharing led to quantifiable benefits on the Andrew Project that included:

- significant reductions in travel costs and expenses associated with bringing vendors on site
- measurable productivity improvements related to more efficient information searches
- more efficient issue resolution
- reductions in duplication and wasted travel time
- contributing significantly to the project meeting its target completion date
- lower offshore costs resulting in a much lower total cost of steadily bringing forward first oil – a principal milestone in the development of a new field.

The Virtual Teamwork programme directors and BP management tend to downplay these figures because they believe the long-term potential of VT to transform the way people work is more important. They are more interested in explosions of creativity than incremental efficiency gains.

Given that aim, they are especially encouraged by the emergence of spontaneous and relatively unstructured uses of the technology. Although the immediate benefits are less clear than the cost reductions and productivity increases of the Andrew Project, these VT explorations are steps towards the kind of fundamental change team members are looking for and suggest that virtual teamworking is developing a life of its own.

For example, VT station users have begun communicating across projects. Members of the Andrew Project in Aberdeen made connections with members of the Miller team, whose experience on the mature Miller oilfield in the North Sea was usefully applied to work on the emerging Andrew field. This type of federal teaming inspired the core team's imaginary headline 'Scottish oil discovered in Alaska!' to suggest virtual teamworking's potential to nullify distance and create a team out of widely scattered individuals.

Business networking centres

The Virtual Teamwork business networking centres are being used once a week for *virtual coffee breaks*. To date, up to twenty people at eight separate locations have joined in video conversations with no set agenda. Like co-workers around water coolers or in the talk rooms provided by some Japanese companies, these team members discuss current work, share new ideas and work through problems. The expectation is that the conversations will pay off in unpredictable ways. Possibly two of the participants will discover a surprising, useful connection between their projects, or a suggestion from an unexpected source will help solve a difficult problem. The conversations may simply give participants a better sense of what is happening elsewhere in the company, but that too is a benefit that may pay off in the future.

Unplanned use of the network showed how quickly VT could be applied to new tasks. Four days before the Quarterly Performance Review in December, an assistant to Rodney Chase, Head of BP Exploration, called the VT core team and suggested using the system to create video presentations to enrich the review. In the past, a few asset managers travelled to headquarters for the meeting and others sent written reports or presentations. The core team contacted the business networking centre hosts and gave each a list of four asset managers. Using the VT clients, the managers created brief video reports that were played at the quarterly review and then published on a CD-ROM and made available to senior managers worldwide.

The success factors

A few key factors were essential to the success of BP's virtual teamworking pilot project.

Support by upper management

Substantial knowledge projects that lack upper management support are almost guaranteed to fail. In addition to approving financial resources, British Petroleum management supported and in part defined the goals of the project. They made clear that virtual teamworking was a mainstream corporate development effort, not a fringe activity or the pet project of a small group of technology and knowledge enthusiasts. Support at the highest level also made it possible to form a core team that crossed department boundaries, an important contributor to the pro-gramme's acceptance.

Full-time, quality project staff

The extensive planning, management and support that made the pilot successful were only possible because of skilled employees who could give all their time to the work. Their successful experience in other parts of the company provided a foundation for making good design decisions and gave them credibility with participants. A part time knowledge initiative is unlikely to work. Besides being poorly supported, it identifies itself as not important to management and therefore safe to ignore. Similarly, assigning work, which needs creative, rigorous and persuasive handling to staff who have not proven themselves and have no 'better' work to do, is a recipe for failure.

Coaching

An initiative which requires participants both to change their work patterns and learn how to use new tools needs to be sup-ported by coaching and training. The responsibilities of the virtual teamwork coaches included countering the scepticism and traditional thinking that could have crippled the project.

Starting with a pilot

Obviously, the investment is smaller and mistakes less costly than for a larger project. Also, choosing a pilot group with clear, measurable objectives that the project can help meet can increase the chances of success.

Measuring and evaluating results

Even for a knowledge project whose ultimate goals are more qualitative than quantitative improvements, measurement and evaluation are essential both to identify strengths and weaknesses and to 'sell' knowledge initiatives on the basis of their demonstrable benefits to the organization. The Virtual Teamwork programme team was able to point to specific cost savings and productivity increases as proof of the value of their approach. More importantly, though, the potential long-term benefits of virtual teamworking, though hard to quantify, were persuasively supported by anecdotal evidence, increased participation and the testimony of participants outside the core team whose experience with VT made them champions for the concept.

Notes

1. This case was prepared by Don Cohen and Laurence Prusak for the Ernst and Young Centre for Business Innovation.
2. Nonaka, I. and Takeuchi, H. (1995) *The Knowledge Creating Company*. Oxford University Press, p. 115.

Chapter 20

Enhancing an alliance with technology at Halliburton Brown and Root[1]

Nada Zdravkovic

New changes for the global organization

Organizations today are faced with immense challenges in a constantly changing environment as they strive to demonstrate that they can provide value-added services to their customers. In recognition of this change Halliburton has realigned all its business units into one global structure, which is supported by a single shared services support organization to share best practices and resources. The key thrust of these activities is to enable the provision of comprehensive integrated services to its customers into the twenty-first century.

Halliburton's goal is to be the world's leading integrated energy services and engineering company. To reach this goal the company is committed to:

- demonstrating operational excellence
- achieving technological leadership
- developing innovative business relationships
- creating a dynamic workplace.

Innovative business relationships through strategic alliances and partners with both customers and suppliers has led to tighter project schedules, improved cost efficiencies and higher product quality. The company has encouraged and supported the use of new technologies, techniques and tools to leverage and develop these relationships.

Larry Farmer, President of Brown and Root Energy Services, one of the Halliburton business units said: 'Our ability to harness and deliver technological change is a key element of our business strategy. Our commitment to using technology more effectively is one of the reasons that our customers come back to us.'

Technology has to be deployed successfully in order to deliver value to the business and this can be achieved through:

- improving communications between and within organizations
- providing access to and enabling information-sharing
- delivering improved working practices
  and in some cases
- re-engineering the business processes.

Effective use of the appropriate tools has significantly contributed to promoting and developing business strategies such as virtual teamworking and strategic alliances.

Tools for alliance enhancement

On the BP Andrew Project, Brown and Root Energy Services was part of an alliance, called the Alliance Companies (a strategic networked organization), which piloted some of the first 'virtual teamworking tools' and developed new and innovative ways of working. This enabled the field to be brought on stream more than six months early and more than £80 million under budget.

Some of the contributory factors to this success were brought about by:

- harnessing the creative influence of the personnel
- developing non-adversarial risk and reward based relationships
- exploiting opportunities created in the value chain (by both customers, suppliers and Alliance members)
- re-engineering business processes

- implementing IT tools which exploited the concept of a 'borderless organization' and allowed the team to work together regardless of the fact that they were physically located in different areas of the country.

Using technologies

Interactive computer-aided design modelling

Brown and Root Energy Services employed a three-dimensional computer-aided design (CAD) system for structural steel work which allowed the design office to produce electronic shop drawings which were issued directly to the plate-cutting machines in the fabrication shop. In total, more than 50,000 hours of work were saved against the traditional fabrication norms because of the direct interface with the design and fabrication teams and systems.

Improved software for pipe support design and for producing spool isometrics directly from the computer model allowed the Andrew team to work from a single set of drawings, eliminating the duplication of work between the engineering office and the fabrication site.

Lotus Notes

The BP Andrew Completions team used Lotus Notes to develop a job card application which allowed all parties involved in the offshore completion activity to develop their full scope including tasks, materials and man-hours for offshore completion activities. The ability for everybody to visibly share and comment on their developing workscope within a 'single-source' live application contributed significantly to both reducing the level of offshore completion and clarified the details on the job cards.

Video- and data-conferencing

Video- and data-conferencing were also used effectively to keep people in 'face-to-face' communication. One of the biggest issues for projects during the design and build phase is the dispersement of teams across many sites. The challenge has always been to develop more effective methods of communication during this critical stage of the project when decisions are needed quickly to maintain momentum and minimize rework.

Transmission of supplier information across the Internet

British Petroleum's Andrew Project saw the first exploitation of the Internet for the transmission of documents between the design office and suppliers. Suppliers were able to submit their documentation electronically to the project for internal distribution and review. At this stage the process was very simple. Once the electronic drawings or documents were received they were printed out and registered in the Project Document Control before being issued on distribution for review and approval. Surprisingly there were still many vendors who were not using the Internet and they submitted their drawings and documents on floppy disks.

The project also piloted the use of EDI implementing configuration tools to register data being transferred between sites. Again the level of usage was small because companies had neither the breadth of experience to implement the technology nor the desire to invest the extra funds.

The Internet experience

The initial level of usage was comparatively small but in the last few years there has been an exponential growth in the use of the Internet in our business activities. Subsequent projects (such as ETAP and Terra Nova) have affected document submission and review procedures as vendors are asked to submit their documentation in an electronic format via the Internet. Why has this happened?

- The universal reach of the Internet.
- The Internet is recognized as a cost-effective transport and communications medium.
- The Internet is a technology enabler for changing working practices.
- Previous tools depended on proprietary software and expensive communication links.

The Internet has reduced costs and communications barriers and provided a competitive and effective method for 'virtual organizations' to openly talk and communicate with each other electronically. For many people security remains an issue and will need to be managed.

People and technology lead the way

The BP Andrew Project won the Overall Project of the Year Award in the 1997 Major Construction Industry Awards. Ash Bakshi, Managing Director, Brown and Root Energy Services, Europe and Africa commented: 'The judges saw that the success of BP Andrew was mainly down to the people on the project and the way they behaved.' This 'can do' and 'pride in achievement' philosophy coexisting with a drive to actively utilize and exploit technology to deliver value is one of the reasons we can develop long and lasting relationships with our customers.

Halliburton Web communications initiative

In recognition of the role which the Web and associated technologies could play in shaping the future of communications within the Halliburton organization, a WorldWide Web initiative (HALWEB) was established to support and promote the vision of the company. Rachelle Bjelde, the Web Communications Manager, considers this initiative, 'one of the key tools we will use to leverage our efficiency and productivity across and within our business communities'.

This initiative will also impact other systems initiatives within the organization. The Siebel Sales Force Effectiveness initiative will leverage the HALWEB, as its central source for sales and marketing literature. The ability to access this type of information from a single source will enhance our knowledge-sharing capability on a global basis.

The real work

The technologies and tools are in place to facilitate 'web-weaving' and to allow virtual organizations, such as the Alliance of Companies, to exist and work together across the globe. What was learned at Halliburton through the experiences of using the latest tools to communicate and collaborate with BP is that real work lies in developing and evolving both working practices and cultural alliances which enable these tools to be used to their maximum potential.

<u>Note</u>

1. Website for information about the organization: http://www.halliburton.com.

Chapter 21

Benefiting on-line alliances with an extranet at Oracle Corporation

Katheryn Potterf

Background

Oracle Corporation, based in Redwood Shores, California, is the world's second largest software company. With annual revenue of around $6 billion, Oracle holds more than 45 per cent of the world's market share for open-systems relational databases. With the indirect sales distribution channel now accounting for more 30 per cent of Oracle's annual revenues, the corporation recognizes the growing importance of its indirect sales forces in meeting the demands of the rapidly expanding general business market.

One of Oracle's stated goals is to achieve 50 per cent of its licensed revenue through its partners. To meet this corporate goal, Oracle has dedicated more services, resources and programmes to its Alliance programme. The Oracle Alliance is a global business network that unites leading information technology companies to deliver integrated customer solutions for network computing. The Alliance provides focused programmes, services, events, marketing and sales support, technology updates and an expansive network that facilitates networking among partners and end users. Alliance partners are typically application providers, complementary software providers, systems integrators, value-adding distributors and resellers. Worldwide, thousands of partners are doing business with Oracle.

New Alliance programme required corporate extranet

When the Alliance programme was founded in 1990, there was a printed directory of partners, but no standard database where Oracle employees could instantly access crucial information about their base of partners and the Alliance programme resources. Nor was there a central repository for partners who needed Oracle product information, pricing, presentations, marketing kits and technical training. Since there were not enough Oracle account representatives to assign one to every partner in the programme, Oracle's help desk found itself inundated with telephone inquiries. Another issue – on both sides – was the lack of clarity about all the technical and marketing services available to partners through the programme. With no standardized profile forms for the partners, Oracle sales and marketing staff could not leverage partner information in their individual and collective marketing efforts. Alliance partners, for their part, often expressed the wish to find out about each other.

Alliance Online

To address this critical need – providing a central locus of information for partners and about partners – Oracle launched the first version of its Alliance Website, Oracle Alliance Online 1.0, in October 1996. Now in its third phase, Alliance Online (http://alliance.oracle.com) is a Web-based service that provides partners with real-time access to key Oracle sales, marketing and technical information. In just one year, it has received more than 8 million hits.

Partners promote themselves

Also through Solutions Online (a component of Alliance Online but a Website in its own right) partners can promote their own solutions and services to the general public. Solutions Online has a sophisticated search engine that can query by various categories, including vertical industry, application type, geography or by operating system – NT or Unix. Oracle partners simply load their own profiles into the central database using their unique company log-in in order to showcase their own Oracle-based solutions and services. Partners also update their own profiles.

'They love it because they control the content and we don't,' says Raghu Viswanathan, Senior Director of Worldwide Business Alliances Marketing.

Solutions Online allows buyers to locate vendors and to preview products and services. The site appears to be doing the job. End users are locating Alliance partners and sending them electronic inquiries for additional information or to schedule sales calls. Customers tend to have more confidence in vendors identified as Oracle Alliance partners, and especially in those whose software applications are certified as 'On Oracle'. Alliance partners, in turn, welcome this trend. 'What we're finding is that CIOs are prequalifying their purchases on the Web. Buying patterns are changing and the Web is becoming more ubiquitous,' says Viswanathan.

Partners can find one another now, too. Alliance Online is just the beginning of a sophisticated, electronic capability linking partners worldwide, assisting them in networking their respective competencies and taking them to market.

True extranet launched

Oracle has now extended the reach of its on-line partner site to transform it into a 'true extranet'. This means that authorized external users can access Oracle's internal databases and download the same information that is used by the Oracle team. By using a password, Alliance Online users can retrieve information from Oracle's corporate repository for product white papers, datasheets, presentations and more.

Further, there is now an end user site where customers and prospects – anyone – can quickly search through more than 11,000 third-party Oracle-based solutions. In other words, the publicly accessible Solutions Online (http://solutions.oracle.com) generates business inquiries, which reflects Oracle's commitment to generating leads for its partners whose offerings are showcased in Solutions Online.

Measuring the success

Alliance Online has been a success and it made Infoworld's Web Hot List in January 1997; Solutions Online appeared on the same Hot List in October 1997. Many Alliance partners have given positive feedback on the site, including suggestions for future directions.

Says Gail Ennis, Vice-President of Global Alliances Marketing: 'Clearly, the WorldWide Web has given us the opportunity to quickly strengthen our marketing support and communication among Oracle and its Alliance community.' Ennis believes that Alliance Online, along with Solutions Online, has increased partner loyalty significantly.

Although Oracle has not yet tracked the direct cost-benefits of Alliance Online, the company does report that the number of hot-line calls to the Oracle help desk for US partners went down by 50 per cent because partners could go to the Web themselves for the information they needed.

For the partners using the Website, the benefits are directly measurable in dollars and dimes. This resource reduces their time to market with the solutions they build; improves access to technical support; increases sales through Solutions Online; decreases cost of doing business, including calls, advertising, marketing and presentations.

How Alliance Online served Global Information Solutions and the Centre for Disease Protection

The search engine provided by Alliance Online has landed a multiyear commitment, including more than $1 million in new business during the first year, for Global Information Solutions (GIS), an Oracle Alliance partner located in Fremont, California, with a development centre in Bangalore, India's 'Silicon Valley'.

Global Information Solutions is in the business of custom software development and systems integration, with its primary competency in ERP, supply-chain management, and document management using Internet (intranet/extranet solutions) and client-server technology. The company builds applications on an Oracle database for any industry sector, including transportation, manufacturing, telecommunications, utilities and medical. In addition, GIS brings in developers from its own Java-based software development centre at Bangalore, India, giving them contract assignments with US companies. Providing these development resources helps to address the current nationwide IT labour shortage.

In March 1997, the Centre for Disease Detection (CDD), a medical diagnostic test company in San Antonio, Texas, located GIS, a California corporation, through Solutions Online. The company's CEO entered 'health care' as the vertical industry and retrieved a list of software integrators doing business with Oracle. The Centre for Disease Detection had a vision: to provide world-class customer support to doctors, nurses and health care workers, affording them instant access to patient test results through the Internet. The company was looking for someone to build an integrated 'paperless' software system that could provide remote access. This included doing the architecture, requirements, business process engineering, design, development, installation, running of the whole enterprise software and providing ongoing maintenance/enhancements for several years – starting from scratch.

Carlos Roca, President and CEO of the Centre for Disease Detection, a company which specializes in testing for sexually transmitted diseases, says he selected GIS after interviewing several integrators. 'I knew doing business with GIS would be less expensive because of its development centre in India and because GIS was on the cutting edge of current technologies in several areas. I also knew GIS had their own very good programming methodology.'

'I was located in Philadelphia and had another office in Connecticut, with my main office and blood lab in San Antonio and customers in all fifty states,' Roca says. 'The Internet now gives us the ability to access test results in a confidential manner literally moments after they have been diagnosed.'

Global Information Solutions President and CEO Kishore Tarachand says:

Looking at his business, we felt it was most appropriate to design in Java. With the browser as the user interface, customers can look up test results on-line, using many different clients, and Carlos and his staff can log in from anywhere to look at activity reports and monitor the business.

Global Information Solutions used its own development methodology called 'PROFET'™ (project life cycle methodology), which provides a seamless 'local' development environment. Global Information Solutions did the architecture and requirements in the USA, with the Indian team doing the detailed design and providing screens for review prior to proceeding to develop the application. The US team picked up the installation and acceptance. PROFET™ is based on best practices in process and project management and enables GIS to identify all requirements in order to provide the right deliverables for approval at every stage (see Figure 21.1). This results in improved quality and ability to meet schedules, so the bottom line is quality projects on time and within budget. Global Information Solutions utilizes this methodology to attain higher levels of the Competency Maturity Model (CMM) with the intention of gaining ISO 9001 certification.

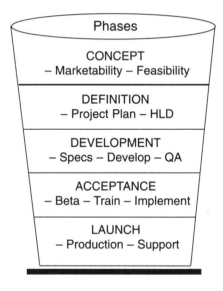

Figure 21.1 Phases of PROFET™

Global Information Solutions is building completely customized applications for Roca's operation. The first phase includes seven modules, which are already in alpha testing, and will be implemented early in 1998. These applications run on a comprehensive customer service module, with invoicing, receivables, operations, complete imaging system (which includes workflow), inventory, human resources and system management modules. Also, all incoming orders will be scanned to make it a completely paperless business.

In the second phase of the project, GIS will build modules for accounts payable, purchasing, general ledger and asset management. As well as an automated computer-telephony interface with automated call distribution (ACD) technology which will identify callers and pop up their records on a screen in front of the appropriate service representative.

Roca is enthused:

Benefiting on-line alliances with an extranet at Oracle Corporation

Once you've been in a paperless office, you never go back. Our staff members now never have to leave their desks. We hire people for their intelligence and creativity, not their ability to push paper. We're going to be the first company without bureaucrats in this industry. We offer better, faster, cheaper services to clients, who are doctors, nurses and health care workers. They have the advantage of having information collected in one central repository, so now they can do 'what-if' type of analyses.

Roca says that his client-doctors will have access to many different kinds of demographic and other statistical information:

They can see people who fit a certain profile for susceptibility to a given disease – whether it is AIDS, gonorrhoea, syphilis. They will have real-time demographics to help guide them in the decision-making process. The system will give them probability statistics for the region where the patient lives. There is a lot of information out there that no one else has access to, but our clients will.

Citing the example of the annual physical, Roca said the doctor might tell a patient to have a certain medical test because national trends suggest that women who fit a given profile, with certain criteria, need to have the test. The information will tell the doctor, 'Test for X, Y, and Z'. Having information like that at the push of a button, Roca believes, will help doctors to understand what is going on:

Sometimes patients should have a test done; sometimes not because it would just be a waste of taxpayer's money and private health insurance. So having information like this can keep costs down for everyone. For example, a certain disease might cost $50,000 to treat if caught one year after its contraction – caught right away, it takes only $5 to cure.

Roca says also that his diagnostic centre can look for genetic codes of HIV. This marks a significant improvement in HIV testing. 'Under the old way of testing, if you have HIV but your body has not yet reacted to it by producing antibodies, the test would not spot it. The new test would spot HIV immediately.'

Although the new enterprise software will not be complete until early 1998, Carlos said that his clients are already happy with the interim work that has been done by GIS. 'It's meant money for us, savings for our customers.'

Kishore Tarachand says that Alliance Online has proven a valuable resource. Not only has it created new business for him, but it has also given him the crucial information for doing business with Oracle, details about products and pricing marketing kits and various promotional opportunities.

Chapter 22

Electronic commerce at Cisco Systems

Arnaud M. Klineberg

The Internet imperative

Over the past decade, no innovation has impacted the way individuals and businesses communicate as dramatically as networking technologies. These technologies have enabled the low-cost development of open, interactive environments that help to break down the traditional barriers to strong business relationships. Yet despite the realization that these technologies can have a real and measurable impact on the top and bottom line, few CEOs and sales and marketing executives understand how to maximize or leverage its deployment. Typically, companies driving e-commerce 'shoot first, and ask questions later' – investing in technology, hiring developers, building sites – only to find down the line that they have no significant return to show for their efforts.

By focusing development on market-based applications, a select few 'early adopters' have realized the golden promises of the Internet: customer loyalty, lower costs and growth. A market-based (customer-centric) application of the Internet derives its function, form, measurement system and infrastructure requirements from the unique characteristics of its target market (see Figure 22.1). Cisco Systems has deployed an end-to-end Internet-based networked commerce application geared toward serving its direct customers and channel partners.

The customer-centric approach has had considerable success: Cisco expects to save more than $535 million a year in recurring business expenses (see Figure 22.2) and at current run rates receives nearly $2 billion in revenues annually through the net. By introducing a new level of depth and value to the traditional vendor–partner–customer relationship, Cisco's Internet strategy has been a source of competitive advantage in the networking marketplace.

Market-based e-commerce applications					
Value Dimension	Markets				
	Key Accounts	Small/ Medium Business	Partners	Vertical/ Horizontal Markets	Consumers
Function	Sales, marketing, coverage, service, support				
Customer Value	Improved service levels, reduce the cost of doing business, improved responsiveness and speed				
Corporate Value/ROI	Shift, lift, acquisition, and cost displacement				
Management Systems	Resource allocation, performance measurement, enabler/sponsor coordination				
Applications/ Infrastructure	Site specific Backbone apps Infrastructure	• Search, content, push technology, etc • Catalogue, payment, database, etc • Gateway, hosting, ERP integration, legacy systems, etc			

Figure 22.1 Internet value matrix

Most organizations recognize they need a strategy for sales and support over the Internet. The real challenge is to define a strategy that fits with the current channel mix and product/ market segments and allows the flexibility to adapt to changing market and customer behaviour. The key to overcoming these challenges, as demonstrated by Cisco, is to centre your strategy and Internet development around clearly defined dimensions of value for specific customer segments.

An e-commerce philosophy: Cisco's Global Networked Business model

Cisco's success can be attributed to its overarching networking philosophy, called the Global Networked Business model, which seeks to maximize the value of information and technology. It is based on three assumptions:

1. The relationships a company maintains with its key constituencies can be as much of a competitive differentiator as its core products or services.
2. The manner in which a company shares information and systems is a critical element in the strength of its relationships.
3. Being 'connected' is no longer adequate. Business relationships and the communications that support them must exist in a 'networked' fabric.

Cost savings	
Category	Savings
• Electronic software distribution	$130,000,000
• Reduced number of customer inquires	$130,000,000
• Others (labour, ordering errors, etc.)	$225,800,000
• Replacing printed manuals	$35,000,000
• More efficient customer support processes	$14,000,000
• Automated commerce applications	$2,000,000
• Total cost savings	$535,000,000

Figure 22.2 Cisco Systems' cost savings

This philosophy advocates a new way of defining information and the ways in which it is shared. 'Instead of defining information as "company information" and the "customer information", we've created a business beyond barriers,' says Cisco's Director of Service Provider Development, Ethan Thorman. 'It's a philosophy that is based on looking at information as a tool for everyone. Because we're most effective when we maximize the information we make available to our customers; the smarter and more knowledgeable we help make our customers, the more successful they will become.' Because the Internet can enable such a transformation, its development has been raised to a CEO-level issue. 'Global networked business sets new standards of effi-

ciency and productivity within business relationships,' says John
Chambers, President and CEO of Cisco Systems. 'By simplifying
network infrastructures and deploying a unifying software fabric
that supports end-to-end network services, companies are learning how to automate the fundamental ways they work together.'
With this philosophy at its core, Cisco deployed the Cisco
Connection Online, a Web-based network, to foster deeper relationships with prospects, customers and partners.

Cisco Connection Online – service/support and sales functions

The 'crown jewel' of Cisco's e-commerce strategy is the Cisco
Connection Online (CCO), the name for the site that houses all
of Cisco's Internet resources. The two main functions performed
by the site are service/support and sales. Through links to
various sites, the CCO provides registered customers, business
partners and employees with open access to the company's
resources and systems, including product and technical information, customer service, technical support, software downloads
and ordering applications. Says Chris Stinton, Director of Cisco
Connection, 'Our objective is straightforward: to streamline business processes and speed up access to critical information and
services'. Additionally, a suite of networked commerce applications help customers and partners manage the entire ordering
process. These valuable service/support and sales capabilities
have driven recent subscription and usage growth:

- By October 1997, the CCO had 50,000 registered users, and
  20,000 registered networked commerce users increasing at an
  average rate of 10 per cent a month.
- Log-ins have increased from 5,000 a month in 1993 to more
  than 750,000 in late 1997, with a typical log-in averaging a
  visit to fifteen pages of information.

Service and support

The use of Web-based applications has enabled a range of customer self-service solutions that has not been possible via traditional customer–supplier interactions. 'The CCO's service and
support site features components that change the relationship

between us, our reseller partners and our customers,' says Peter Solvik, Cisco's Chief Information Officer. 'We're out to shrink time, reduce manual effort and link the various companies together more closely than ever before.' One of the most valuable sections of the CCO is the Software Library, where customers and partners can download beta programs, upgrades, patches and utilities. Another hub of Cisco's Internet-based service and support strategy is the Technical Assistance Library, where users get on-line answers to technical questions and manage cases without having to call the support centre.

Sales

E-commerce takes advantage of the Internet's low cost of connectivity and the network's capabilities to streamline and automate many daily selling tasks of a business. The CCO's e-commerce engine is the Internetworking Products Centre (IPC), located in the Cisco MarketPlace. The IPC allows customers and partners to price, configure, route and submit electronic orders for over 12,800 Cisco products and parts. As of November 1997, 32 per cent of all transactions were being conducted on-line, representing $5 million a day in revenues. It is principally Cisco's largest partners and direct customers that are driving this revenue and transaction sizes are very large. While only 650 of Cisco's 20,000 registered networked commerce users have full procurement authority, all users can price, configure and transmit product purchase orders internally. This requisition routing feature enables the order to be routed electronically through the user's organization, facilitating all appropriate approvals prior to order completion.

These ordering and supporting applications offer significant advantages over EDI by giving users a highly interactive method of order entry. While EDI provides a set of standards for data exchange on value-added networks, users typically have only a one-way communication capability. They submit a request for a specific product, push a button, and hope the order is received and processed correctly. However, if the supplier's customer service representative or server detects an error, the order is returned to the customer and critical time is lost in correcting and resubmitting the order. The IPC, on the other hand, instantaneously checks that all orders are submitted correctly and returns those that are not within seconds of its receipt. And customers can track the order through Cisco's Status Agent, using PO numbers to access order dates, expected ship dates and shipping carriers. Furthermore, customers can link to Federal Express to find out exactly when their product will arrive. 'What Cisco is doing is extremely exciting: they're using customer service and distribution as a strategic weapon,' says Federal Express Vice-President of Electronic Commerce, Mike Janes.

Quantum leap results of a global networked business

Whether it is providing customer service or facilitating transactions, Cisco is looking for what CIO Solvik calls, 'Quantum-leap results: lower costs, higher customer satisfaction, and leadership in service and support'. To achieve these results, Cisco has deployed Web-based tools that deliver customer and corporate value along the dimensions in the e-commerce value matrix (see Figure 22.3). Customer value on the Internet is measured along three dimensions: information/speed, service and economics. Corporate value derived from the Internet can be measured by the shift and lift of revenues and costs.

Dimension of value	Cisco direct customer/partner e-commerce application	Quantum leap results
Information/ speed	• 24 x 7 customer support, service and ordering • Faster delivery on most products	Loyalty/ efficiency
Service	• Simplified and integrated procurement process • Control of decentralized buying through preconfigured offerings	Loyalty/ efficiency
Economics	• Lowest prices immediately reflected on the site • Reduced procurement cost and cycle times	Efficiency
Shift	• Leverage for field resource and reduced telechannel requirements • Displaced marketing and demand generation and fulfillment costs	Efficiency/ growth
Lift	• Coverage of more buyers • Increased purchase frequency • Increased face-to-face and selling resource productivity	Growth

Figure 22.3   Electronic-commerce value matrix

Each dimension of value delivers certain 'quantum-leap results' for the vendor, including: loyalty, efficiency and growth (see Figure 22.4). These benefits are impossible to achieve without first creating both customer and corporate value.

e-Commerce quantum leap benefits		
Loyalty	Efficiency	Growth
• Improve communication with customers and partners • Increase customer productivity • Increase customer satisfaction • Reduce problem resolution times • Reduce cost of doing business with Cisco	• Increase customer service group • Decrease current and future customer support calls • Save time on each support call • Minimize document and software distribution costs	• Keep pace with product and service demands of customer • Develop greater knowledge base of information • Increase sales

Figure 22.4   Electronic-commerce quantum leap benefits

Customer value: information/speed, service and economics

In June 1992, Cisco introduced Cisco Information Online, a text-based bulletin board system that allowed customers and partners to access technical information and download software. The site, Cisco's first concerted push on to the Internet, aimed to improve customer satisfaction and loyalty by speeding the delivery of service and support to customers and partners. Over the years, the content and functionality of its Internet site has changed, but Cisco has maintained its focus on delivering tools that drive customer and partner loyalty by improving communications and by eliminating inefficiencies in the sales cycle.

Information/speed and service

Numerous testimonials highlight the positive impact the CCO has had on its customers and partners, particularly in the areas of improved speed of communications and self-service benefits. 'We get immediate results in terms of knowing about compatibility and workability,' says Charles Miano, Purchasing Manager for Cellular One. 'It breaks down many communications barriers. Before when we would send things to our account manager or customer service rep and it could take two to five days to get an answer.'

Cisco's self-service model provides distributed access to information worldwide, twenty-four hours a day, seven days a week. Usage patterns suggest that many customers prefer on-line communications and service to other vehicles:

- More than 75 per cent of registered CCO customer requests are sent on-line.
- Each day the site is resolving between 60 and 70 per cent of these requests without direct human interaction.
- These requests include the download of nearly 25,000 technical cases per month from the Technical Assistance Centre.
- The Software Library section, where customers can download upgrades and utilities, registers 16,000 downloads a week.

The ability of Cisco to provide information and service to its customers, with speed and accuracy, has had a measurable impact on customer satisfaction. Cisco's 50,000 registered users give the Internet site an average satisfaction rating of 3.9 out of 5.0 and overall customer satisfaction has risen 30 per cent over the past few years. Improved customer satisfaction is driving loyalty to Cisco and its products and creating barriers to entry in key accounts for its competitors. For example, in early 1997 Cellular One decided to standardize on Cisco products, and subsequently increased its purchases of Cisco routers and hubs thirteenfold. According to Cisco, Cellular One was motivated by the up-to-the-minute pricing, faster delivery and remote access to order status made possible by the Cisco Connection.

Economics

In addition to convenience benefits, the networked commerce applications offer appreciable economic advantages as well. Supported entirely by the CCO infrastructure, Cisco's networked commerce applications require no development efforts by users. The system is available twenty-four hours a day, 365 days a year and is accessible to anyone authorized when a networked commerce agreement is signed. It is not necessary for a dedicated information services representative to oversee the application. Orders submitted correctly the first time flow directly into Cisco's system without rekeying; those not sent correctly are returned immediately, meaning greatly reduced rework efforts and significant savings. Using Cisco's networked commerce applications can reduce product delivery lead times by an average of two to three days and improve productivity by 20 per cent. 'We're saving an average of three days on delivery and the errors are almost nil,' said Jamie Burton, an account manager at Data Systems West, a Cisco reseller.

In another move destined to drive partner loyalty and efficiency through improved service and economics, Cisco has allowed its partners to give their customers access to CCO online. The Partner-Initiated Customer Access (PICA) programme, as it is called, allows partners to offer these on-line services to their customers. Providing basic self-help support solutions through CCO frees staff to address more difficult questions and problems. Customer issues, in turn, are resolved more quickly. Through PICA, partners may also provide customers with real-time access to the latest software releases.

Corporate value: shift and lift

Most executives today are faced with the challenge of growing sales while using fewer investment resources. In a sense, this is like trying to 'eat more and lose weight'. Today many companies are studying ways to use networked technology to reduce the cost of sales and leverage sales resources to maintain closer relationships with customers and partners. Two concepts of value have been developed to frame the benefits of e-commerce to a corporation – 'Shift' and 'Lift' (see Figure 22.3).

Cisco's Internet site has delivered on these two measures of value, shifting costs and lifting revenues to drive corporate efficiency and growth.

Shift

When the Cisco Information Online was introduced, Cisco did so because it needed to find a way to maintain high levels of customer satisfaction even while growing at speeds that would make building a call centre impossible. Cisco realized that if its rate of growth continued, it would be impossible to maintain high customer satisfaction rates through traditional customer support operations. There simply was no way Cisco could scale its traditional labour-intensive infrastructure to support its growing customer base. The Internet provided a support medium that was scaleable to the rest of its operation. It allowed Cisco to shift specific sales and service activities away from its direct sales and telecentre resources to this low-cost channel (see Figure 22.5).

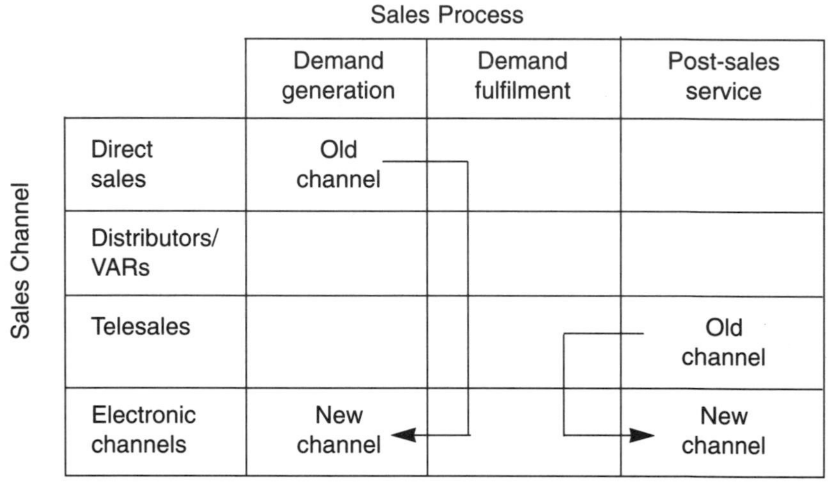

Sales Process

		Demand generation	Demand fulfilment	Post-sales service
Sales Channel	Direct sales	Old channel		
	Distributors/ VARs			
	Telesales			Old channel
	Electronic channels	New channel		New channel

Figure 22.5 Activity shift

In service and support alone, the efficiencies gained are enormous. Says Cisco's CIO:

Cost savings are here now. During one recent month, we had 50,000 log-ins to the Web that eliminated the need for phone calls to our technical assistance centres. Each phone call costs us an average of $200, so 50,000 fewer calls meant $11 million saved in one month. That same month, we had 50,000 software downloads. We saved $500,000 in FedEx charges alone.

And customers and partners consider the benefits of on-line communications to outweigh the disadvantages. Increasingly, customers and partners are accepting and using more of the company's networked commerce tools. For the same reason people prefer using an automated teller machine card over a bank teller for speed, accessibility and control, so too are they turning to the Web.

Lift

Cisco's first commerce tool was the Status Agent, released in August of 1995. Cisco found quickly that the on-line tool was being used by Cisco sales representatives, business partners and direct customers to check on the status of orders. This tool reduced the time sales representatives were spending on low value-added activities and allowed customers to check their orders on demand. Today, over 300,000 status queries are received per month. Cisco's direct sales force and partner representatives say that the CCO has given them more time to build relationships, cover multiple buyers in accounts and explore new business opportunities. It has also pushed them to develop consultative skills, designed to add value to the product sale. See Figure 22.6.

Examples of Sales Rep Leverage Gained by e-Commerce Applications	
Features	Benefit
Configuration agent	• Provides convenient, immediate access to current configuration information • Saves configuration information for later use and order verification • Reduces lead times
Pricing agent	• Provides current, immediate access to current pricing information • Allows saving of information for later access
Order status agent	• Provides convenient, online access to current status Cisco orders • Improves communication and increases productivity • Improves order management

Figure 22.6   Direct/channel sales representative productivity tools

Beyond improving sales rep productivity, the CCO has motivated some partners and customers, like Cellular One, to standardize on Cisco gear. This trend should continue, adding to
Cisco's share of its customers' and partners' networking investment.

Lessons learned: discipline and customer focus

It many ways it makes sense for Cisco to be a leader in e-commerce. As the supplier of 80 per cent of the networking infrastructure that runs the Internet, you would hardly expect
otherwise. Cisco's innovations and leadership in e-commerce
contain instructive points for companies in many industries. The
two most important lessons to be learned are the value of discipline and customer focus when setting and executing an e-commerce strategy.

Cisco has had success on the Internet in large part because
it has been disciplined about the investments it has made in
infrastructure and technology. Unlike many corporate Websites,
Cisco has eschewed 'whiz-bang' technology in favor of capabilities that support its Networked Business philosophy. Cisco has
also excelled because of its unrelenting focus on creating value
for its customers and partners. While it measures the impact of
its Website on internal efficiencies, the true measure of success
for Cisco is customer satisfaction. 'The goal is not to generate
dollars. It's to reduce cycle times and to increase customer satisfaction,' says Cisco CIO Solvik, 'We know we're doing that on
every on-line order we take.' To this end, Cisco has been a leader
in identifying those capabilities that impact its customers' and
partners' businesses and launching them with great speed.

Chapter 23

Reality bytes

Steven B. Weissman

Introduction

Stepping aside momentarily from all the previous cases of connections between people and technology that wove fabulous results, this chapter is a light-hearted 'reality check'. It makes the case for improving connections by providing real-life examples of situations in which processes failed because critical communications were missed. While these are true stories of just one customer's personal experiences, they represent familiar situations any of us may have experienced when systems and processes go awry and illustrate how poor connections can damage a business directly on the bottom line and indirectly by causing customer dissatisfaction.

'Mi casa es su casa': a hotel experience

Day one

I had reserved a suite with adjoining rooms at a prominent midtown hotel in New York for myself and a colleague, Ms B. I checked in first and the desk clerk told me that Ms B had not yet arrived. My wife was joining me later, so I accepted two electronic keys to my room and went upstairs. [Front desk interactions: 1. Key count: Mr W: 2, Ms B: 0.]

An hour later, the bellhop came into my room with Ms B and her luggage. The front desk had told the bellhop that Ms B and I were sharing a single room and given her two keys to my room. The front desk was informed of the error, Ms B was given two keys to the adjoining room and she gave me her two keys to my room. [Front desk interactions: 3. Key count: Mr W:4, Ms B: 2.]

We soon discovered that Ms B's keys did not work and called

the front desk, who said Ms B's keys were for the room adjacent but not adjoining mine. She was told to move. (Why? Because she had requested two twin beds – her sister was joining her for one night – and the adjoining room contained only one.) Her luggage had to be moved again – then we found out it had to be moved out next morning as the adjoining room was reserved for the following night! [Front desk interactions: 4. Key count: Mr W: 4, Ms B: 2.]

Day two

Ms B and her sister awoke, repacked their bags, and moved them into my room, because they could not yet check into the reserved adjoining room. The plan was at the end of the workday to pick up the keys to her room, which would be her home for the rest of the trip. When the time came, the keys the desk clerk gave her did not work in her door! However, they did work in mine, where she waited while I called the front desk to talk to a manager. [Front desk interactions: 6. Key count: Mr W: 6, Ms B: 2.]

The manager was very solicitous and explained that the computer indicated Ms B and I were sharing a single room. I told her the computer was still wrong and was asked to explain the situation from the beginning. Ten minutes later, she delivered new keys for both rooms. [Front desk interactions: 7. Key count: Mr W: 8, Ms B: 4.]

Day three

The next morning both keys operated properly. However, upon returning late that night Ms B's keys once again did not open her door! This had long since ceased to be funny so I went down to the front desk and spoke with a different manager, who was equally solicitous and personally delivered and checked two new sets of keys. [Front desk interactions: 9. Key count: Mr W: 10, Ms B: 6.]

End results

Besides being very aggravating to the customers, the situation was costly to the hotel, which suffered in several ways:

- *Cash flow* The second manager waived all our incidental

expenses and gave us a large fruit basket and a bottle of champagne.

- *Efficiency* Significant human resources were expended as each
  interaction with the front desk involved several people to
  answer the phone, check the computer, and produce and
  deliver the new keys.
- *Reputation* We did not receive the high level of service we
  expected and therefore would think twice about staying in that
  hotel the next time we visit New York.

While in the end the problem was resolved, poor connections
between people, their room tracking system and other processes
had prolonged it far beyond reason. Clearly, the hotel did not
have very effective systems for communication and collaboration,
and these systems repeatedly left its customers 'out in the cold'.

Making a spectacle of making spectacles

It seemed like an excellent deal: buy one pair of eyeglasses and
get a second pair for free! The timing seemed perfect, my prescription had changed slightly, so I went to the optical store.

I made my selection: two sets of wire-rim frames, one for
regular glasses and one for sunglasses. Then the questions began:
glass or plastic lenses? Scratch-resistant coating? Grey or green
tint for the sunglasses? The shop assistant painstakingly wrote
down my answers on a form to be sent to the off-site laboratory,
where a technician would grind my lenses and put them in the
frames I had picked out. I was told the glasses would be ready in
two weeks. [Pairs of glasses ordered: 2. Pairs received: 0. Time
since ordering: 0 weeks.]

After three weeks of silence, I called the store and was told
my glasses would be ready in a week. On the appointed day, I
drove to the store and discovered that only my sunglasses had
come in. Worse, the lenses were the wrong colour – I had ordered
grey, but these were seaweed green. The attendant duly noted all
of this and prepared a new order form for the laboratory. To my
surprise, she handed me the wrong-tinted sunglasses to take
home and said the right glasses would be ready in two weeks.
[Pairs of glasses ordered: 2. Pairs received: 1. Time since ordering: 4 weeks.]

After two more weeks of silence, I called the store again and was told that my glasses would be ready in two days. I called ahead to check both pairs had arrived from the laboratory, drove over and discovered that the sunglasses – grey this time – contained two right lenses; but my regular glasses were OK. We repeated the process: a new order form for the lab, one pair to take home and another waiting period far longer than the one required to purchase a hand gun. [Pairs of glasses ordered: 2. Pairs received: 2. Time since ordering: 6 weeks.]

A week later the shop called and proudly announced my sunglasses were ready. A trip to the store confirmed that the laboratory finally had got everything right and I was ready for the outdoors at last. [Pairs of glasses ordered: 2. Pairs received: 3. Time since ordering: 7 weeks.]

A happy ending? Certainly. But it gets even better: four weeks after picking up the properly prepared sunglasses, I was told that my regular glasses were ready. Curious, I picked them up and found them to be a duplicate of the pair I collected seven weeks before. Not a bad deal! [Pairs of glasses ordered: 2. Pairs received: 4. Time since ordering: 11 weeks.]

End result

So what was the cost to the optical store?

- Two-for-one became four-for-one. Surely a loss was made on my transaction?
- The store's order processing and quality assurance procedures were abject failures. What was the real cost of the time and materials involved in making and shipping the extra glasses?
- The many mistakes and the slow turnaround thoroughly undermined the store's claims to customer service. Besides receiving twice the product I paid for, why would I ever go there again?

Instead of weaving excellent links between the shop assistant and laboratory technician, and between shop assistant and customer, the optical store's communications meant every problem was a surprise, and the situation took months to resolve because no one seemed to be paying any attention to it. Furthermore, my angry exchanges with the store staff were heard by other in-store patrons so hearing my experiences probably affected that web of connection as well.

'Dollars and sense': do not forget the business logic!

I ordered some automotive accessories from a catalogue company noted for the quality of its products and service. Unfortunately, I miscalculated the sales tax on my order (user error!) and inadvertently wrote a cheque for 15¢ less than the amount actually due. Consequently, I received a notice several days later about my shortfall and asking me to send a cheque for the difference, which I did.

Think about it. I owed 15¢, but what did the company have to pay for the stamp on the envelope? And what did it pay for the envelope itself? And how much expense did it incur when the system did the database lookups and printed the notice, and when it processed my follow-up cheque? And I wonder what it cost my bank and their bank to process a check for only 15¢? All together, certainly more than 15¢.

The point here is that although the process worked perfectly, it was imperfect because it lacked a key piece of business logic: the ability to suppress shortfall notices when the amount due is less than or equal to the processing costs. Details like this are often overlooked – and the cost of ignoring them may adversely affect the bottom line.

Conclusion: poor connections, serious consequences and some considerations

Poor connections

While many companies are weaving better connections and improving systems, these do not always translate into better experiences for the customers. The above examples are still typical of many organizations today. While the tendency may be to shrug off these incidents as being 'inconvenient but unimportant', the real cost of such failures may surprise you.

The consequences

For example, my New York experience probably cost the hotel $250 in uncollected incidental expenses, plus another $50 for the fruit basket and champagne. Three hundred dollars may not be a big figure, but I am only one business traveller in a nation where some 289 million trips are taken annually. If only one person in 1,000 has a similar experience, then the hotel industry stands to lose some $86.7 million!

Some considerations

The way to avoid this kind of pitfall is to focus as much attention as you can on the personal and procedural interactions that make your organization run, and to make sure they are as efficient and effective as possible. Please note that this exercise does not have to involve new technology (such as the Web) though systems implementation often follows as a result. The trick is to develop a solid understanding of how your people do, should and will communicate, and then build on this knowledge to forge the best connections you can in order to avoid failing your customers.

Chapter 24

Improving global communication at Global Office Network

Kevin Tea

Introduction

The Global Office Network is an international association of high-class, independent business centres in fifty-eight locations spread across eighteen countries, over multiple time zones, and run by people of different cultures, language and technical skills levels. Communications between members has been problematical because of the very global nature of the association.

At the simplest level it meant that phone calls often had to be made at socially difficult times, i.e. in the early hours of the morning. Distribution of agendas, minutes and other paper-based information was expensive in terms of materials and personnel time with staff standing for hours in front of fax machines, feeding in reams of paper and punching in countless long international telephone dialling codes. At a more complex level, effective decision-making was slowed down as many small, almost trivial, matters, tied up much valuable time when members physically came together for meetings, condensing the time for serious discussions on matters of greater importance.

At a more general level, the association needed to enhance the referral procedures between members and look at ways of promoting itself in the global marketplace.

Early steps

In 1995, one of the Global Office Network (GON) members –
Virtual Office based in London – was working with a system
operator who introduced GON to the benefits of CompuServe. It
seemed an ideal solution. The CompuServe libraries could hold
all relevant files which members could browse and download at
their leisure, while discussions on GON matters could be carried
out in the messaging section.

If a discussion needed a decision, a simple system was established with the prefix DISCUSS being placed before a topic and
a time scale inserted into the message body. When the allocated
time ran out an associated thread was started, this time with the
word VOTE prefixing the topic and people responded with their
views and a decision eventually reached.

Running in parallel with the GON section on CompuServe,
GON began creating the association's first WWW site. It was
decided to adopt an economic 'suck it and see' approach and the
first site was a relatively simple affair, with a brief explanation of
the association and a directory of GON members with hyperlinks
to e-mail addresses and, where applicable, their WWW site
URLs. The site was hosted by a Unix-based ISP and although it
contained an easy to use CGI-based form, the level of technical
sophistication was fairly low.

Growing discontent among GON members with the
CompuServe solution and the speed of progress being made with
Internet technologies were pivotal in deciding on a change in
direction for the Global Office Network.

Getting up to speed and running on NT

Following an informal 'council of war', the site was moved to a
different ISP which ran Microsoft NT servers. As well as enabling
the use of FrontPage extensions, the transfer also enabled the
association to use a new breed of Web messaging software which
permitted not only threaded messages, but also real-time conferencing providing the user's browser was Java-enabled.

The site was redesigned utilizing some of the Java script
facilities to enhance navigation and allow visitors to find their
way quickly and intuitively around the site. The first of these was
a simple to use, but powerful site search engine whereby the

script would search the site – not the rest of the Internet – for keywords such as city names, etc. The second was a drop down box facility which enabled visitors to select a country of their choice and jump straight to that directory, bypassing the directory of countries where members were based further into the site.

The enquiry form was enhanced and other cosmetic and design changes were made, but the major new development was the Web forum. This gave GON ten sections dedicated to threaded messaging. The first areas were dedicated to a general welcome area, a closed section where GON members could message confidentially, an open GON section where visitors could ask questions about locations, facilities, services, hotels, accommodation, etc. and a section devoted to travellers' tips where visitors could pass on the benefits of their expertise to others. Another open section is dedicated to the Global Office Network's US partners, the Alliance Business Centres Network, which operates executive suite centres through North America.

Another significant task was to educate the members to make better use of the site, to improve the content of their respective pages and to provide substantially more information about the facilities and services in their geographical area. For example, a UK businessperson who is to set up a German subsidiary in Bonn not only wants to know about the size of offices, secretarial support services and mail and telephone facilities, but also the best hotels and restaurants in the vicinity, ground transport routes, car hire, theatres, museums and other cultural pursuits for his or her leisure time. Female executives wish to know which hotels specialize in providing special facilities for women, such as separate dining areas, all female bedroom areas and the like. This additional information is especially important when Europeans are visiting the Far East and have queries about visas and health inoculations and also cultural queries so as not to unintentionally offend the standards and norms of their host country.

Expansion of this information also provides greater opportunities for GON members to increase revenue. By offering incoming clients assistance through hotel and car hire booking, for example, the member can receive an agent's fee. But probably more important is that by offering a one-stop shop to the incoming business executive, the perceived 'cuddle quotient' and goodwill generated will mean the difference between securing a contract or losing it to another centre.

Summary

Over the past two years the Global Office Network has made great inroads into using electronic messaging. All but one member now has an e-mail address, either through CompuServe or an independent ISP of their own choice, and communication between members and the GON officers has improved dramatically. Global Office Network members have the choice of having a link to their own WWW site or having a 'subpage' beneath the national directory, outlining the services their centre or centres provide. One UK member who has taken up the latter option at a nominal charge reports a substantial amount of enquiries being generated.

The GON initiative must not be seen as an electronic Utopia, however. As with all things linked to the Internet and the WWW, the pace of change is terrifyingly fast and the learning curve is steep. The pro-Web enthusiasts are often at odds with other members who, while appreciating the benefit of e-mail, cannot appreciate the long term benefits that the WWW site or electronic messaging in its broadest sense can bring. However, the pride that GON enjoys in having a superior set of electronic messaging facilities to its American partners is another driving force that will ensure that more time and effort will be devoted to advancing this marketing and communications tool.

Chapter 25

Team syntegrity

Raul Espejo

Introduction

This chapter describes the process of producing a book in honour of Stafford Beer, a pioneer of organizational cybernetics. The idea was to use systems ideas in its production. Since Beer himself is one of the outstanding systems thinkers of our days, nothing is better than applying his own work for this purpose. The book, *To Be and Not To Be, That Is the System: A Tribute to Stafford Beer*,[1] was produced using one of his own inventions – team syntegrity.[2] This protocol made it possible for a group of thirty people from all around the world to work together in collaboration.

The group tested the team syntegrity communications protocol as a means of creating a common, highly integrated, knowledge product. The usual solution, when the purpose is bringing together multiple contributors to one book, is making the task manageable by decoupling participants and asking them to produce independent contributions. However, in this case the production of the book followed a truly integrative protocol, which permitted the rich tension between the individuals' desire for a genuine personal contribution and the group's desire for an integrated solution. Indeed, this is a common collaborative problem which applies to many social contexts.

The book's twelve chapters, their names, purpose and content, were created together by the thirty participants in a non-hierarchical process. The chapters were organized, following team syntegrity, as the twelve vertices of an icosahedron, something which permits the reader to navigate, discovering state-of-the-art applications of cybernetics to organization and society in a truly systemic fashion.

Complexity and the integration of multiple views

Conceptually our problem was to create a process, that at the same time of giving the opportunity for people to express their own views and contribute to the best of their abilities, permitted them to integrate these views and knowledge in a genuinely synergistic product, with its own identity.

Faced with the problem of managing the interactions of a relatively large number of people, a common strategy is to reduce their complexity. This may be achieved in different forms, but the cost of these strategies is reducing mutual influences and the synergy of the group, thus reducing its overall performance.

The strategy used in this project was very different. Its emphasis was in amplifying the participants' capabilities. Rather than finding an existing common denominator it provided a context for people to create different foci for their interactions. These foci were used to organize the participants' individual thinking. Rather than operating in a hierarchical structure the strategy was to use a truly non-hierarchical communications protocol, which allowed all participants to relate to each other even if they did not talk to each other. The overall process relied on creating lateral communication channels to allow the reverberation of ideas throughout the group. The actual design of this strategy is explained below.

A protocol for collaboration: team syntegrity

Team syntegrity is a meeting protocol to support the encounter of about thirty people in a non-hierarchical set up. It supports a strong exchange of personal knowledge and experience, giving all participants the chance to contribute to the best of their abilities to the purpose of the project. The steps of the protocol are:

1. Proposing an opening question and the constitution of an Infoset. The opening question emerges from the purpose of the meeting. The Infoset is the group of people contributing to the meeting.
2. Participants are asked to contribute individually with 'statements of importance' (SIs) relevant to the purpose of the collaboration.

3. Based on these SIs, participants elaborate aggregated statements of importance (ASIs). These are statements emerging
   from participants' interactions, supported by several of them,
   rather than by single individuals. This is achieved in a marketplace of ideas. Participants jostle and achieve support of
   four or five people to what they consider relevant to the
   purpose at hand. This way hundreds of SIs may be reduced to
   tens of ASIs.
4. The participants are then asked to relate ASIs in triplets and
   doublets of associated ASIs, that is, the ASIs are combined in
   groups that seem to address the same topic. The purpose is to
   reduce the ASIs to twelve consolidated statements of importance (CSIs) by a process of elision. These are the twelve
   topics for discussion in the meeting.
5. A voting procedure follows to enable each participant to
   express his/her preferences for the twelve topics.
6. Based on the voting, topics are allocated to participants using
   a computer supported algorithm. Each participant becomes
   member of two discussion teams, that is, is member of two
   teams of five, responsible for the elaboration of two topics,
   and becomes a critic of two other teams. Team members
   discuss the topics and prepare 'final statements of importance' (FSIs). Critics observe a team's discussion and contribute as requested to improve the quality of this discussion.
   Critics are free to discuss with the team members during their
   allocated times, commenting on either the content of the discussion or on the process of the meeting.
7. Teams discuss the topics in three meetings, moderated by
   facilitators, who may also support the documentation of these
   discussions, e.g. using flip-charts. Each meeting ends up with
   a summary. The last of the three 'outcome resolves', as these
   meetings are called, ends up with the teams' FSI.
   Intermediate outcome resolve statements are made available
   to all participants to enhance the reverberation of ideas in the
   Infoset.

Process design

Team syntegrity was used to define the book's contents and to
make possible the creation and reverberation of ideas in a non-

hierarchical set-up. In this case the twelve topics were the twelve chapters of the book. The whole process took place between September 1995 and September 1996.

The collaborative process was supported by distant and local communications among contributors. It started with an electronic exchange of ideas (electronic syntegration I), it was followed by a face-to-face meeting (local syntegration) and it ended up with an electronic process during which the book was written (electronic syntegration II).

Electronic syntegration I (pre-local syntegration)

The decision was made to use electronic media for the processes of creating the book's content and allocating chapters to participants.

The opening question was formulated as follows: 'What is the (actual and potential) contribution of cybernetics in general, and Stafford Beer's work in particular, to organization and society?'

After constituting the Infoset, most of the interactions were via e-mail. However, by October 1995 we had a WWW site on the server of City University, London (http//:www.city.ac.uk/sbfp). At that stage, participants could input their SIs directly via the Web on to the homepage.

In the following three months, diverse inputting, signing and voting procedures were handled via WWW to produce ASI and CSI. At the same time, multiple lateral communications took place, mainly via e-mail and phone. The end result was the definition and names of the chapters and their allocation to participants.

Local syntegration (24–27 March 1996)

The local syntegration was organized by the University of Lincolnshire and Humberside in the UK, with the technological support of Team Syntegrity International, from Toronto. They provided the protocols to run concurrent meetings and the continuous logistic support of meetings. Most of the technology for the local Syntegration was non-computer based; flip-charts, boards, copying machines. As all the sessions were video-recorded, this implied the activity of two camera operators.

Electronic syntegration II (post-local syntegration)

The hub for the post-local syntegration activities was at the University of Wales in Bangor. Activities were supported by First Class, a communication software package from SoftArc Inc., Canada, which runs under Windows. This package permitted fast and easy interaction between the members of the Infoset. It also allowed each one of us to keep an overview of progress in the discussion and production of chapters in the different teams.

Most of the production of the chapters was realized on Word for Windows, version 6.0. Substantial use of co-authoring facilities was made. Also, several graphics packages were used – e.g. Designer 4.1, PowerPoint, etc. The multimedia production of the book was realized by Roy Stringer in England. Extensive use of scanning and digitalization of video materials and documents was necessary.

Experience: the unfolding of the process

About forty people joined the electronic syntegration. However, the composition of this Infoset changed over time. There were some participants who, despite their commitment, did not succeed in solving technological communication problems, and therefore did not become as active as they wanted to be. There were others who showed active participation in the electronic syntegration, but were unable to join the local syntegration. Eventually, for the local syntegration we had exactly thirty participants, who constituted the final Infoset. They came from sixteen different countries in four continents.

Electronic syntegration I – pre-local syntegration

The Infoset produced about 150 SIs. In general there were no problems in prompting the production of SIs; the flow was good. The facilitators encouraged Infoset members to organize the SIs into categories, to gain an overview of the contributions. Participants were then supposed to create their own ASIs, and for that they were stimulated to engage in lateral conversation with other members of the Infoset. Eventually, a page was made available for each member to input ASIs. With some persuasion by the facilitators, it was possible to have thirty-five ASIs supported by four or more members of the Infoset, at the end of the process –

12 February 1996. It was then necessary to reduce the thirty-five statements to twelve topics (CSIs). The next step was to open a voting page in the website. The outcome of this step was the following list of twelve CSIs, which constituted the topics for the local syntegration (its agenda and a preliminary list of chapters for the book):

1. Developing cybernetics methodology.
2. Communication and information.
3. Syntegration: an architecture for democracy.
4. Cybernetics and ethics.
5. Diffusion of cybernetics
6. Spirituality and self-transformation.
7. Adaptive ecological organizations.
8. Humanizing society.
9. Management knowledge and knowledge management.
10. Recursive organization.
11. Second order cybernetics.
12. Community and cybernetics (public management/policy).

Participants voted for the topics they most wished to participate in and with the support of a computer algorithm their wishes received a 94 per cent of satisfaction.

Local syntegration – 24–27 March 1996

The twelve groups of five were engaged in three meetings or outcome resolves. The first iteration was mainly an ideas shower, the second was focused on finding a kernel for each chapter and developing its conceptual model and the third to reach agreements for the detailed implementation of the chapter. The three iterations were developed over three days, the first two in sessions of seventy-five minutes each, the last with forty-five minutes per session.

During the earlier parts of the process one of the participants suggested to end the local syntegration with a strong statement integrating all the views expressed during the three days. However it became clear that the complexity of thirty people was much higher than any synthesis of one viewpoint and therefore the outcome of these meetings was the debriefing of all the videotapes produced during the three days. These debriefings provided the platform to write the chapters.

Electronic syntegration II – post-local syntegration

The idea was to maintain communication within groups in ways similar to the iterations of the outcome resolve, and to give critics a chance to exercise their editorial, quality assurance role. This idea worked only partially. The team structure for the production of the *festschrift* was mapped in First Class, where the twelve nodes and their critics had independent but related folders (see Figure 25.1).

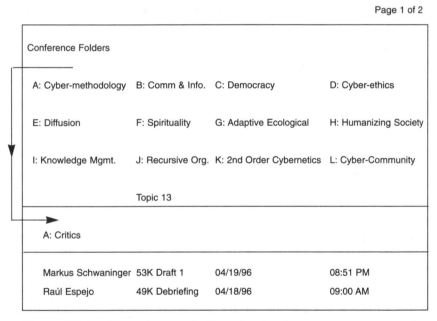

| Title: SB Festschrift | | | Friday, April 26, 1996 11:01:25 AM |
| | | | Page 1 of 2 |

Conference Folders

A: Cyber-methodology	B: Comm & Info.	C: Democracy	D: Cyber-ethics
E: Diffusion	F: Spirituality	G: Adaptive Ecological	H: Humanizing Society
I: Knowledge Mgmt.	J: Recursive Org.	K: 2nd Order Cybernetics	L: Cyber-Community
	Topic 13		

A: Critics

| Markus Schwaninger | 53K Draft 1 | 04/19/96 | 08:51 PM |
| Raúl Espejo | 49K Debriefing | 04/18/96 | 09:00 AM |

Figure 25.1 The software platform for the electronic outcome resolve

This phase was characterized by an interaction which was much more intensive and competent than the communication in the electronic syntegration I. This indicated that the local syntegration had achieved a steep increase in group cohesion. The modes of operations were very different among the teams. At one extreme, we had a couple of teams adhering strictly to their schedules and to the production rules. At the other extreme, one team had no clear idea what to do or how to organize itself. In between we could observe multiple forms of cooperation, which are reflected in the content of the book. The chapters were wholly self-produced. No one interfered in their content.

In the end, after a year, we created a global publication. It was a genuine exercise in computer supported co-operative work (CSCW).

Comments: project assessment

This was a classical example of collaborative work between people working in different locations and at different times. All the twelve teams produced their contributions as promised. Much was learned in the process. This project has made it clear – and the evidence is in the videotapes – that strong checks and balances are likely to emerge during a local syntegration, when participants are communicating in the same space and time.

These checks and balances, are much weaker when people operate in different places and at different times. While First Class permitted participants to see in real time each of the conferences in progress, and also permitted critics to see in real time the files sent to them by the teams for their inspection, in practice this powerful capability had only a limited use. Not only did several of the active participants experience difficulties in accessing First Class, but even some of the successful users did not experience in the flesh the pressures of an ongoing interaction.

This psychological effect of distance made interactions much less effective than in the local syntegration. The powerful effect of being in the same place at the same time with four others became diluted during the electronic process. Perhaps the pressures of daily life and the concreteness of many other physical real interactions made much less relevant these distant, future-oriented, virtual interactions. It was not until the time for producing the final drafts for the book that people started to bridge the distance barrier. It could be argued that the problem is their lack of commitment and/or the limited resources available to them. However, our experience suggests that there is much to be learnt about how to make more real a virtual space of interactions. At least, space and time became much less of a problem when people realized the immediacy of the task.

While we reserve our judgement about the book's quality, we are left in no doubt that the twelve CSIs were highly interrelated and that treating them in isolation, even if individual contributions could have been of higher quality, would have meant a less comprehensive and rich approach to the total situation. At least in our case there was an underlying coordination and integration of the CSIs which offered the potential for a holistic view of social issues. We considered that integration of the content was fundamental to our endeavour. Not a rational, one-viewpoint integration, but an experiential integration based on real-world interactions. We learnt a good deal about cooperation in these circumstances, but we also had to accept that we were a long way from knowing how to facilitate good levels of cooperation.

Quite naturally, people felt ownership for what they were producing and there were difficulties in the integration of different contributions. Often the implicit view was that integration meant diluting individual thinking into the minimum common denominator. However, there were participants who were not prepared to dilute their thinking. It became more and more clear that collaboration meant to express individuality around a common kernel, not to dilute it for the benefit of common authorship. In the end, the chapters have different configurations of authorship. Chapters are owned by individuals and teams and they are fully responsible for their content.

Preparing a book following the syntegration protocol made apparent at least two problems. First, it implies communication requirements far beyond those that would be necessary to produce a book of weakly related chapters. Therefore it makes sense to use it only if the interest is in producing a highly integrated book in a collaborative venture between several or many authors. Second, the need to produce a highly integrated book depends on the nature of the issues at hand. If these issues are highly interconnected then it makes sense to map them with the requisite network of interpersonal interactions. In this case our foci were on a variety of highly interrelated organizational and societal issues, suggesting the value of integration.

Notes

1. Espejo R. and M. Schwaninger (1997), *To Be and Not To Be, That Is the System: A Tribute to Stafford Beer.* Karl-Auer-Systeme Verlag. Distributors in the UK: Syncho Ltd, Aston Science Park, Love Lane, Birmingham, B7 4BJ.
2. Beer S. (1994) *Beyond Dispute – the Invention of Team Syntegrity.* Wiley.

Chapter 26

Generous networks of productive connections at BrainPool

Isabel Willshaw

Networking IS intelligence gathering, IS knowledge creation.

What is going on?

Industrial Era organizations and belief structures are crumbling, and giving way to – what? New infrastructures, new ways of organizing, but they are not quite here yet. We are caught in the very real pain of disintegrating relationships at all levels of our lives – families, communities, religions, the workplace, politics both national and international. Add to this the accelerating effect of mass media, where the death of Princess Diana or the collapse of share prices are experienced in millions of living rooms as part of our own lives, and it is small wonder many experience stress and chaos.

From the chaos emerge new forms

In the wake of old structures disappearing, new forms of organization and new behaviours are becoming easier to distinguish. A new vocabulary helps us see the emerging reality – e.g. portfolio workers, self-organizing systems, networks, employability, personal pension plans. Some governments and companies are starting to explore new ways of thinking and to encourage new behaviours – as understanding of this transformation deepens, we start to see amazing new possibilities for cooperation across boundaries, for a quality of connectivity that takes human beings to new levels of personal and organizational capacity.

The big shift in Western cultures is that individuals are waking up to the recognition that they, and they alone, are responsible for their lives. There is no kindly parent or organization who is going to take care of them. They now need to ask – what kind of life am I intending to live? What is my unique contribution? What do I need to do to realize this potential? Nobody will provide them with a lifelong career, the government will not take care of them from the cradle to the grave. Many people for the first time are waking up to the fact that they are operating in a marketplace and they cannot articulate what they are selling.

As you tread your seemingly lonely, or self-reliant, path, it becomes clear that the social networks which exist within and beyond organizations are no longer sufficient. For those working inside organizations, it becomes crucial to be more widely networked – to be more successful in current employment, and to ensure that word of future work opportunities will reach you effectively. For the growing numbers of self-employed, being networked is not an option – it is vital to financial and psychological survival.

Overheard on the Edinburgh to Glasgow train: 'Who are your connections in the BBC/Channel Four/Glasgow Development Agency/etc. Who do we need to get on board this project? Who has decision-making powers? What's this person like?' This is high-level networking or intelligence-gathering – essential to getting projects off the ground. It cannot be found in books or on the Internet and you do not get it by passing exams. The only way to gather such intelligence is to build information-sharing relationships with other people, based on trust – a process that is accelerated by access to suitable opportunities, clear personal integrity, and the willingness to put in the time and effort necessary to building and maintaining those relationships.

Getting to know you

Who are you, really, and why should I trust you? We are educated to promote ourselves using our qualifications and track record, but our decisions to trust, and therefore to do business with, others are based on how we feel about them. We have been trained to reveal only part of ourselves through CVs and our behaviour in professional circumstances. But the information we need to form trust-building (and information-sharing) relationships is not supplied.

Boasting about your achievements, name-dropping, game playing – activities experienced every day in workplaces, kill trust. If you choose to stay in the brittle world of superficial chat, if you have to make a joke to avoid answering deep questions, you will find it difficult to build relationships of trust.

One of the most important tasks for each of us is to state clearly who we really are. Not just our work track record and how well we do certain things, but also what is important to us as a whole person. What values do we work from? What do our friends and colleagues value us for? What do we really care about? Another real challenge is to suspend our rush to judge others before we can appreciate who they really are.

BrainPool

BrainPool was founded in 1994 in Edinburgh as a generous network for people exploring new ways of working and new ways of being. Members are architects, IT consultants, lawyers, senior managers, designers and many more. Many are based in Scotland, but the network stretches around the world. What they all have in common is that they want to contribute to and participate in a learning community that is constantly changing and growing. It is a 'pool of endless possibility', where people are supported to take new leaps in their lives and encouraged to have an open mind towards other people and to new activities and beliefs.

Key activities include a weekly breakfast with no agenda other than to be there and make productive connections. Workshops and social get-togethers are offered monthly, and often led by members. There is an extraordinary buzz, and cynical or sneering exchanges are noticeably absent. We are getting better and better at creating the structures and opportunities that people need to make productive connections. Members are learning new behaviours, such as quickly getting to trust-building conversations through revealing more of their personal selves and offering to be of help to others. It is a network where the main attraction is the sharing of ideas.

Organizationally BrainPool is small but the linkages to global networks, and its capacity to enhance the lives of individuals at work, are immense. Operating from a small office, it could be labelled a microbusiness. In the café, what you see might be a group of friends talking. At another level, however, BrainPool is (for those who can see it) a vast network of warm resources, interconnected through work and personal relationships which can be mobilized instantly to bring a project into being.

Recently a member bought a small publishing company and was able to source writers, designers, editors immediately, as well as creating many new strategic partnerships.

What makes BrainPool work?

Attractor and filter

The language BrainPool uses in its literature, the nature of the activities it offers, act as a powerful attractor for those who are open to new ideas and new ways of working and as an equally strong filter to discourage those who might sabotage or drain the energy.

Dedication and drive from the centre, plus a belief in creating the space for others to flourish. An understanding that the most important job for a network coordinator once the occasion is set up is to get out of the way and offer barrier-free connection. At its most effective the efforts of the coordinator are invisible, like the feeling you have when you have been to a really good party or event. You had a good time, you met some really interesting people, it felt like time well spent – and it felt effortless.

A new way of being

We are now being challenged to help each other create intelligence, to become intelligent agents for each other. By that I mean that we create a web of relationships where we make it our business to find out what information is of most value to others – information that is relevant and timely, and that delights the other. The hallmark of an intelligent organization is its commitment to creating space where people can think and connect, where knowledge creation is rewarded. The key characteristics of an effective network host are selflessness, generosity and constant attention to the quality of connections being formed.

Watching *Casualty* or *ER* on television, one is assailed by the tensions of workplaces where staff are constantly stretched to the limit, under so much pressure that there is no space to build and nurture the relationships that lead to information-sharing. Band-Aid solutions are sought, and potentially fatal mistakes are waiting to happen.

Poolside Learning Café

BrainPool launched Poolside Learning Café at the Edinburgh Festival in 1996. The Cafe has grown in scale and significance as a safe space for people from a wide variety of backgrounds to try out new and crucial skills of connecting and personal learning. The core design structure of the Café encourages people to discover their full creativity and stretch their potential in a friendly, welcoming atmosphere. The Café becomes a community of explorers, who learn to be together in a new and caring way, confidently. They experience unique quality and depth of learning and networking.

Workshops on 'Trust and Passion in Work', 'Come and Meet The Most Interesting Person in the World', 'Creativity', 'Think the Unthinkable' are eagerly attended by people from Yorkshire, Portsmouth, Italy, Monaco, Brighton, Aberdeen, London, Australia, Canada, from Edinburgh suburbs and Glasgow housing estates. Musicians, secretaries, managers, solicitors, beauticians, chief executives, artists, students, civil servants, with ages ranging from 20 to 84 years – a glorious, unique brew.

Poolside Learning Café is a place where we know you will make productive connections. You will meet someone you never expected to meet, someone will say something that changes your life, you will have insights that change the way you work, and most importantly you will make new connections with your self. *It is about significant, whole person learning.* People learn skills to help them thrive in the new Knowledge Era, and more importantly they discover hidden facets of themselves which they can develop in their work and their personal lives.

Direct results have included grand romances, new business partnerships, new projects and the development of new workshops (which are now being offered more widely in the marketplace) and new behaviours at work.

Electronic community

When you combine deep spiritual commitment and integrity with advanced facilitation skills (invisible coordinator, intelligent agent, motivator, highly developed ability to synthesize data) and a grasp of what the technology currently can support, it is possible to create peak experiences on-line.

My own experience is of a Lotus Notes 'Community of Inquiry and Practice Into Meaning and Wholeness At Work', convened by groupware pioneers Peter and Trudy Johnson-Lenz in 1996. Peter and Trudy crafted with great care an on-line community which lasted for five months. Their highly developed ability to host, facilitate, and to know – without being asked – what was needed, encouraged people to contribute in deep and personally meaningful ways.

Peter and Trudy experimented with a number of devices used in face-to-face meetings, in order to explore which would work particularly well in a virtual community. Talking sticks, Dialogue, Open Space, Café tables, and digests of the learning were on offer, plus a Wants and Offers section and personal introductions by each member, complete with photograph. Some of the areas, like the Café and Open Space, were very busy, and I found the number of messages overwhelming. Other spaces, like the Council Circle, where each person has one opportunity per round to contribute, offered more space for reflection. The offerings were very personal and thoughtful.

More recently I took part in the Berkana Conversations, an e-mail community exploring the works of Margaret Wheatley on self-organizing systems. Once again, when careful attention is paid to structure, values, language and quality of facilitation, a very deep level of connectedness can be established.

I firmly believe that we only create intelligence when we create trust-building relationships with others. Groupware and other technologies support this process, but do not on their own deliver intelligence. The companies and individuals who will thrive in the Knowledge Era are those who are clear about their values and their purpose, and who are able to foster trust building relationships, both internally and externally.

We are living in times when our ability to be contributing members of networks and communities is being called on. The ability to repeat rote-learned data will not build intelligence. Increasingly the need is for a skillset which has barely been made visible. I look forward to the day when I read an advert in the recruitment pages that goes something like this:

Wanted
Web-Weavers and Intelligent Agents

Go-ahead company seeks Weavers, Facilitators, Catalysts, Coordinators, Hosts with the following qualities:

- Ability to initiate rich information exchanges
- Ability to synthesize complex information
- Generosity, selflessness, integrity
- Ability to feel comfortable with any group of people
- Ability to see the bigger picture and make connections across boundaries
- Always out to lunch and on the phone
- Well-maintained large and diverse personal networks
- Presence – ability to make the business case for creating space and structures to support intelligence building
- Ability to think laterally
- Superb communication skills

Critical success factors:
- A noticeably higher flow of energy and enquiry throughout the organization
- New, productive, cross boundary relationships
- Marked decrease in territorial disputes
- Strong, caring interpersonal relationships at all levels
- A network of skilled facilitators and hosts
- Efficiency savings
- New products, new projects resulting from higher quality relationships
- Greatly enhanced relationships with customers and suppliers

We offer:
- High-level backing, freedom to roam, financial support for key connection building initiatives.

Rewards are high for such rare individuals, who are our key Intelligence Creators.

Chapter 27

Trading Post: a safe place for champions

Peter Lloyd

If you are reading this book, you are probably someone who is interested in keeping track of the latest IT trends coming over the horizon and what impact they will have on your organization. So you will appreciate that tracking technology is time-consuming and almost a full time job. Maybe you wish there were other people like you to talk with about the issues behind the trends, to discuss what is hot and what is not, and to help you consider what will be the best combination of products and services for your business. While you know you are not alone and that there are more ways than ever before to connect with your peers, you are probably too busy to find these people. Of course you could reach out through the Internet to one of the discussion groups or attend one of those conferences which are popping up every week – but the value received for the time invested in these 'chance' meetings is low.

  If there was a better way to trade experiences and examine new ideas and share questions with your opposite numbers in large and complex organizations, would you participate? Well, about three years ago I felt there was a need for such a group and so I created one in the UK. Trading Post is designed as a safe place for technology and organization development pioneers to meet their peers in other corporations and exchange knowledge with each other; just as the traders and trappers used to do in the old days of the Wild West.

The first Trading Post meeting took place in London on 18 November 1994. Those who attended that meeting came from my travels and my contacts, but the main source was the many conferences on groupware, which were being held at the time. Although they came from a wide variety of different organizations, they had a similar focus.

What is Trading Post?

Trading Post is a closed network of information technology and organizational development watchers, especially those concerned with groupware and collaborative technologies – such as intranets, virtual teams and knowledge management. The members come from a broad cross-section of large and complex organizations in both the private and the public sectors.

Our logo (see Figure 27.1) is a geodesic dome in the open with the woods behind. The geodesic dome was the invention of R. Buckminster Fuller and it represents his belief in the importance of sound technological design combined with a holistic and humanistic philosophy. It is the only practical kind of building which has no limiting dimensions and can be set directly on the ground as a complete structure.

Figure 27.1   Trading Post's logo

Fuller is regarded as one of the most original thinkers of the second half of the twentieth century and according to the *Encyclopaedia Britannica* he was perhaps the first to attempt to develop, on a global basis, comprehensive, long range, technological and economic plans designed 'to make Man [sic] a success in the universe'. As we progress ever faster towards the new millennium and our organizations become even more complex, so we need more thinkers like 'Bucky' and we need safe spaces to incubate their ideas.

About the members

Trading Post is for the people who are described as the 'champions' or visionaries, and their enthusiasm for the benefits of exploiting new technology is infectious. Quite often these people do not have substantial power, budgets or staff; but they do have significant influence within their organizations. They have usually been with their current employer for several years and have held a number of different posts – often both inside and outside the IT department. This deep understanding of the organization is valued by the senior management and so they are tolerated as mavericks within their companies.

Many of them do not regard themselves as IT people as they have come from 'the business side' of their employers. In addition to IT, members may come from areas such as human resources, quality assurance and general management staff; they all recognize that IT is a key enabler and agent of change.

The members tend to take a holistic view on most things and they realize successful system implementation needs the integration of human and technology factors to be taken into consideration. Accordingly, the Trading Post network has become a safe place for IT, HR, total quality management (TQM) and general management people to explore together successful strategies for organizational transformation.

The members can best be described as those who are in the 'crow's nest' of their organizations. That is to say they are the ones who are responsible for monitoring future trends in IT and the likely impact these will have on their own organizations. These are the people who are the ones most likely to have brought to their Board of Directors' attention the emergence of the Web, intranets and knowledge management.

However, by definition this position is a lonely one. By choosing this role within the organization they turn their backs on the traditional career paths. Like the trappers in the old days they have become self-reliant and independent, so they have very few people they can talk to within their own companies who understand them. They tend to be driven people who care deeply about their companies and have high standards. This in turn means that they have very little time for socializing, especially outside their own companies.

This group recognizes that it is a full-time job keeping abreast of the latest developments within this fast-moving technological field, while it is also a full time job doing whatever it says on their business card. In addition there is the time-consuming, but essential for survival, process of tracking the changes and politics within one's own organization; another full time job! Time is at a premium for these people and so a network which enables the members to turn to each other for fast answers and unbiased opinions on emerging trends and the latest products and services is worth a lot to them.

Members pay an annual subscription per person per organization per annum and the rate varies in different countries. For companies wanting multiple memberships, up to a maximum of five, there is a sliding scale of discounts. Subscriptions are not tied to any nominated person within a member organization, so member organizations can send the person most appropriate for each topic or location.

Why do they join?

Today's members were each personally invited by me to attend an initial meeting and subsequently to join Trading Post (TP). The network has grown organically and we do not believe in advertising or direct mail. We are building a community and we think that it is very important that the right people are invited in the right way and introduced to the group in the right way.

What we mean by 'right' is that they like the ambiance, relate to the other members and the topics being discussed. It has little to do with their job title or seniority within their own organizations. If they participate, then it is clear they are getting value from the meetings and are making productive connections. However, if it is not directly relevant to their needs, then they usually know who is the more appropriate person in their organization and they usually give us their name to be invited to the next meeting.

One of our members, Ron Eagle of Perot Systems, described the value they get from their membership as:

Our company strives to be a true 'learning organization' and in this spirit subscribes to a number of 'user groups' and IT learning communities. Each of these does in their own way, of course, contribute to increasing the critical mass of technical and experiential knowledge, which is then made generally available to be shared by all the members of our teams. The 'groupware' technologies that allow us to share in this way are intranet, cc:Mail, databases, etc.

What makes TP uniquely valuable is that it is hybrid:

- It offers the conviviality of a 'user group' with individuals (Note individuals … not just company delegated attendees) who are genuinely enthusiastic about their subjects;
- It offers a calibre of speakers, researchers and associated members that really do provide cutting edge technical insights.
- It provides its services in the spirit of a 'learning organization', i.e. barrier-free sharing of information and experiences, but with a focus on empirical usefulness to members.
- It is both academic in scope of subjects, but also practical in application since most members actually do implementations of groupware in some form.

Applying the key performance indicator, no company will continue to subscribe to a mere talk shop if its employees' time would be better spent elsewhere. If my own experience is typical, then every hour spent with TP has been recouped several times over in adding quality to my real work. I therefore have no doubt that TP will not only survive, but expand as this experience is shared and communicated.

We have reached the point where our members are now going to conferences and mentioning Trading Post to the people they meet, who naturally want to come to the next meeting and assess it for themselves. In the long term the challenge will be how to keep the quality of the network as it expands numerically and geographically, which is why our logo is a geodesic dome.

The meetings

Since the very beginning the group has been run for the benefit of the members and they dictate what topics they want to talk about. My function has been to act as a facilitator – to discover what they want and then to make it happen. Every time I think I know what the group wants, I get it wrong and yet in the process I learn more about myself and the group, so that ultimately the group grows and gets better all the time. We started with an intention to meet four times a year, which turned out to be the right frequency of face-to-face meetings.

After three years of these meetings in London, I took the decision to hold our first regional meetings – one in Bristol and one in High Peak, in the glorious Derbyshire Dales. These were very successful and now the UK Trading Post meets fourteen times a year – four times in both the West Country and the Midlands and six times in London/the Home Counties. Between meetings, there is a moderated Internet mailing list and a directory of members to enable individual networking.

The range of topics we have discussed is quite broad and past meetings have featured the following subjects:

- The anywhere office.
- Virtual teamworking: case study by BP.
- Collaborative computing – is it worth it?
- Sedgwicks: case study of Lotus Notes.
- Intel: case study of Notes adoption.
- Nationwide: case study in multimedia design and usability.
- Managing information as a resource.
- Lotus Notes vs Intranets.
- Café society and the development of an information-sharing culture.
- Change, complexity and leadership.
- Dying for information.
- Supporting the commercial manager: information management for business streams.
- How to make money via the Web.
- Changing the culture of the MIS department.
- Business benefits of technology adoption.

The Trading Post community

The group functions rather like a user group in that the meetings are hosted by one of the members, who either gives a talk or an outside expert is invited to give a presentation. This is followed by general discussion and then a buffet lunch. Almost half of the time is allocated for 'mingling'. This significant proportion of the meeting time is important for attendees to get to know each other and exchange contact details.

We take great care to look after people the first time they come to one of our meetings. For example, we always circulate a list of attendees just before the meeting and the final version at the meeting. Then at the beginning of a meeting I always go round the whole room and briefly introduce each person to the group. This is a good 'ice-breaker' and it means new people can discreetly make a note of who they want to meet over the buffet lunch.

Our members value the time they spend with each other and so great emphasis has always been placed on the face-to-face meetings. Electronic communication was only added in the second half of 1997. We experimented with different Web-based computer-conferencing systems, but in the end we found you cannot beat a simple e-mail list. Every one checks their e-mail, but conferencing systems are just one more thing to do.

Expanding overseas

Although Trading Post began in the UK, it was not long before interest was expressed in holding meetings in other countries. Meetings have already been held in Portugal and the South of France and there are plans to launch it in the Netherlands. In addition coordinators have been identified in a number of other key cities around the world, such as Boston, Washington, San Francisco, Singapore, Toronto, Geneva and Perth.

What is next for Trading Post?

The ultimate vision of Trading Post is to create a network of coordinators in a hundred different cities around the world and each one would arrange at least four meetings a year for twenty members in their locality. This would mean a global network of some 2,000 large corporations and public sector organizations and at least 400 meetings a year – more than one a day! Assuming that the content of all meetings is captured and stored in a secure Website, we will build up an incredibly valuable resource for our members. This archive will be a treasure trove on a wide range of subjects and will represent different cultures at different stages of technological adoption.

But the really valuable resource will be the network of members in the different countries and no doubt members will drop in on each other's meetings when they are passing through each other's countries.

For the coordinators the opportunity to be part of this network will undoubtedly greatly enhance their personal networks and give them access to an exceptional global community of fellow pioneers.

Today's members

As at February 1998, the members in the UK include ISI (Mars group), Royal Mail, Post Office, HM Customs and Excise, Department of Trade and Industry, Dixons, the Greenalls Group, KPMG, Perot Systems (SBC Warburg), Halifax plc, Eastgate Insurance, Harlow Butler Broking Services, Ericsson, Orange, Asea Brown Boveri, BP, Shell, Burmah Castrol, Halliburton Brown & Root, Schneider Groupe, T & N, Surrey County Council, DiverseyLever (Unilever), GlaxoWellcome, Napp Pharmaceutical Group, SmithKline Beecham, Rhône-Poulenc Agricultural, Scott Bader, Linklaters and Paine, the Greenalls Group, Northern Foods, Avon Cosmetics, Imperial Tobacco and the RAC.

Tomorrow's members

Dear reader, I invite you to discover this group. If you are a pioneer currently working for a large and complex organization, which does not understand you, and are interested in membership – or if you are interested in exploring the possibility of becoming a coordinator, please see our Website – www.trading-post.org.uk.

Part Three

Web-Weaving – What Next?

Our finale on web-weaving is really an overture of tomorrow's world. We asked our contributors to 'fast-forward the video' and describe what the world might look like in the future. Here we step aside from looking inside, outside and in-between and instead look at:

- developments in information technology, which will affect strategic business decisions
- changes in the shape of organizations and the role of the individual
- people issues and the social effects of information technology.

In Chapters 28, 29 and 30 we listen to the voices of information technology leaders from Hewlett-Packard Laboratories, Microsoft and the WorldWide Web Consortium as they describe their visions of the future.

In Chapter 28 Joel Birnbaum describes a future in which there will be a digital utility, which will turn what is today a capital investment, into a competitive service similar to the utilities for electricity and water. He believes the digital information infrastructure will create new industries in a similar way to those created by the public highway infrastructure when the automobile became pervasive – such as car insurance, car rentals and service stations.

In Bill Gates's chapter, his basic premise is that all companies have a 'nervous system' (the way that a business deals with planned or unplanned events) and the excellence of which determines a company's competitiveness. Due to technological breakthroughs, it is now possible to have dramatically more responsive nervous systems, which he terms the 'digital nervous system'. He believes the boundary of what you do inside your company and what you do outside the company needs to be reconsidered once these nervous systems are in place.

In Chapter 30, Tim Berners-Lee, the creator of the WorldWide

Web, describes the Web of tomorrow. Starting with his original dream, he goes on to raise important issues such as trust systems, a common language for machines to communicate over the Web, and a resource description framework (RDF) which will simplify the exchange of information about documents around the world.

In Chapters 31, 32, 33 and 34 four leading thinkers consider different aspects of the changing shape of the organization and the role of the individual.

Meredith Belbin, who pioneered the principles for building successful management teams in the 1980s, points out that organizational hierarchy can be considered a natural extension of a common biosystem that affects much of the living world. He then describes how current organizations need to change to cope with networks and draws upon the order of social insects, which appear individually stupid but are collectively wise, whereas humans are individually intelligent but prone to mass stupidity.

Don Tapscott is an acknowledged visionary, author and speaker. This abridged chapter from his seminal book, *The Digital Economy*, describes a cascading model of business transformation enabled by new technology and media in which the 'internetworked business' is the new model for wealth creation. But there is a contrary view of Tapscott's theory from Michael Wolff in Chapter 33, who is a pioneering practitioner of teleworking in the Scottish Highlands. Michael puts forward the hypothesis of personal transformation, where the individual knowledge worker becomes empowered by the network and therefore will be free from the need to give his or her power to a hierarchy, such as Tapscott's 'internetworked business', and can build his or her own hierarchies at will. With open access to all the resources of the network, they can choose when, where and how to work. At all times they will be in charge of their own destiny and creating their own meaning and purpose. So he believes the 'empowered individual' will achieve for oneself personal security and satisfaction, which ultimately changes the markets which rely on such workers.

In Chapter 34 John McIntyre, an Honorary Member of the Centre for Tomorrow's Company, continues the theme of the independent role of knowledge workers, whom he describes as playing roles similar to independent lawyers and doctors of today. He thinks we are on a threshold of a new world and quotes Peter Drucker as saying this transformation may take until 2010 or 2020 to be completed. He extends Charles Handy's 'shamrock organization' (core of management and essential staff; long-term contractors; and temporary workers) through William Bridges' four-segment square (adding the customer) to his own

Maple Leaf model (adding education). This leads to the *inclusive approach* – a philosophy of business leadership based on the deliberate and constructive management of *all* the organization's key relationships, typically the stakeholders.

Chapters 35, 36 and 37 conclude by looking at the people issues and social effects of web-weaving.

Nelson Thall, Research Director of The McLuhan Centre for Media Studies, expresses his unique perspective of the 'global village' and 'internet-man' [sic], 'who wears his brain outside his skull and his nervous system on top of his skin. He is like an exposed spider squatting in a thrumming web, resonating with all other webs. But he is not flesh and blood; he is an item in a data bank, ephemeral, easily forgotten and resentful of that fact'. He believes, 'All technologies hypnotize the user and we are machines serving machines – and not vice versa. To survive today, we must strive to understand the power of technologies to isolate the senses and thus, to "hypnotize" society'.

Susanna Opper, groupware pioneer and author, follows this line with a comparison with life in a walled town in France in the year 1151, in Chapter 36. Coming back to the present she notes that, 'Somewhere along the way we've lost touch with a part of our humanity; we will need to reclaim it in the years ahead. We need an antidote to the "too much" of our lives today. An antidote is defined as a remedy to counteract the effects of poison or of anything noxious taken into the system.'

Finally, in Chapter 37, Dr Robin Wood, proponent of New Sciences in management, coins the expression 'symplectics', which means a set of frameworks, methods, models and tools used to bridge the distances between people with very different backgrounds and life experiences. He stresses the importance of becoming more aware of world views (which we and others hold and the actions we take as a result) and how they influence the kinds of futures we set about creating.

Chapter 28

The digital utility[1]

Joel Birnbaum

How the coming digital utility may reshape computing and telecommunications

I am convinced that the Internet and the WorldWide Web built upon it are the earliest form of what will become a digital information utility. Technological barriers as well as issues of public acceptance and national policy stand in the way, and it may not happen for ten to fifteen years, however, I believe that irresistible market forces will cause these barriers to be overcome. The digital information utility will create a new style of computing and will both demand and enable a new type of communications infrastructure.

Pervasive computing, appliances and digital information utility

I have been pursuing a dream for about twenty years. The precursor of the illustration in Figure 28.1 was originally made in 1982–83 and it used to be regarded as fanciful. The dream was that the Internet would become pervasive.

Towards pervasive information systems

By a pervasive technology, I mean one more noticeable by its absence than its presence – in just the same way that automobiles, television sets, telephones and many other technologies have become part of everyday life for most people. Figure 28.1 shows the progression of computing technology over several decades; computing elements are shown below the S-curves; how they are interconnected is shown above. A key point is that in the beginning of this decade making the devices small had finally led to the ability to specialize them according to their function in sufficient volume so that they could be priced for mass markets. Another important point is that the architected interface between the requesters and providers of services, the so-called clients and servers, which produced open systems, is the enabling transition for computing technology to become pervasive within the next decade.

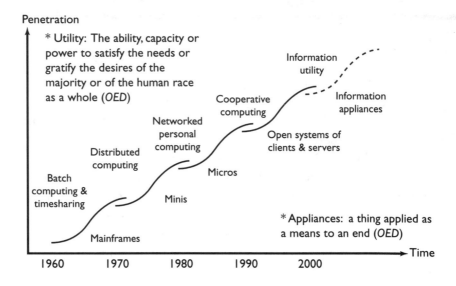

Figure 28.1 Towards pervasive information systems

People born after a technology has been invented think of it as part of the environment. Tomorrow's children will think of computers the way today's think of telephones and television. In order for true pervasiveness to happen, the technology must transcend being merely manufacturable and commonplace and must be intuitively accessible to ordinary people, delivering value sufficient to justify the large investment in supporting infrastructure.

In the next century, computers will often be embedded in devices dedicated to performing a particular task, which will allow people to think in terms of the task being performed and not in terms of how the tool which performs it operates. The analogy with electric motors and consumer appliances is instructive: we think in terms of the function of a washing machine, electric toothbrush or videocassette recorder (VCR), not of the motors within; in fact, we do not know, nor care, how many motors we own. The same will be true for computers.

Information appliances

This is what we usually refer to as an information appliance; a device which is a means to a particular end and whose usage seems quite natural to a great many people. It differs greatly from a small, mobile, general purpose computer in what it does and in the much smaller learning overhead imposed on the user. We expect appliances to evolve to hide their own complexity, just as the one-button automatically tuned television set of today has replaced its less complex, but harder-to-adjust ancestor; and because of continued advances in semiconductors and software, the information appliances of tomorrow will be able to do the same. These appliances need not be small or portable – think of furnaces and refrigerators – and the greatly enhanced bandwidth of the utility will allow the more demanding processing to be done non-locally. They conform to a simple model of usage, like the 'neutral–drive–reverse' of automatic transmissions in cars.

A successful infrastructure

Like all successful infrastructures, the digital information infrastructure will have to be so dependable that we only notice it when it fails; it must be secure, endure over generations, be found everywhere and serving a purpose important to almost all of the population. Just like other pervasive infrastructures, it will catalyse new industries; for example, the public highway infrastructure, which made the personal automobile a pervasive technology, created the auto insurance, car rental, driver training and gasoline station industries to name just a few.

Why client-utility computing?

In such a world in which clients (general purpose computers or appliances) connect to this utility, people would pay for their computing by usage, modulated by response requirements, a change that turns what is now a capital investment into a competitive service, like electricity and water. This is not the same as time-sharing, which was proprietary, not open, and often location-dependent. In client-utility computing, open resources, located arbitrarily, are combined as needed. It will no longer matter where the computers are located or which manufacturer makes them. The suicidal obsolescence schedule of today will be replaced by the capacity requirements of the service provider, with upgrades undetectable by the end user within a given performance envelope. Just as people pick up a phone and expect a dial tone so, too, will people expect the information utility to be available, ready and waiting, and quality of service will be a crucial competitive differentiator at the systems level.

The emerging Information Superhighway

A key aspect of this utility is that it will be digital. Of course, this is the basis of multimedia; but more importantly, I think, this means that devices that send and receive information can be independent of each other, instead of having to be designed in matched pairs, like fax machines or television and radio transmitters and receivers are today. Given the appropriate interchange standards, your fax machine, for example, could begin communicating with your television, which could also receive your newspaper and diagnostic information from your car.

Many of the decisions that are made at the transmission end can now be done at the receiver end. Once information interchange standards are in place, appliance and peripheral families will emerge and many of these will be able to communicate directly, without the intervention or invocation of a general purpose computer and the attendant cumbersome operating system. In fact, many, if not most of the computers of the next generation will be enormously powerful, non-reprogrammable, invisible processors, such as the several dozen hidden in a modern car, which control the ignition, suspension, braking, steering, engine management, climate control systems and provide diagnostic information to the driver and the mechanic. No one has ever asked a car dealer whether the computer runs Unix or NT. The interface is the steering wheel or brake pedal. Function is augmented without the need to introduce an unfamiliar interface.

Everything has a Web page

It is already practical to embed a Web server in individual devices, which means that everyday appliances can have a Web page at negligible cost. So you can inspect and control – visually and simply, using a conventional browser – things like home security and heating/cooling systems or individual appliances like a bath or a toaster, from anywhere that you can click on a Web page (see Figure 28.2). We may even make it possible for ordinary adults to programme a VCR! In fact, any instrument's front panel, or a subset of it, can be viewed from anywhere by people with access rights, making it possible for engineers and scientists to collaborate across vast distances at very low cost and making remote maintenance for low-cost devices practical. Notification capability can be incorporated; for example, imagine a printer that signals a supplier automatically for replacement of toner or ink cartridges, when some usage threshold is crossed.

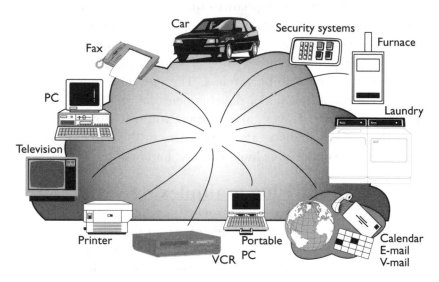

Figure 28.2   Everything has a Web page

If the communications pipe is fast enough and cheap enough, this also means that you can do things far away that appear to be done locally. Distributed computing power, remote distributed measurements, very rich user interfaces in small inexpensive devices, remote printing and scanning become meaningful and practical, and will enable applications at a scale and cost unthinkable today.

I believe that client-utility computing will provoke as great a change in the computing industry as open systems did in this decade. The new paradigm will do for computation what the Web did for data and will produce such dramatic decreases in cost of ownership, with concomitant increases in up-time and accessibility that those companies that do not react to the opportunity will not be able to satisfy customer expectations. History tells us that this can have dire consequences.

The Information Age (the Tera Era)

We are entering a period that some people at Hewlett-Packard Laboratories have begun to call the 'Tera Era' because of the very demanding technical requirements to support inexpensive, high bandwidth networks. The viability of the digital infrastructure for multimedia documents, appliance-utility computing, and distributed remote measurements depends upon a number of key technologies coming together. Particularly critical is being able to have high bandwidth at very low cost. For some applications, the end user access will need to be wireless. The question then becomes, are there technologies under development that will address these needs? The answer is 'yes', and I expect you will soon be hearing a lot more about many of the contenders in the wireless sweepstakes and the options for huge wireline bandwidth.

Wavelength division multiplexing

For example, important developments are taking place in optics technology that could have a huge effect on the telecommunications system. The theoretical capacity of the fibre is vast – something on the order of 25,000 GHz – though, we typically do not take advantage of anything but a tiny fraction of that, just a few gigahertz. Thus, if we can find a way to send and switch more signals through a fibre optic cable, we could increase the system's capacity by at least two or three orders of magnitude. It would mark a radical change in such systems: for the first time the electronic switching systems become the bottleneck, instead of the transmission lines connected to them. This suggests that an all optical system is needed, and the most promising approach is called wavelength division multiplexing. This is not a new idea, but it is now becoming realistic to think of such systems being deployed in the next decade or so.

The communication network of the future

Fibre technology has advanced over the last twenty years to the point that the distance across which a usable light pulse can be sent has grown from a fraction of a kilometre to hundreds of kilometres, and cost has plummeted concurrently. If we could transmit and then select all the theoretically possible frequencies, then the system could work the way that a radio does. That is, at one end, a particular station chooses its frequency and, at the other end, the user has what amounts to a big dial. Depending on whom you want to be connected to, you turn the dial and change the frequency of the receiver. Sometimes a movie comes over the pipe, sometimes a newspaper, sometimes the result of an economic model from a distant supercomputer.

Wavelength division multiplexing over existing fibre infrastructure

This is, of course, a lot more easily said than done. If these technology problems could be overcome, the results would be fabulous, the breakthroughs dramatic. Just one strand of fibre, in principle, could carry 2.5 billion separate audio telephone calls – all the phone calls for a large city. Many users of the digital information utility will want enough bandwidth for high resolution, real-time, multimedia – say a 100 MHz-wide channel – that is ten times an entire ethernet for each user. With wavelength division multiplexing, a single optic fibre could carry 250,000 of these superbandwidth channels.

Network measurement and management

Besides greater bandwidth, the digital utility will also require much more sophisticated network management. This is because users will expect the quality of service they now get from their telephone system. The Internet as we know it today is nowhere close to this.

Management approach

To manage applications end to end, there can be no alternative to making distributed, continuous measurements of performance, capacity and usage statistics, and relating them to a model of the system, or part of it. By measuring what is actually happening across the entire system, you can adjust its capacity, detect many types of fraud, predict where performance bottlenecks are likely to occur, locate outages and identify unused parts of the system for reserve capacity. Once again, Internet technology will reduce the complexity and lower the cost; in fact, Hewlett-Packard has built a very successful prototype of such a system that is operational today in a London cellular phone trial.

Network management and measurement are the Achilles heel of the robust, flexible infrastructure that operator and user both want. I think these will be the pacing core technologies of the Information Age and they demand the immediate attention of telecommunication and computer manufacturers alike. It will be important to develop international standards; and while the technology will be similar in some ways to that now used by distributed computer systems and the telephone networks, it will have to solve problems of scale and speed that people have not had to deal with before. Systems with millions, or even tens of millions, of nodes will be commonplace, and the heterogeneity of the hardware and software will be unprecedented.

Distributed measurement systems
Once developed, this core capability of measuring and managing the evolved Internet itself will be extended to enable a vast range of distributed measurement applications that today would require specialized, far-too-expensive systems. The utility provides the infrastructure to link distributed sensors at very low cost and in an ubiquitous way. Many industries will be radically transformed by this ability to operate on a continental basis.

Security
Security is a difficult problem because we are on a difficult tightrope – we want maximum interoperability for authorized, authenticated users among all computers, all appliances and all nations – which means no barriers to interconnection. This interoperability goal is in direct tension with the issues of access control, privacy and system integrity. Citizens' rights to privacy are in direct conflict with the needs of national security and criminal justice agencies. Building a truly open global system is antithetical technically with a secure system with good performance

and attractive cost, and so a set of difficult technical, social and political trade-offs are inevitably involved.

My opinion is that the security issue will be solved more easily than the bandwidth and management ones. Most of the world's computing and communication companies are working feverishly on this. Although no perfect solution is likely to emerge, I believe that an acceptable *de facto* standard – based on an acceptable range of trade-offs and compromises – will emerge because of the overwhelming financial and market forces driving it.

Summary

The telephone system that we know today, and the Internet and Web technology built upon it, are precursors of a global digital information utility. The Internet is delivering today, at low bandwidth and relatively high cost, entirely new classes of information and services. As the bandwidth and usage grow, and as the costs inevitably come down as a result, the resulting information utility will dramatically change computing as well as telephony and the delivery of multimedia information. In time, we will think of today's systems as quaint.

I see the major obstacles as providing high bandwidth at low cost, managing a network of this scale and resolving many security issues. It will take time to solve these problems, but many talented and energetic people are working on these issues, and I am confident that most of the barriers will be overcome in the next ten or fifteen years. The world will never be the same again.

Note

1. This chapter is taken from a speech at the IEEE (Institute of Electrical and Electronic Engineers), 17 October 1996.

Chapter 29

The digital nervous system[1]

Bill Gates

Introduction

When I say 'nervous system of a business', what I am talking about is the way that a business deals with events – planned events (like yearly budgeting or sales results) or unplanned events (like competitive activities or unhappy customers). And there are all the different systems – the meetings, the paperwork, the way the information workers are organized, the way that information about customers is stored, the budgeting system, the coordination system. All of those are the nervous system of the company.

No matter what business you are in, it is my claim that the excellence of that nervous system determines your competitiveness. In the past, companies were virtually all alike in terms of how well they managed these things. The tools were well known and so there was not much differentiation. But my thesis is that with the incredible advances in technology, it is now possible to have dramatically more responsive nervous systems. And I term this the digital nervous system.

The first factor of a million

The rate and scope of technological change has been pretty unbelievable. When Microsoft got started, computing was a million times more expensive than it is today. And computing was simply a central tool, a tool for keeping track of business accounts or reservations. And only the largest organizations could have this tool. In fact, it was a clear advantage for very large companies. But once the computer reached over a million users, things changed.

That factor of a million did more than simply drop the price. It changed the very character of how we think about computing. It changed computing to be a tool of communication. It enabled people to individually think about how they manage information so that everybody has a machine and great flexibility in dealing with that information.

The next factor of a million

Over the next twenty years, the cost of computing will fall again by a factor of a million. Now, the good news here is that the demand elasticity for computing is quite amazing. Other markets where you find efficiency anywhere near this, you have a tendency to shrink the market. When radial tyres came along, they lasted longer and so they were quite a bit cheaper in the long term. But people did not respond by driving around a lot more and so the total revenue of the market shrank.

When people looked at computing and the exponential impact of Moore's law, the doubling in performance every two years, they were really worried about what would happen to the computer industry. Would it also shrink? In fact, the computer industry has grown because the ways that we can use this power have proliferated even faster than the performance improvements. And my belief is again that this next factor of a million will be absorbed in the same way. So it is very different than any other industry on the planet.

As we use these devices for communications, we need to think about more than just the speed of computation or even the size of the memory or the size of the disk. We need to think about how these machines are connected together. And if there is anything that will slow down the pace of revolution, it is if we do not get these high-speed, low-cost connections in place.

High speeds, low costs

I am very optimistic about the demand elasticity for high-speed connections. I believe that the phone company investments in ISDN and ADSL will pay off in a major way, even more than they expect to. I also think that PC cable modems are providing users with additional choice and that this is a very positive thing that will spur more competitiveness in this area. These important movements to provide high-speed, low-cost connections are fundamental and, unfortunately, also subject to a great deal of government regulation.

Inherently, networks have a problem of needing to be shared to be economic. And so you will see a lot of differentiation from country to country in terms of how this is managed. Does a country create an atmosphere where these investments are encouraged? And because the quality of these nervous systems depend on that, and because the very competitiveness of the firms in the countries depend on that, it will make a huge difference in terms of who leads in world competitiveness.

Unlimited potential
Now, when we take the improvement in speed and the improvements in communications and put that together with what the software industry is doing, I would say that there is an opportunity to do almost anything businesses are interested in doing with information. If you can imagine how information would flow in your company, how it would automatically be analysed and compared and summarized and brought to the attention of the people who need to know about it, I would say that building a system that can fulfil your wildest dreams is possible today.

Not only is it possible, but it is possible with development costs that are really quite modest. We no longer talk in terms of many-year projects – two, three, four years of development or a huge backlog of activity. Today, if the right infrastructure is in place, people can build applications in as little as four to eight months.

Tomorrow's computers
If we think of what the computer system will look like ten years from now, it will be radically different, because the way we interface with the machine will have changed. It will not just be the keyboard and the mouse. We will be talking to our computer. We will be typing in sentences. If you want to find things on the Internet, you will not use keywords, where you get back thousands of things that you have to wade through. Instead you will say the same thing to your computer, either by typing or speaking, that you would to a human assistant. And all the richness of

linguistics and common sense will be applied in helping perform that operation.

And so we will be using that next factor of a million in extra performance to change the way that we interact with the system. The operating system of the future, over 90 per cent of its code, will relate to speaking, listening, recognizing handwriting and understanding linguistics. And the things we think about in the operating system today will still be there – graphics, menu management – but they will actually be the smaller part of the code.

Nervous systems examples

Well, let us talk about excellence in these nervous systems. How are you to know whether you are managing this in the best possible way? There are lots of questions you can ask that get at this issue. First is to examine the use of paper. How much paper is flowing around the company? I did an exercise recently where I had every paper form at Microsoft brought to me. And I looked at them and said: 'Why do we have this paper form? Everybody's got a PC. We're really connected up. We're ready to use electronic mail.' And very quickly we were able to eliminate the majority of them. Within a year, we will have got rid of virtually all of them.

Paper-trapped systems

A symptom of a bad nervous system is where you find that you are printing out a lot of information, such as when you have lots of printed sales reports. When you have data on a piece of paper, you cannot delve into it. You look at it, and let us say it is a sales number that really bothers you. The sales are not high enough. What do you want to do?

Do you want to call somebody up and talk to them about it and have them find the same piece of paper and look at it and have them say, 'Whoops, we'll dig into that'? Or would you like to just point to it and click on it and see it broken down by geography, by time period, by product type and really try to get at the bottom of what is going on? Is it a volume change? Is it a price change? And as you go in and see something that catches your attention, then you want to be able to send electronic mail to the right people in the organization and enclose exactly the view of the data you have. So everybody is sharing the same thing.

A less-paper system

An example of moving to a good system, one that removes some paper is what AIG, the insurance firm, did in terms of interfacing with its brokers and agents. They used to use paper systems to send out reports, pricing and commission structures and it took a lot of time. And over 25 per cent of the time was spent correcting errors and just dealing with the overhead of getting the information back and forth.

When that was moved to be solely an electronic system up on the Internet, not only did that 25 per cent go away, so the cost of running the system was much lower, but also the ability to target information and get it to the broker is improved. The information is completely up to date in the middle of the day, and they can analyse which brokers were doing things particularly well and make recommendations to them. It was a whole new capability that the paper system never would have allowed to operate. We will be moving away from these paper systems.

Customer systems

Perhaps the most important system in this nervous system concept is customer information. Where do you store customer knowledge? Can you go to one place and see everything about a customer? I think that is an imperative. If you do not have it all in one place, how can somebody make a decision very quickly for that customer? How can they know whether a great job is being done there?

Let us say your company finds out that you are about to lose a customer. How long does it take to put the people together who can relate to that? They may be all over the globe, so you have to have them brought together electronically. They have to see a common basis of what is going on. This customer database is fundamental. It is the summaries of the customer database that really give you the sales analysis to make decisions. It is dealing with the individual records that decide how responsive you are.

Companies have allowed systems to go up that are really stovepipes, where information about the customers is captured based on the product or the division. Even the taxonomy of who the customer is and tracking the key individuals there, and tracking the contacts or events for that customer, that are very diffuse within a company. Driving to have a single system and all customer information brought together is very important, particularly as you bring in electronic interaction.

My claim is that there is almost no unique investment required to connect the customers through the Internet, because even if there was not an Internet, you want to bring this information together in an easy-to-understand fashion. Then what you want to present through the Internet to the customer, to let them bank on-line, to let them order on-line, is simply a subset of what you have to have internally for your employees in dealing with that customer. There are not two investments here, one for the internal, intranet customer information and another to finally get out there and have a Website where you can connect up and do transactions. That is all one effort that brings the customer database together.

Systems and surprises

Another test of a nervous system is how it deals with surprises. The human nervous system has evolved to be very sophisticated, even processing data locally when you need superquick response times and really integrating everything that is necessary. A good test for Microsoft was when the Internet phenomenon came along. It was a little bit of a surprise to us – how use was going up and who was using it. And the symptoms were seen by different parts of the company. Some of our salespeople would see something going on. Some of our engineers would go to a conference and see something going on. It was only by having use of rich electronic mail and discussion groups that this came to a fever pitch very rapidly, and it was recognized as a crisis that required quick change.

Then, by using the digital nervous system we were able to quickly communicate to people that the project plans are going to change and new versions of software have been scheduled, without long meetings or anything. We decided we were going to put more Internet standards into key products, the schedule was very different and we were going to price things very differently. All of this got compressed into about a forty-five day period. That could not have happened if we had had a classic nervous system.

A company acquisition system

Another great example, I think, is the way that Cisco is able to acquire new companies. It is very complex to bring those employees in and get everybody working together. And unless you have good systems, that becomes very, very difficult.

Companies that do this well are able to use acquisition as part of their strategy. Companies that do not have these systems often do acquisitions that just never come together. The people never seem to be getting the synergies that were imagined at the high levels when it was put together. In the world of technology, there are many examples of mergers that were not handled properly. I think it is more than just a business strategy question. I think it comes down to the mundane specifics of these information systems.

A digital sales system

I want to give a few examples of how in the digital world the way this all works can be a lot better. One thing we have got here is a site called CarPoint that shows how you can actually tap a lot of rich information. You can let somebody get in a car and look around. You can take information about the person and make recommendations to them. The interactive nature of the information is very, very important. It is not just reading things that are out there. It is letting people contribute and bring in all of their work together.

Another example is what Dell has done with their Website. They are selling over a million dollars of equipment a day. That number is not really the thing that gets me excited. It is very easy to take orders that used to be sent in by paper and move them to the Internet and get some big number and call up the press and say: 'Okay, we've got a billion dollars of electronic commerce here.' If you are just shifting the paper form to electronic, that is not interesting. Two things are interesting. First, is a much richer interaction where the person can configure their systems in a better way and get better advice. Dell has done this where they create unique pages for their corporate customers and so the configurations that you buy are up there.

They have also taken the approval process that you have in your company and built that into their logic. So if an arbitrary employee comes along and orders, it understands who to send electronic mail to and who has to approve that before the order gets processed and sent directly to that person. You bring together the individual's desires, the corporate standards and the approval process without a single piece of paper, all just happening in a matter of minutes. A transaction can be placed, approved and on its way in a very efficient system. So, as you ship the orders, you can make them a lot better.

A second thing you can do is match buyers and sellers that never would have found each other before. And that is very exciting, the idea that somebody who is searching on the Internet can see goods and services that are out there that might apply to them. It becomes a new distribution system, not just a way of sending in the order information.

A digital health care system

Another pioneer in using technology is Columbia/HCA. Here in health care, they are using the fact that the Internet lets you send video and screen information very inexpensively. With NetShow, they have a doctor who does an operation, and talks about the right way to do it. And that is available to all of their medical centres. They can watch it when it is being presented and even come in and ask questions. Or it is stored away so if they are not available until later, they can call it up and play it across the Internet.

They also use what is called Net Meeting, where you can take and share a document, share a spreadsheet or a presentation. No matter where the two people are who are working on that document, because they are connected to the Internet, they can see each other's changes. This even works across corporate boundaries, so if you have your law firm and you are working on a contract, you do not need a face-to-face meeting. You can sit there and edit together and make sure it comes together. And that is just free software that works easily on the Internet today.

A tax data-sharing system

A final example is what Ernst & Young has done. They take all their information about tax advice and put that into an SQL database. They scan things. They type things in. And they make it easily accessible so that around the world, the people who care about it can call up all of that tax information. There are people who are getting access who would not have had any way to come in and see that information.

Conclusions

Let me close by making a few predictions here. These are not just predictions aimed at getting people anxious about whether are they doing the right thing, but real beliefs I have about where this is going. The first point is that I think there is a real tendency to overestimate how much things will change in the next two years; but also, and dangerously, a tendency to underestimate how much things will change in ten years.

When somebody sits down to write an article, they want to say it is going to be different tomorrow. When your consultant says, 'Well, it's good you hired me, because there's imminent disaster here', they want to write up that it is going to change very quickly. And then when it does not change, when you have that prediction that it would happen overnight and it does not change, you can be lulled into a sense of security, thinking, 'Well, nobody's ever going to use the Internet. Geez, what was all that all about?'

The Web lifestyle

In fact, year by year, the factors are driving it into the mainstream. The user interface will be dramatically better. The bandwidth will be much better. More and more people will be used to it. Children who go to college in the USA today live what I call a Web lifestyle. That is, for any major thing they want to do – plan a trip, make a purchase, coordinate things with their friends – they are going to use the Internet as part of the process.

Even if they do not actually place the car order through the Internet, they will know before they go into that car dealership exactly what the dealer paid for that car, so they will certainly be better at negotiating what has to go on there. And so as more and more people like that move into the workforce, as we get the ease of use and manageability to be far better, slowly but surely electronic mail and all these information systems will become the mainstream.

I think it is safe to say that within ten years the majority of all adults will be using electronic mail and living a form of that Web lifestyle. And they will begin to ask, 'Why can't I file my taxes that way?' Well, of course, you will be able to. 'Why can't I ask my doctor a question or schedule an appointment easily electronically?' Some professionals will jump at that opportunity and make that possible.

Rethinking a company's boundaries

Another prediction is that the whole boundary of what you do inside your company and what you do outside your company needs to be rethought once you have these digital nervous systems. I think the average size of a company will be less than it is today.

There will be more things you decide can be outside the company than things you decide that are outside today that need to move in. And, of course, the boundaries will not be as hard as they have been. Because you will be able to reach out to some-body who is far away and not only find them when they are far away, but also do work with them when they are far away, your flexibility will be much greater.

Customers are primary assets

Another prediction is that many companies will think of their customer assets as their primary asset. And the world of the Internet has a lot of things where the barriers tend to come down. Distribution systems for lots of products are not as complex, not as much of a barrier. The thing people have is a customer rela-tionship. It gives them their scale. It gives them their brand iden-tity. And the way they process that information to make customized offers to those customers will be very important.

At Microsoft, we are measuring how many customers for whom we have their electronic mail address, and how many have given us permission to mail to them on a monthly basis informa-tion we think they might be interested in. Electronic mail, where you just take e-mail names and send people mail that they are not interested in receiving, will end up being blocked out. It is not worth a person's time to just receive arbitrary mail. And so their mail client will be set up to indicate who they are interested in –

their colleagues, their friends. Mail that is not in a predesignated category will end up in a folder you never have time to read.

For most people, the only way they will read it is if it comes with a monetary reward; that is, if it is marked as saying: 'If you read this piece of mail, we will pay you 10 cents or a dollar.' It is advertising without the intermediary. Instead of paying the money to the content creator, who then creates something that is worth your time to watch so you are willing to watch the advertisement, it goes to the consumer direct.

That mechanism will be built into the software. If a car dealer sold you a car three or four years ago, you might be ready to buy the new model. It is probably worth quite a bit for them to send you an expensive communication and let you know what the latest choices are. That will happen. That interaction with the customer will define how effective a business is.

Empowering knowledge workers

A final prediction is that I think companies need to think about the environment they create for their knowledge workers. Knowledge workers are not like factory equipment. They are not cogs in a process. When you give them empowering tools, when you let them see the information, when you let them have the context of knowing what your company is planning to do and how their job relates to that, it can make an incredible difference.

People who talk about taking away the PCs from the people, who are not continuing to invest in giving them great flexible systems, I think that is a mistake. There will be a shortage of good knowledge workers. Getting them jobs that are interesting, because these tools make it that way, will be important both for recruiting and for getting the most value out of the worker.

It is an exciting time. It is a time of great change. And I am certainly looking forward to how this unfolds over the next ten years.

Note
1. This chapter is an extract of a speech given at the Microsoft CEO Summit in Seattle, Washington on 8 May 1997.

Chapter 30

Realizing the potential of the Web

Tim Berners-Lee

Introduction

The first phase of the Web is human communication through shared knowledge. We have a lot of work to do before we have an intuitive space in which we can put down our thoughts and build our understanding of what we want to do and how and why we will do it. The second side to the Web, yet to emerge, is that of machine-understandable information. As this happens, the day-to-day mechanisms of trade and bureaucracy will be handled by agents, leaving humans to provide the inspiration and the intuition. This will come about through the implementation of a series of projects addressing data formats and languages for the Web, and digital signatures.

The original dream

The Web was designed to be a universal space of information, so when you make a bookmark or a hypertext link, you should be able to make that link to absolutely any piece of information that can be accessed using networks. The universality is essential to the Web: it loses its power if there are certain types to which you can't link.

There are a lot of sides to that universality. You should be able to make links to a hastily jotted crazy idea and to link to a beautifully produced work of art. You should be able to link to a very personal page and to something available to the whole planet. There will be information on the Web which has a clearly defined meaning and can be analysed and traced by computer programs; there will be information such as poetry and art which require the full human intellect for an understanding which will always be subjective.

And what was the purpose of all this? The first goal was to work together better. While the use of the Web across all scales is essential to the concept, the original driving force was collaboration at home and at work. The idea was, that by building together a hypertext Web, a group of whatever size would force itself to use a common vocabulary, to overcome its misunderstandings, and at any time to have a running model, in the Web, of their plans and reasons.

For me, the forerunner to the Web was a program called 'Enquire', which I made for my own purposes. I wrote it in 1980, when I was working at the European Particle Physics Laboratory (CERN), to keep track of the complex web of relationships between people, programs, machines and ideas. In 1989, when I proposed the Web, it was as an extension of that personal tool to a common information space.

When we make decisions in meetings, how often are the reasons for those decisions (which we so carefully elaborated in the meeting) then just typed up, filed as minutes and essentially lost? How often do we pay for this, in time spent passing on half-understandings verbally, duplicating effort through ignorance and reversing good decisions from misunderstanding? How much lack of co-operation can be traced to an inability to understand where another party is 'coming from'? The Web was designed as an instrument to prevent misunderstandings.

For this to work, it had to be not only easy to 'browse', but also easy to express oneself. In a world of people and information, the people and information should be in some kind of equilibrium. Anything in the Web can be quickly learned by a person and any knowledge you see as being missing from the Web can be quickly added. The Web should be a medium for the communication between people: communication through shared knowledge. For this to work, the computers, networks, operating systems and commands have to become invisible, and leave us with an intuitive interface as directly as possible to the information.

Re-enter machines

There was a second goal for the Web, which is dependent on the first. The second part of the dream was that, if you can imagine a project (company, whatever) which uses the Web in its work, then there will be a map, in cyberspace, of all the dependencies and relationships which define how the project is going. This raises the exciting possibility of letting programs run over this material, to help us analyse and manage what we are doing. The computer enters the scene visibly as a software agent, doing anything it can to help us deal with the bulk of data, to take over the tedium of anything that can be reduced to a rational process, and to manage the scale of our human systems.

Where are we now?

The Web you see as a glorified television channel today is just one part of the plan. Although the Web was driven initially by the group work need, it is not surprising that the most rapid growth was in public information. Web publishing, when a few write and many read, profited most from the snowball effect of exponentially rising numbers of readers and writers. Now, with the invention of the term 'intranet', Web use is coming back into organizations. (In fact, it never left. There have always been since 1991, many internal servers, but as they were generally invisible from outside the companies' firewalls they did not get much press!) However, the intuitive editing interfaces which make authoring a natural part of daily life are still maturing. I thought that in twelve months we would have generally available intuitive hypertext editors. (I have stuck to that and am still saying the same thing today.)

It is not just the lack of simple editors that has prevented use of the Web as a collaborative medium. For a group of people to use the Web in practice, they need reliable access control, so that they know their ideas will only be seen by those they trust. They also need access control and archival tools that, like browsing, do not require one to get into the details of computer operating systems.

There is also a limit to what we can do by ourselves with information, without the help of machines. A familiar complaint of the newcomer to the Web, who has not learned to follow links only from reliable sources, is about the mass of junk out there.

Search engines flounder in the mass of undifferentiated documents that range vastly in terms of quality, timeliness and relevance. We need information about information, 'metadata', to help us organize it.

As it turns out, many of these long-term needs will hopefully be met by technology, which for one reason or another is being developed by the technical community, and agreed upon by groups such as the WorldWide Web Consortium (W3C), in response to various medium-term demands.

The WorldWide Web Consortium (W3C)

This consortium exists as a place for those companies for whom the Web is essential to meet and agree on the common underpinnings that will allow everyone to go forward. (There are currently over 230 member organizations.)

Whether developing software, hardware, networks, information for sale, or using the Web as a crucial part of their business life, these companies are driven by current emerging areas such as Web publishing, intranet use, electronic commerce, and Web-based education and training. From these fields medium-term needs arise and where appropriate, the consortium starts an activity to help reach a consensus on computer protocols for that area. Protocols are the rules that allow computers to talk together about a given topic. When the industry agrees on protocols, then a new application can spread across the world and new programs can all work together as they all speak the same language. This is key to the development of the Web.

Where is the Web going next?

Avoiding the worldwide wait

You have heard about it, you may have experienced it, but can anything be done about it? One reason for the slow response you may get from a dial-up Internet account simply follows from the 'all you can eat' pricing policy. The only thing which keeps the number of Internet users down is unacceptable response, so if we were to suddenly make it faster, there would almost immediately be more users until it was slow again. I have seen it: when we

speeded up an overloaded server by a factor of five, it once again
rose to 100 per cent utilization as the number of users increased
by a factor of five.

Eventually, there will be different ways of paying for different levels of quality. But today there are some things we can do
to make better use of the bandwidth we have, such as using com-
pression and enabling many overlapping asynchronous requests.
There is also the ability to guess ahead and push out what a user
may want next, so that the user does not have to request and then
wait. Taken to one extreme, this becomes subscription-based distribution, which works more like e-mail or newsgroups.

One crazy thing is that the user has to decide whether to use
mailing lists, newsgroups or the Web to publish something. The
best choice depends on the demand and the readership pattern. A
mistake can be costly. Today, it is not always easy for a person to
anticipate the demand for a page. For example, the pictures of the
Schoemaker-Levy comet hitting Jupiter taken on a mountain top
and just put on the nearest Mac server or the decision about Louise
Woodward which Judge Zobel put on to the Web – both these generated so much demand that their servers were swamped, and in
fact, these items would have been better delivered as messages via
newsgroups. It would be better if the 'system', the collaborating
servers and clients together, could adapt to differing demands, and
use pre-emptive or reactive retrieval as necessary.

Data about data – metadata

It is clear that there should be a common format for expressing
information about information (called 'metadata'), for a dozen
or so fields that needed it, including privacy information,
endorsement labels, library catalogues, tools for structuring and
organizing Web data, distribution terms and annotation. The
consortium's resource description framework (RDF) is designed
to allow data from all these fields to be written in the same form,
and therefore carried together and mixed.

That by itself will be quite exciting. Proxy caches, which
make the Web more efficient, will be able to check that they are
really acting in accordance with the publisher's wishes when it
comes to redistributing material. A browser will be able to get an
assurance, before imparting personal information in a Web form,

on how that information will be used. People will be able, if the technology is matched by suitable tools, to endorse Web pages they perceive to be of value. Search engines will be able to take such endorsements into account and give results that are perceived to be of much higher quality. So a common format for information about information will make the Web a whole lot better.

The Web of trust

In cases in which a high level of trust is needed for metadata, digitally signed metadata will allow the Web to include a 'Web of trust'. The Web of trust will be a set of documents on the Web that are digitally signed with certain keys, and contain statements about those keys and about other documents. Like the Web itself, the Web of trust does not need to have a specific structure like a tree or a matrix. Statements of trust can be added exactly so as to reflect actual trust. People learn to trust through experience and through recommendation. We change our minds about who we trust for different purposes. The Web of trust must allow us to express this.

Hypertext was suitable for a global information system because it has this same flexibility: the power to represent any structure of the real world or a created imagined one. Systems that force you to express information in trees or matrices are fine so long as they are used for describing trees or matrices. The moment you try to use one to hold information that does not fit the mould, you end up twisting the information to fit, and so misrepresenting the situation. Similarly, the W3C's role in creating the Web of trust will be to help the community have common language for expressing trust. The consortium will not seek a central or controlling role in the content of the Web.

'Oh, yeah?'

So, signed metadata is the next step. When we have this, we will be able to ask the computer not just for information, but why we should believe it. Imagine an 'Oh, yeah?' button on your browser. There you are looking at a fantastic deal that can be yours just for the entry of a credit card number and the click of a button. 'Oh, yeah?', you think. You press the 'Oh, yeah?' button. You are asking your browser why you should believe it. It, in turn, can challenge the server to provide some credentials: perhaps, a signature for the document or a list of documents that expresses what that key is good for. Those documents will be signed. Your browser rummages through with the server, looking for a way to convince you that the page is trustworthy for a purchase. Maybe it will come up with an endorsement from a magazine, which in turn has been endorsed by a friend. Maybe it will come up with an endorsement by the seller's bank, which has in turn an endorsement from your bank. Maybe it won't find any reason for you to actually believe what you are reading at all.

Data about things

All the information mentioned above is information about information. Perhaps the most important aspect of it is that it is machine-understandable data, and it may introduce a new phase of the Web in which much more data in general can be handled by computer programs in a meaningful way. All these ideas are just as relevant to information about the real world: about cars and people and stocks and shares and flights and food and rivers.

The Enquire program assumed that every page was about something. When you created a new page it made you say what sort of thing it was: a person, a piece of machinery, a group, a program, a concept, etc. Not only that, when you created a link between two nodes, it would prompt you to fill in the relationship between the two things or people. For example, the relationships were defined as 'A is part of B' or 'A made B'. The idea was that if Enquire were to be used heavily, it could then automatically trace the dependencies within an organization.

Unfortunately this was lost as the Web grew. Although it had relationship types in the original specifications, this has not generally become a Web of assertions about things or people. Can we still build a Web of well-defined information?

My initial attempts to suggest this fell on stony ground, and not surprisingly. Hypertext markup language is a language for communicating a document for human consumption. SGML (and now XML) gives structure, but not semantics. Neither the application, nor the language, called for it.

With metadata we have a need for a machine-understandable language that has all the qualities we need. Technically, the same apparatus we are constructing in the resource description framework for describing the properties of documents can be used equally well for describing anything else.

A crying need for resource description framework (RDF)

Is there a real need for this metadata and is there a market in the medium term that will lead companies to develop in this direction? Well, in the medium term, we see the drivers already – Web publishing, education and training, electronic commerce and intranets.

I have mentioned the vicious circle that caused the Web to take off initially. The increasing amount of information on the Web was an incentive for people to get browsers, and the increasing number of browsers created more incentive for people to put up more Websites. It had to start somewhere and it was bootstrapped by making 'virtual hypertext' servers. These servers typically had access to large databases – such as phone books, library catalogues and existing documentation management systems. They had simple programs which would generate Web pages 'on the fly' corresponding to various views and queries on the database. This has been a very powerful 'bootstrap' as there is now a healthy market for tools to allow one to map one's data from its existing database form on to the Web.

Now here is the curious thing. There is so much data available on Web pages, that there is a market for tools that 'reverse engineer' that process. These are tools that read pages, and with a bit of human advice, re-create the database object. Even though it takes human effort to analyse the way different Websites are offering their data, it is worth it. It is so powerful to have a common, well defined interface to all the data so that you can program on top of it. So the need for well-defined interface to Web data in the short term is undeniable.

What we propose is that, when a program goes out to a server looking for data, say a database record, that the same data should be available in RDF, in such a way that the rows and columns are all labelled in a well-defined way and that it may be possible to look up the equivalence between field names at one Website and at another, and so merge information intelligently from many sources. This is a clear need for metadata, just from looking at the trouble libraries have had with the numbers of very similar, but slightly different ways of making up a catalogue card for a book.

Interactive creativity

I want the Web to be much more creative than it is at the moment. I have even coined a new word – intercreativity – which means building things together on the Web. I found that people thought that the Web already was 'interactive', because you get to click with a mouse and fill in forms! I have mentioned that better intuitive interfaces will be needed, but I don't think they will be sufficient without better security.

It would be wrong to assume that digital signature will be mainly important for electronic commerce, as if security were only important where money is concerned. One of my key themes is the importance of the Web being used on all levels from the personal, through groups of all sizes, to the global population.

When you are working in a group, you do things you would not do outside the group. You share half-baked ideas, reveal sensitive information. You use a vernacular that will be understood, you can cut corners in language and formality. You do these things because you trust the people in the group, and that others will not suddenly have access to it. To date, on the Web, it has been difficult to manage such groups, or to allow one to control access to information in an intuitive way.

Letting go

So, where will this get us? The Web fills with documents, each of which has pointers to help a computer understand it and relate it to terms it knows. Software agents acting on our behalf can reason about this data. They can ask for and validate proofs of the credibility of the data. They can negotiate as to who will have what access to what and ensure that our personal wishes for privacy level be met.

The world is a world of human beings, as it was before, but the power of our actions is again increased. The Web already increases the power of our writings, making them accessible to huge numbers of people and allowing us to draw on any part of the global information base by a simple hypertext link. Now we image the world of people with active machines forming part of the infrastructure. We only have to express a request for bids, or make a bid, and machines will turn a small profit matching the two. Search engines, from looking for pages containing interesting words, will start indexes of assertions that might be useful for answering questions or finding justifications.

I think this will take a long time. I say this deliberately, because in the past I have underestimated how long something will take to become available (e.g. good editors in twelve months).

Now we will have to find how best to integrate our warm, fuzzy right-brain selves into this clearly defined left-brain world. It is easy to know who we trust, but it might be difficult to explain that to a computer. After seeding the semantic Web with specific applications, we must be sure to generalize it cleanly, leaving it clean and simple so that the next generation can learn its logical concepts along with the alphabet.

If we can make something decentralized, out of control, and of great simplicity, we must be prepared to be astonished at whatever might grow out of that new medium.

It is up to us

One thing is certain. The Web will have a profound effect on the markets and the cultures around the world: intelligent agents will either stabilize or destabilize markets; the demise of distance will either homogenize or polarize cultures; the ability to access the Web will be either a great divider or a great equalizer; the path will either lead to jealousy and hatred or peace and understanding.

The technology we are creating may influence some of these choices, but mostly it will leave them to us. It may expose the questions in a starker form than before and force us to state clearly where we stand.

We are forming cells within a global brain and we are excited that we might start to think collectively. What becomes of us still hangs crucially on how we think individually.

Chapter 31

Changing the organization to meet the needs of networks

Meredith Belbin

Overestimating the role of time

Web-weaving today is making knowledge accessible to ever-growing numbers of people. But to what overall effect tomorrow? It is easy to assume wrongly that it will result in many benefits to be achieved simply and naturally over time. Consider the enterprising employee: encased in a highly structured company, one can surf around the world of networks collecting knowledge as avidly as a stamp collector. But what value has that scrapbook of knowledge for the organization? Does it lead to a greater readiness and capacity for action?

In 'The digital nervous system' (Chapter 29 in this book), Bill Gates affirms that it does and he maintains that networking raises the scope for empowerment. He also says these rewards require *time*. Certainly time is a parameter that mediates the impact of any technical innovation. But time on its own is scarcely a force which enables empowerment. In a sense, empowerment cannot wait for time. Granted that collecting greater knowledge over time can lead to greater *potential* for empowerment; but what is the impediment which blocks the way forward to actual empowerment, to actual utility? *Not time.*

The real challenges of empowerment

The utility of any technological advance, such as the Internet, *demands* an appropriate cultural setting without which it leads nowhere in particular. For example in Islamic fundamentalist societies, where boy never meets girl before betrothal, romances flourish on that great technical innovation and channel of communication – the telephone. Yet the parties still retain their distance and so remain in accordance with the cultural canons of respectability. Similarly, tapping knowledge on the network may take on the character of an enthralling romantic adventure, but there may be no happy ending.

While the technological advance of distributed networking creates a *climate* for change, empowerment does not necessarily follow nor evolve in cultures such as those rooted in a closely controlled hierarchy. In such cultures, there is no active force to bring out its utility or even to facilitate the process of seeking the value of such networked systems. Outside the realms of the solo entrepreneur or the small-scale enterprise, there is also a notable lack of organizational role models.

This lack of models makes it difficult to compete with the established pyramidal hierarchies in managing the avalanche of new information provided by a network and the opportunities it can create. Therefore, while it appears that in such a climate for change there is the *potential* for individual knowledge gathering to lead on to empowerment for the whole organization, this opportunity is contingent on an organization's culture and willingness to consider alternative models.

Surprisingly, there is a growing awareness of this challenge. The deadening effect of large hierarchical organizations on enterprise innovation is a commonly expressed concern today. The signs of this concern are appearing in numerous managerial discussions about how to create conditions which favour openings for 'intrapreneurs' in such large companies. However, such solutions are being focused on incentivizing individuals rather than on changing organizational patterns and culture. Clearly there is still a big problem that remains to be resolved before such large organizations can reap the rewards of a network of individuals empowered by shared knowledge.

Hierarchy and other structures

In order to change organization patterns and culture to be more receptive to empowerment, a change in corporate *structure* is often required. Yet for many large hierarchical organizations, the basic human problem of responsiveness can be considered biogenetic:

- When humans congregate in large groups they share with all mammals a common mode of behaviour; that is to say, males who vie for supremacy govern them.
- The alpha male rules the pack and there is a constant struggle between the lesser males for dominance in their particular territories, struggles that prepare them for becoming the supreme pack ruler.

Therefore, in accordance with the above observation of nature, organizational hierarchy can be considered a natural extension of a common biosystem that affects much of the living world. Therefore, the structure of hierarchy can be considered natural and inevitable, were it not for the fact that *the basis for the structure has little to do with efficiency of delivery*. In fact, multitiered hierarchies generate bureaucracy and are notoriously inefficient.

We are blindly bound to the principles that underlie the big systems of organization because it is so immensely difficult to escape from the genetic inheritance that determines herd behaviour. Fortunately, there are other models in the natural world which can inspire us if only we can learn to adapt it to our new needs. One relevant model is to be found among the social insects, notably bees, ants and termites.

It is significant that these unrelated creatures have been guided by evolution to a common set of principles of organization. There is no hierarchy as such: the queen is a misnomer for a specialist breeder with no power outside her reproductive function. Instead, an arrangement of interlocking castes and a complex and extensive communication system provides the capability to rapidly adapt to a wide range of changes in the environment. Lateral communications underpin the effectiveness of social insect communities[1] and generate far more points of interconnection than the linear, top-down communication system which characterizes human collective efforts.

The use of web-weaving as an enabler of lateral communication has closer parallels to the world of the social insects than to the processes endemic in human organizational hierarchies. The real significance of these models is to open our eyes to a realization that it is possible to escape from these organizational prisons. Yet, we need a new social formation if we are to perfect an escape plan. In place of castes (to use the language of social biology) we have the nearest human equivalent, *roles and functions*.

Changing the role and function of management

In the new rapidly developing world of complex information we no longer need a large alpha male to dominate our affairs any more than our diminutive cousins need a big insect.

Talents for vision and strategy are not so ill-distributed among humans that they are to be found only in a single person who sits at the apex of the hierarchy. These talents can be built into small, specially selected teams. Such teams, when properly balanced, are less subject to the massive blunders to which self-centred leaders are so susceptible.

Such a conclusion is not to decry the role of management. Managers play a crucial role in assigning tasks, responsibilities and contracts to others and for making certain types of decision. Ideally, in the language of the social insects, managers:

- may be likened to members of a special caste who contribute to the success of the whole
- should be viewed as essential for the dynamic operation of a system rather than as privileged members of a group arranged in some pecking order.

In other words, the world of the effective working community is about optimizing networks and interrelated roles and functions and is a far cry from the world of ranks and grades that prop up a static, non-evolving structure.

Bioprocesses and radical changes

Networks are ushering in an organizational revolution and computers are changing the way we think and act. Ironically, the computers which humans have invented are closer in their mode of operation to insect brains than to human brains. The brains of the social insects, large in proportion to their body areas, act at great speed and they integrate information from a wider range of senses than humans could possibly handle, all at the same time. For example, their perception of odour and taste (senses that humans have difficulty in distinguishing between), touch, sight, the sensing of temperature differences and above all response to the range of pheromones (the chemical agents affecting behaviour) emitted by other castes can all be processed at the same time to result in a finely attuned pattern of action. The brains of humans, in contrast, operate in a different fashion and are limited by what is known as single-channel processing. The bottleneck is the restricted capacity of attention.

Experimental psychology has generated evidence that information is handled in only one modality at a time and in a step-by-step process. Attention to an increasing range of stimuli has an exponential effect in slowing response time and in accelerating confusion. When a large number of people meet, the bottleneck of collective attention acts as an additional brake on the outputs of the group, both in terms of speed and depth of thought. The focus of the group then moves towards consensus attention. The consequence, in terms of a loss in effective intelligence, has given rise to what Professor Janis, as a result of his studies, has termed 'groupthink'.[2] These different bioprocesses, belonging to different parts of the natural world, may explain why it is that social insects appear individually stupid but collectively wise, whereas humans are individually intelligent but prone to stupidity in the mass. Yet, if we break away from the rules that underlie current human organization, the prospects may change.

Horizontal accountability

Communications technology is pushing the door ajar to beckon in horizontal accountability. Humans, just like the social insects, can communicate with others through advanced networks and become better informed, and so rapidly arrive at joint decisions without need for further referral. Such a mode of operation is far removed from communicating only through a boss.

Yet horizontal accountability demands certain conditions if it is to succeed. The rules are the interests of the group take precedence over the interests of the individual – or in the familiar language of sport, the team comes before the player. As in soccer, what counts is scoring goals. By bringing in useful information the capacity of the system is improved, just as a team can improve its goal-scoring rate by transferring in players from other clubs. Since players can also be transferred out, the process is fluid.

With vertical accountability the team creates its own pressures to improve its balance and its performance to ensure that the sum is always greater than the parts. The problem is that the desired resources belonging to another system cannot be assimilated at will. As they are not actually owned, they can be incorporated only by negotiation on terms that both parties find acceptable. But all this takes time. Strategic alliances between partners with independent systems are liable to flounder unless general codes of practice and contract come into being. Progress needs to be made on this ethical front to allow assumptions to be made, trust to be established and the problem of excessive secrecy to be overcome.

A transformation ahead

The following questions now arise: will it happen? Can large organizations begin to act against their very nature? Is such a transformation a biological impossibility? It is easier to reach a pessimistic rather than an optimistic view. Nevertheless, the prospects for progress are real enough.

First, power in the world is gradually shifting from the centre to the periphery. It is becoming more difficult for the centre to exercise effective control, to know exactly what is going on and to discipline miscreants. The Internet and the growth of regional autonomy are examples of this process in action.

Secondly, senior executives are learning that dominant

behaviour is not effective. *Results matter* and if more productive patterns emerge, humans will learn to adopt them, even if it appears to go against their nature. The growth of horizontal communication widens the prospects for new models to be on the management agenda of tomorrow's organization.

Notes

1. The details of these complex communities are worthy of study and I have given further attention to this important subject elsewhere: see Belbin, M. (1996) Lessons from a diminutive masterclass. In *The Coming Shape of Organization*, ch.4, Butterworth-Heinemann.
2. Janis, I. L. (1972) *Victims of Groupthink*.

Chapter 32

The internetworked business[1]

Don Tapscott

The nature of knowledge work changed little throughout the industrial economy. It is true that for some specialists, such as doctors or engineers, there has been considerable improvement in tools throughout the twentieth century. But for most people – managers, teachers, salespeople and others – the nature and tools of their work have remained fundamentally the same. The host-based mainframes and mini-computers of the 1960s and 1970s automated existing business processes with the goal of reducing costs. A by-product of those systems was the printout (or the truckload of printouts). Such reams of paper may have provided management information and other side benefits, but did little to improve overall individual

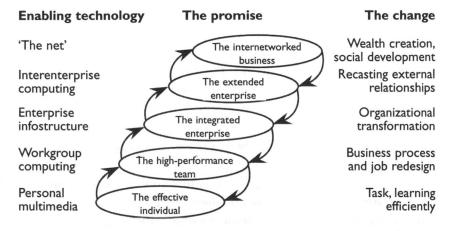

Enabling technology	The promise	The change
'The net'	The internetworked business	Wealth creation, social development
Interenterprise computing	The extended enterprise	Recasting external relationships
Enterprise infostructure	The integrated enterprise	Organizational transformation
Workgroup computing	The high-performance team	Business process and job redesign
Personal multimedia	The effective individual	Task, learning efficiently

Figure 32.1 Business transformation through the new media. © New Paradigm Learning Corporation, 1996

effectiveness or individual job fulfilment. (Even today companies rely strongly on printed output – as Hewlett-Packard's Vice-President of Research and Development Joel Birnbaum says, 'Ink from the inkjet printer is the embalming fluid of information'.)

Multimedia is changing this picture dramatically. Personal computing is becoming multimedia computing as the rich and natural power of audio, image, and video become more integrated into compound digital documents and humanized styles of computing. By 1995, most personal computers were sold with a CD-ROM drive, which can store vast amounts of information in various media. Most new computers are powerful enough to handle new forms of input beyond the keyboard – such as microphones, scanners, and cameras.

Efficiency (doing things better) results in time savings which can in turn be reinvested in personal effectiveness (doing better things).

The high performance team

For a decade, companies have been working to organize themselves into team-based structures. As Peter Drucker explained in 1988: 'Traditional departments will serve as guardians of standards, as centres for training and the assignment of specialists; they will not be where the work gets done. That will happen largely in task-focused teams.'[2] Some diehard defenders of the old approaches have clung to hierarchy as, 'The most efficient, the hardiest and in fact the most natural structure ever devised for large organizations.'[3] But most companies have chosen to work toward team-based approaches. Business teams can enable faster responses to changes in the business environment and increasing customer demands. Teams can help to bring the right people together from many disciplines and parts of the formal structure at the right time to battle competition at home and abroad. Business teams can help organizations to dramatically change their cost structure through the elimination of traditional bureaucracies or by avoiding the creation of new ones. Even re-engineering theorists have been forced to recognize that teams are an effective way to execute horizontal business processes.

However, because of the power and capacity of the new media to open dramatically the channels for human communication and collaboration within an office, across geography and across time, knowledge work is becoming collaborative work, taking place in teams on high-capacity networks. Such teams interoperate with one another, thereby enabling distributed team-based structures that are the antithesis of the old hierarchy.

In the traditional hierarchical organization with its multiple layers of management, accountability and bureaucracy, information flow was vertical. Host-based islands of technology corresponded to the old structures. But through internetworked work group computing tools, the corporate pyramid can be replaced with internetworked teams. The focus shifts from the individual, who was accountable to the manager, to teams that function as service units of servers and clients. Teams are both clients and servers for other teams who are both internal and external to the organization. As clients, they receive deliverables and other inputs from supply and support teams and add value to these for the purpose of serving others. This value-added output is consumed by other clients. The new model, first explained in the book, *Paradigm Shift*, is derived from Michael Porter's concept of the value chain, but extended into our notion of a value network. The provision of value is not something chained in a linear way, but rather something that is generated through an ever-changing open network. It is a model designed to encourage flexibility, innovation, entrepreneurship and responsiveness.

The 'killer application' to launch work group computing was the software product known as Lotus Notes. Notes saved Lotus as a company after its previously popular spreadsheet application for the PC (1-2-3) had lost leadership – creating the value for IBM to justify its acquisition of Lotus. More important, Lotus Notes showed thousands of companies how technology could enable work groups to form and be effective. The business team was a half-baked idea before Notes came on the scene. Notes has been applied to a wide range of problems from product planning to sales.[4]

The team approach to designing automobiles used in Japan initially popularized the team concept. Each new car project was headed by a project leader with genuine power. The team consisted of people from all necessary disciplines – power-train engineering, body design, purchasing, marketing, finance and manufacturing, among others. The project manager was more than a coordinator who traipsed from department to department making or collecting decisions; the project manager became a synergistic focal point, a leader for change. Better, faster, cheaper designs and quality Japanese automobiles devastated the competitive dominance of the American Big Three.[5]

However, the American manufacturers came to understand something beyond teams – the power of work group computing – and, as a result, are clawing back gains. Chrysler, for example, was the first to go beyond the Japanese approach to implement a technology-enabled team approach to design. Based on work-group computing tools for designing an automobile, Chrysler created the 'platform' approach – the jeep platform, the large cars platform, the small-cars platform and the minivan platform.

True, this approach embraced the Japanese system of empowered teams. For example, designers did not have to go up the hierarchy to get key decisions made. But the Big Three went beyond the Japanese. In fact, when planning began for the Neon, Chrysler designers were simply given several criteria (mileage, cost, etc.) and told to create a vehicle. In the old world, Lee Iacocca was actually brought into design decisions. Because Iacocca liked cars with wire wheels and red seats, Chrysler vehicles always had these as options even though few buyers chose either of them, In the new world, designers were freed up to design without worrying about the boss's personal preferences.

Unlike the Japanese approach, the new basis of the platform is technology. Designers collaborate around workstations to engineer a new design concurrently rather than in a serial fashion. In simple terms, that means many functions can happen simultaneously; individuals are not waiting for someone else to complete a task before they can add their input. Concurrency also enables better synergies across the various design teams. The technology is interactive multimedia – a computer-assisted design system that enables the creation of three-dimensional designs.

Bottom line? Chrysler has reduced the time from concept to production of a new car from six years to two. The high-performance team structure has meant that they are beginning to take market share from Ford, General Motors – and the Japanese.

The Ford Motor Company responded with an integrated

work group computing network linking engineers throughout the world to design the 1994 Mustang. Design chief Jack Telnack has dubbed the process 'virtual collocation'. Computer models take rough sketches and create realistic vehicles that can be viewed from all sides on the screen, as if the designer could actually walk around the vehicle.

The integrated organization

Business process re-engineering (BPR) was useful because it highlighted the importance of designing business processes that are horizontal, that is, they cut across old organizational boundaries. However, in practice, most new processes are of a fairly low level; they are restricted to one department or perhaps span two or three departments. Because of the rise of standards and the feasibility of implementing something we call an enterprise infostructure, it is possible to think bigger – to create entire businesses that are integrated.

The key is for business leaders to define a target information technology architecture and devise a migration path to get there. Because of the maturity of technology standards, it is now possible to plan an entire enterprise architecture rather than just adding another room on to the farmhouse.

The new architecture is based on principles defined by business people, not technologists. It includes models of the business, applications, information and technology. The architecture also defines a number of standards for systems within the organization. As it becomes implemented, the enterprise has an enterprise infostructure upon which it can become an integrated enterprise.

The enterprise infostructure provides the backbone for the new enterprise. It enables an organization to move beyond the old hierarchy because layers of management are not required when information is instantly available electronically. An infostructure can enable the enterprise to function as a cohesive organization by providing corporate-wide information for decision-making and new competitive enterprise applications that transcend autonomous business units or teams.

At the same time, such architectures provide a platform for entrepreneurial innovation in the use of computers by business teams while maintaining an enterprise capability. Business units can become viewed as networked clients and servers, working in a modular, flexible organizational structure. That is a very different concept from the stovepipes of the old hierarchy.

Chemical Bank and the Canadian Imperial Bank of Commerce are two of the first financial institutions to work towards an enterprise infostructure. Both have developed a principle that states that, 'All customers will be treated as a customer of the bank', rather than treating individuals as customers of one branch or users of one product or a single service. This principle will result in far-reaching changes to both banks – changes that will go beyond business process re-engineering. This thinking involves new ways of interacting with customers, for example, through an information appliance; new virtual services that combine old ones; new customer-focused organizational structures; new roles for employees freed from the deadening bureaucracy of old redundant processes; and new ways of delivering new services to customers of the banks.

Union Pacific's nightmare was far-flung: knowing the location of each and every one of its 1,000 trains that were rolling on rail lines. Once the company built an enterprise architecture, it could transform business operations. Now, all cars are barcoded and can be tracked by using sensors that are in turn connected to fibre optic cables along the tracks. What was once a boxcar business has been transformed into an information business that satisfies customers with an on-time delivery success rate that has doubled from 48 per cent to 94 per cent. 'Fast info-movement is the only way to run a railroad,' says Union Pacific CIO Joyce Wrenn.

One of the early examples of an integrated organization is Federal Express (FedEx). Through pursuing and measuring quality, a strategy of innovation, and an enterprise infostructure, FedEx has become the dominant force in the package delivery business in North America with 50 per cent of the market share. In this business, companies must strive to deliver packages correctly 100 per cent of the time. If they fail once, they may never recover that customer. In 1986 FedEx changed its mission statement to reflect the importance of information technology in achieving quality. The mission includes the words: 'Positive control of each package will be maintained by utilizing real-time electronic tracking and tracing systems.' A service quality index was developed to define quality and an integrated computing architecture enabled its measurement. Such integrated systems placed FedEx on the ground floor of tracking parcels in real time. Detailed information regarding minute-by-minute parcel movements also enabled the proactive improvement of quality – service to the customer. Federal Express was able to build an integrated enterprise in which people work together across the organization with the tools to deliver customer service and quality. This is a far cry from re-engineering business processes. Punishment is swift for those who fail to transform themselves through the new technology. While Federal Express revenue soared, the US Postal Service was unable to break free from the old paradigm. The ultimate irony? From time to time the post office has been forced to subcontract overnight delivery to FedEx.

'The command-and-control organization that first emerged in the 1870s might be compared to an organism held together by its shell,' says Peter Drucker.

The corporation that is now emerging is being designed around a skeleton: information, both the corporation's new integrating system and its articulation. Our traditional mind-set – even if we use sophisticated mathematical techniques and impenetrable sociological jargon has always somehow perceived business as buying cheap and selling dear. The new approach defines a business as the organization that adds value and creates wealth.[6]

The extended enterprise

Wal-Mart and Target Stores have transformed their businesses and become successful retailers through interenterprise computing – again by linking their computer systems with their most important suppliers. Interenterprise computing enables suppliers to forecast demand for their products as well as to help the retailers strengthen their supply networks, reduce inventory, and improve product availability on the shelves. Today when you buy a jacket at Wal-Mart, a stream of computer bits is sent across the value network all the way to the factory that mills the cloth, putting in motion a series of events that results in the jacket rack being replenished. The new jacket, however, did not go into a central warehouse. It was sent directly to the store from the manufacturer, just as 97 per cent of all Wal-Mart's goods never pass through a warehouse. This enables what Sears new CIO Joe Smilowsky calls, 'The strategic efficiencies that have transformed the nature of retailing'.

Just as the walls within organizations are falling, so the walls among organizations are falling too. The result is what has been called the 'virtual corporation'. Rather than staff up, you partner. You understand your core competencies and unite with companies having other talents. You forge a series of ever-changing alliances to achieve competitive success. Most advocates say that information technology is the most important enabler of such virtual structures. But how?

The fact is that interenterprise computing is already beginning to blur lines among organizations, enabling new kinds of business relationships. Networks are extending the reach of companies in ways previously unimagined, transforming the nature of business interactions and raising far-reaching issues of business strategy.

The Boeing 777 was designed as a digital aircraft because it was more than a digital set of drawings. The 777 can fly in digital space, where its velocity, wind resistance, handling characteristics, and responsiveness can be tested. Because it was digital, customers, such as the airlines, could be effectively brought into the network to contribute to the design, helping to ensure that their requirements and innovative ideas were incorporated and that the digital plane worked.

Furthermore, most of the pieces of the plane were manufactured by suppliers to Boeing – hundreds of them – who were also brought on to the network. Because designs, specifications and other information are bits rather than atoms, the cluster of companies was able to work together differently. By using a network, Boeing created an extended enterprise that ensured that designs met customer requirements and that the plane was manufacturable, largely by business partners.

Consortia and partnerships based on interenterprise computing are flourishing. The Insurance Value Added Network Services (IVANS) links a group of insurance companies with thousands of agents. In the auto-parts industry, used parts suppliers cluster around AUTONETWORK to exchange information and make their industry competitive against new parts manufacturers who have united to connect to retailers through MEMA/ Transnet, a group initiated by the Motor Equipment Manufacturers Association. A number of electronics companies in Silicon Valley, California, are creating a virtual partnership called CommerceNet. Companies will be able to communicate, access product information and exchange software and even consulting services over the network. In Toronto, a company called the Virtual Corporation provides a network and other services to enable independent consultants and software developers to partner on projects.

Interenterprise computing is causing new economic dynamics in many ways. as follows:

Accessibility of partners

Information not previously available can become available when digitized, in turn enabling new kinds of access between partners. For example, computer databases of government information, ranging from land and geographic data to road safety information, provide various stakeholders with access to information that manual searches or manual communications may never be able to satisfactorily address. This enables governments to create new partnerships in providing such information as well as classes of information users.

Similarly, companies can conduct new product launches over a global video-conferencing network. Car rental customers are able to enter their destination on an airport computer and get a printout of a customized map. Computer-driven voice response systems grant customers access to information that previously was too expensive to provide. Hotel guests review their accounts on their in-room television. Vacationers learn about opportunities for holidays through an interactive screen that shows actual video footage about alternatives.

New interdependencies

Early systems, such as the American Airlines SABRE reservation system and the American Hospital Supply customer order system, have become legends in how to use technology to create mutually beneficial interdependencies. In each case the company provided customers with direct access to computer systems in order to strengthen relationships, thus locking-in the customer.

However, such systems were really the tip of the iceberg. Today insurance agents link electronically with insurers. Auto dealerships configure car orders on a screen, which in turn are transmitted to the manufacturer. Various companies cooperate to create frequent flyer, renter, buyer, user and guest points. In each case, the technology is enabling new beneficial interdependencies.

Interorganizational metabolism

The port of Seattle took business away from the port of Vancouver when Seattle began using electronic data interchange to speed up the process of a ship clearing the harbour. The metabolism between a shipping company and the Seattle port was much faster because the voluminous information exchange activity between the two was electronic rather than through manual documents, forms, checks and meetings. Vancouver has now caught up by implementing a similar system.

Cooperative competitiveness

Sounds like an oxymoron, but every time you use a banking machine you are helping banks compete through cooperation. The banking networks, built through cooperation among competitors, currently handle billions of interbank transactions per month, enabling banks to provide new services and compete effectively with domestic and international rivals. Today, competing hotel chains have built a common reservation network. And competing research laboratories cooperate in the USA to implement a massive research network.

Interorganization value creation

Interenterprise computing enables new kinds of partnerships to create new products and services. Later in the chapter we will look at how a housing consortium has attacked the Japanese marketplace.

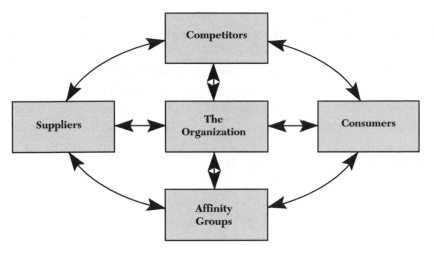

Figure 32.2 The digital value network (information flow digital: value generated)

All this is being done by using the information garden paths of today. But consider what kinds of opportunities will exist as the network becomes a highway and its capacity – bandwidth – increases a hundred or a thousand times.

The value chain is becoming a digitally based value network for enterprises to reach out through technology to their customers, suppliers, affinity groups and even competitors. Virtual corporations on the I-Way are competing in a digital economy.

Punishment is swift for the laggards. Wal-Mart and Target transformed themselves for success. Sears – the greatest retail empire of all time – stuck with the old model and fell behind. The half-vacant Sears Tower is a monument to tradition. But Sears learned and is staging a comeback that threatens to leapfrog its new competitors.

The internetworked business

Beyond the virtual corporation, commerce must move on to the public I-Way. For example, there is a huge housing market in Tokyo where the average age of a construction worker is 55 years and there are no raw materials available. How could an extended enterprise exploit this opportunity? Create a cluster of companies on the I-Way. The cluster could include architects, forest products firms, appliance manufacturers, and various building trades such as plumbing and heating, carpentry and masonry, roofing and flooring, and all the other elves and shoemakers required to complete a family dwelling.

In the first step by an internetworked building group, the prospective homeowner and the architect create a house on a computer workstation. Working with aspects from several basic designs, the client chooses a floorplan, decides on the number of bedrooms and bathrooms, then picks the other main features such as a fireplace or rear deck. To test the 'feel' of what is being created, they go for a walk together through the virtual house on the screen. The client can see how the dining room looks from various locations and can make changes to the ceiling height. Do not like the way the kitchen table is visible from the front hall? Alter the placement of the door opening. As the design is finalized, the cost of the end product is calculated in real time. The completed drawings are then transmitted over the Internet to the other partners in the cluster who go into action and fabricate the structure in various locations where the expertise and materials exist. Three weeks later, the house is in a shipping container on its way to Tokyo for final assembly on site. Without the partnership, there would be no timely way to respond to this opportunity. And without the Internet, it would take months rather than weeks to create the house. The technology enables this new interenterprise.

Far-fetched? Plans are under way to do exactly that. Such clusters are currently being organized in San Francisco and Calgary. The evidence is mounting that this type of technology-based arrangement is not a fad but, rather, a part of a fundamental change in the way we do business and work.

The final dimension of transformation is a new kind of internetworked enterprise that makes the virtual corporation look like child's play. We are on the threshold of a new digital economy in which the microprocessor and public networks on the Internet model enable fundamentally new kinds of institutional structures and relationships. The firm as we know it is breaking up. What is happening instead is this: effective individuals, working on high-performance team structures; becoming integrated organizational networks of clients and servers; which reach out to customers, suppliers, affinity groups and even competitors; which move on to the public Internet, changing the way products and services are created, marketed and distributed. In economic terms, this means new models of wealth creation. In social terms, it means new systems for sustaining social development and improving quality of life.

As Alliance collaborator Carl Thompson puts it: 'I think the ability to integrate internal and external information services with the Net represents the next major wave of change.' He argues that the promise of widespread use of EDI, for example, will finally be realized through the simplified and more ubiquitous services on the Internet. Transforming internal information and transaction-based systems to integrate with the Internet represents a major opportunity for many organizations to transform themselves and their relationships with outside entities.

Buckle up – look where this is going

Digital markets are different from physical markets in a number of ways. Because physical constraints are eliminated, comparison shopping has no boundaries. Companies with truly different products or better price performance will more quickly rise to the surface and those without will fail. For example, what happens when a number of companies with the slogan 'We will not be undersold' enter a digital market? Alliance contributor Steve Caswell says: 'It is like the four service stations at an intersection launching a price war. Either they put themselves under or they decide [on] some rules regarding how to deal with each other.' In digital markets, all companies are at the same intersection.

Every industry will be unrecognizable in a decade. Musicians who cannot get their creations recorded by a record company can already place their song or video or score or musical on the Internet through the Internet Underground Music Association (IUMA). As a 'listener' you simply download the file on to a CD or digital tape and play it on your information appliance or home stereo. Any Website with music on it becomes a directory for other sites, effectively creating a new world of music accessible by anyone on the Internet. Even a star like Madonna already has selections on the Internet. Given that there will be a billion people on the Internet by the end of the decade, why would anyone market any other way? What is the role of the retail outlet in such a world?

The IUMA is an example of a entire industry in which production, distribution, marketing and sales are all moving from the physical world of bricks and mortar, big company organizational charts and high-paid executives to an electronic world on the I-Way. In doing so they will, in the words of musician Bob Dylan: 'Shake your windows and rattle your walls.'

Notes

1. This chapter has been published previously in *The Digital Economy: Promise and Peril in the Age of Networked Intelligence* (McGraw Hill, 1995).
2. Drucker, P. (1988) The new organization. *Harvard Business Review*, January–February. For a more complete presentation of Drucker's views, see Drucker, P. (1989) *The New Realities*. Harper and Row.
3. Jacques, E. (1990) In praise of hierarchy. *Harvard Business Review*, January–February.
4. Lotus Notes is seen by most as a work group collaboration tool, but hundreds of companies like CCTC are using it as a delivery system.
5. Womack, J. P., Jones, D. T. and Roos, D. (1990) *The Machine That Changed the World*. Rawson Associates.
6. Drucker, P. (1995) *Harvard Business Review*, January–February, p. 62.

Chapter 33

The empowered individual

Michael Wolff

Tapscott and the effective individual

Don Tapscott, author of the best-selling *Digital Economy:, Promise and Peril in the Age of Networked Intelligence*,[1] has developed a model of business transformation in the Information Age. His main argument is that the new economy will become a 'networked' economy and that in business we are looking at the emergence of the 'internetworked business'. By 'networked' Tapscott is referring to the interconnection of desktop end users, whether connecting from home, office or elsewhere.

In Tapscott's hierarchy, he sees the 'internetworked business' as the highest form of organizational structure. Below this is the 'extended enterprise', followed by the 'integrated enterprise', the 'high-performance team', and at the lowest level, the 'effective individual'. (See the previous chapter for definitions of these terms.)

Tapscott sees the effective individual as the basic building block of the networked economy and describes his effectiveness in terms of learning efficiency through the enabling of personal multimedia. By failing to appreciate both the need and the effect of the required psychological transition, Tapscott underestimates the full potential of individual empowerment and therefore quite understandably places the effective individual at the bottom of the networked hierarchy. He has perhaps unwittingly fallen into the same paradigm that prevails for conventional organization without realizing what is actually happening in practice.

In conventional business, we rightly see the largest organizations as being the most successful and the examples of best

315

commercial practice. They would not have grown so large if they were not doing the right thing. However, within the organization the individual thrives only in so far as he aligns his sense of meaning and purpose with that of his organization. At the point where this alignment fails, the individual becomes expendable. It may be true to say that the organization stands on the shoulders of its employees, but the organization serves its own purpose, not necessarily that of the individuals employed by it.

In this sense, employees at all levels within an organization allow themselves to be disempowered for the good of the organization. In the hierarchical structure, each individual divests his or her power in favour of the next level of authority. In return, the individual derives income, social status, meaning, purpose and security. Especially with respect to job security, this organizational contract is now under increasing stress. It is also arguable that this type of hierarchical structure is becoming both pathological and dysfunctional as it ceases to fulfil the needs and aspirations of its members.

In the networked economy, this paradigm is stood firmly on its head. The empowered individual, free from the need to give away his or her power to hierarchies that serve their own purpose and supported by the huge self-organizing networked economy, is free to build his or her own hierarchies at will. With open access to all the resources of the network, the individual is spoilt for choice. The potential is almost infinite. He or she can choose when, where and how he or she works. At all times the individual is in charge of his or her own destiny. He or she creates his or her own meaning and purpose.

The empowered individual, the first level of integration, is able to create one or more core business services in which the end-to-end value chain is fully integrated electronically. These processes involve the client, the suppliers of information and value enhancement services and the coordinating empowered individual. This is the second level of integration.

At the next level, functional support services such as sales, marketing, IT support, accounting and many other functions can be integrated as end-to-end value chains.

Each of the individuals supplying services within these chains needs to be empowered in the same way, as will be shown below.

We now begin to see a model of the networked economy in which the empowered individual is supported by a network of empowered individuals, each fully in control of his or her own destiny.

While Tapscott does not play down the seismic upheaval that is presaged by the emergence of the networked economy, his thinking is still tainted by the old-paradigm notion that higher levels of organization are more effective than lower levels. Teams are more effective than individuals, integrated enterprises more effective than teams, the extended enterprise more effective than the integrated enterprise, and so on.

Tapscott does not distinguish in any detail the difference between the employed and the self-employed effective individual. His underlying assumptions suggest that the effective individual is an employee. The employed knowledge professional becomes more effective with his or her understanding and practice of the technology, which will in itself act as a trigger for the psychological transition. As the awakened individual strives for further empowerment and discovers a new sense of purpose and meaning, there will be an inevitable divergence between the purpose of the individual and the organization.

Not only is there a tension of purpose, but also the individual's greatly improved commercial effectiveness – combined with an increasing psychological robustness – pose a considerable threat to the organization's competitiveness.

The structure created by the empowered individual will inevitably evolve to become the most competitive economic unit. Therefore it would appear that it is in the interests of both individuals and organizations to work together to support and facilitate this process.

Individual empowerment is not in itself a modern concept. One historical example is the notion of the Japanese samurai warrior. For the samurai, his tool was his sword. For the empowered individual, it is his desktop. To master the use of his sword, the samurai developed not only his technical skills, but also his mind.

Of what use was a sharp, well-balanced sword, or an intricate and technically elaborate method of using it in combat, if the samurai who had to be prepared to face death every day had not also developed a stable, inner platform of mental control from which to act or react according to the circumstances of an encounter? The relationship between this condition of mental stability – which made it possible for the martial skills expert to assess a situation quickly and coolly, simultaneously deciding upon the proper course of action – and a coherent and powerful execution of that decision had been perceived by almost every martial arts instructor in Japan.[2]

In the unstructured networked economy, the empowered individual needs to combine technical, commercial and entrepreneurial skills with an aspiration for personal development that takes him or her beyond the stage that has enabled him or her to be successful in the conventional economy.

I intend to illustrate this point with a brief description from my own research.

The transition to individual empowerment

I have identified five levels of technical and one level of transformational competence, all of which are required to some degree for an individual to make this transition successfully. It is assumed that the individual already has a well-developed set of commercial, managerial and entrepreneurial skills.

The five technical skills include the abilities to:

- use all the common and latest desktop application software packages and to be able to manage the desktop environment
- navigate the Internet and the Web, using all its resources, with the ability to communicate and share information
- have access to sources of on-line business intelligence as appropriate
- build, manage and maintain one's own Website, and to use this as a means for building relationships with clients, suppliers and associates who are potential work partners or information sharers
- build and manage a virtual office, which involves the management of the core business competency and all the other business functions that support it, such as marketing, sales, IT support, billing, collection and accounting.

The empowered individual has the potential to operate as a self-contained microbusiness, integrating and coordinating the value chain between suppliers and customers, and the functions needed to support this process, all from his or her single desktop.

The enabling technology, as with information, is easily accessible, universally available and usable by any intelligent person.

In a networked environment where information is universally accessible and infrastructure costs are the same for all participants, the potential to gather, organize, synthesize, evaluate – to generally add value and leverage intellectual material to produce a higher-value asset – still remains.

However, this asset cannot be realized unless the individuals engaged in the process are prepared to share information. A very high degree of information-sharing has been enabled by the technology, facilitating wholly distributed processes, that is, individuals being able to live and work anywhere. However, true information-sharing requires a high degree of mutual trust. Furthermore the development of mutual trust between individuals who may never meet each other face to face, requires an ability to build and maintain relationships that are quite different to those necessary for successful operation in a conventional organization.

In a conventional organization, the successful manager needs to be able to exercise power and control. In the networked economy, the professional bases success on personal empowerment and mutual relationships built on trust. The exercise of power and control just does not work. In fact the empowered individual can organize him or herself so that he or she is never in a position where another individual – whether an employer, customer or vendor – can exercise power or control over him or her. At the same time, the individual has no need to use this mode on others.

The culture of conventional organizations, however flat the structure, is still rooted in the concept of hierarchical power. Personal fulfilment and identity are determined by the complex reward structure, which tells a person who he or she is by how he or she performs in relation to the purpose of the organization. Personal financial security and sense of fulfilment are totally geared to this process. Inevitably the individual's level of psychological development must remain stuck at this level, because moving to another level threatens to undermine not only his or her financial security, but also social status and, most importantly, *the sense of who he or she is.*

In any networked relationship, most of the functions that give us meaning in a conventional organization are no longer valid. Status, role, authority, earnings level, social position, gender, age, physical appearance – none of these have any relevance. So how do we need to change in order to orient ourselves in this new and potentially bewildering environment? The psychological transition is now well understood and discussed below.

Employment status and motivation

The networked economy is global and with the universal availability of information, there is a high degree of transparency relating to the prices of products and services. For almost any product or service, a global price is emerging.

For an individual to sell his or her services in the networked economy, he or she needs to be competitive within the global pricing structure. This means that he or she needs to take a hard look at the value of his or her services, distribution channels, income needs and underlying cost structure.

If the individual works for a large successful organization he or she may have a high sense of security. He or she has the rights of an employee, derives a regular income from one source and the chances are still reasonably good that if he or she were to lose his or her job, another employer could be found.

However, as the networked economy gathers momentum, the individual will become increasingly aware that his or her level of security is diminishing rapidly and that the window of opportunity to make the transition to self-empowerment is closing fast.

With any luck he or she will not become a victim of the downsizing in his or her industry and will manage to survive each successive merger and subsequent rationalization that takes place.

According to Find/SVP, a US research group that tracks workplace developments, the number of workers telecommuting, at least part-time, has nearly tripled, jumping from 4 million in 1990 to 8 million in 1996 and to 11.1 million in 1997. While most of these are still employees, an increasing number are becoming self-employed. It is clear that as individuals develop and hone the skills outlined above, self-employment and home-based working will become the norm for knowledge professionals. In a recent conversation with the head of an executive outplacement service, I was told: 'Three years ago we were able to find full-time employment for all our clients. Today we are placing 80 per cent, but in three years we are forecasting that we will only find jobs for 50 per cent. The remaining 50 per cent will have to be considering alternative forms of employment.'

Individuals with high-quality skills and operating from a low cost base with few fixed overheads will inevitably prove to be highly competitive in knowledge-based markets. This applies to a high percentage of white-collar professional jobs.

The motivation for these people is that they can maintain their current standards of living and at the same time improve their overall quality of life and sense of well-being. This may be achieved at the expense of very high earning levels, major capital accumulation and/or power in the conventional sense.

Quality of life is achieved primarily through the individual's ability to choose

- where to live and work
- what to do
- with whom to work.

In this structure, the development of high-quality relationship and mutual interdependence (albeit virtual) is the basis for achieving his or her goals.

Also in this structure, the whole notion of information takes on a different significance. Back in the early days of the telegraph, information was used as a tool for achieving financial leverage and power through the process of differentiation and still is. I have it, you do not. I win, you lose. In the networked economy, information has become a universally available resource and the possibilities for leverage are limited. In this situation information becomes a means for harmonization and integration. A tool for building relationship as well as adding value.

Individual transformation

Understanding this point is critical to understanding the process of change from the conventional to the networked economic structure. This will become clearer when looking at the psychological transition that is required:

- An individual in life goes through various stages of development and these do not stop at adulthood.
- At each stage of development the individual sees the world in a certain way and that this changes as one moves from one stage to the next.
- At a certain stage of development an individual can become conscious of his or her own consciousness, that is to say, he or she can achieve a certain level of self-knowledge that enables him or her to observe him or herself and understand his or her own patterns of behaviour and motivations.
- Having reached this stage of 'metaconsciousness' an individual is able to progress to further stages of self-knowledge and psychological development.

In this respect we are only concerned with the level of psychological transformation required that enables the individual to achieve maximum adaptation in the emerging networked environment. Why the individual needs to change will become clearer as we proceed.

There are many schools of psychology that interpret this process in slightly different ways. A concise exposition can be found in Robert Kegan's book, *The Evolving Self: Problem and Process in Human Development*.[3] Kegan, a senior lecturer at Harvard Graduate School of Education, has identified five major stages of personal development and has described in detail the process of transition from one stage to the next.

What is relevant to our discussion is his description of the transition from the fourth level (the institutional) to his fifth level (the interindividual). The thrust of our argument is that the institutional level – which corresponds in this case with the individual's successful adaptation in the conventional power and control world of business – must progress to the interindividual level, in order to become empowered and build trusting relationships in the networked economy.

Kegan shows first that at each stage of development, there is a tension between the individual's need for differentiation and his or her need for integration. At the first and last stages of development, integration becomes the dominant mode, whereas in the intermediate phases, including the fourth institutional phase, differentiation is the main requirement for the individual.

Kegan describes the transition from one stage to the next in terms of three main phases. The first, *holding on*, involves the confirmation of the stage that has been reached and a desire to hold on to this stage. However, having assimilated and started to grow out of this phase, the individual moves towards *contradiction*, which initiates the process of letting go. The final phase, which Kegan calls *staying put for reintegration*, involves the need for continuity to provide a safe bridge from one major stage to the next.

In the institutional stage, the individual's identity is very much determined by his or her social and organizational status. Identity is determined by job titles, earning levels, power, property, financial wealth. It is less a question of who you are, but what you do, how much you earn and what you own. In order to be successful in this stage, the individual is willing to become the role that he or she has defined for him or herself and has allowed others to define for him or her. Role models are other successful individuals in the organization or chosen social niche. In the *holding on* phase, the individual achieves his or her career goals, a certain level of authority. Through his or her career he or she gets a sense of personal enhancement, fulfils ambitions and achieves a number of goals. The individual is motivated by need, especially respect and acceptance within his or her social group. Personal goals are adjusted within the organizational and social structure. He or she engages in a high degree of socialization.

To succeed in the networked economy, it is clear that the individual must move out of this phase or fail. In the networked world, there are no job titles; there is no organizational status, no social position, fewer opportunities for face-to-face socialization.

There is no scope for authority, no opportunities for personal enhancement, no peers against whom to measure one's performance. Without these identity props, the individual has to redefine his or her whole identity. In this stage, he or she must discover, know and define him or herself. The centre of his or her universe becomes him or herself, not the institution or social grouping to which he or she belongs. The individual needs to let go of the organizational and social trappings. He or she becomes motivated by choice, his or her personal goals are self-actualization and social goals are liberation. He or she is searching for autonomy. His or her measure of success is authenticity, the ability to speak his or her truth, his or her overall sense of well-being.

Kegan describes this phase as the acknowledgement and capacity for interdependence, for self-surrender and intimacy, for interdependent self-definition. This is also the stage at which, being centred in him or herself, the individual can build the 'stable inner platform of mental control' which is essential when the individual has no other means by which to define him or herself.

Key issues

I have outlined a situation in which highly skilled, entrepreneurial and psychologically developed professionals can embrace the opportunities emerging through the networked economy and achieve a high degree of personal security, competitiveness, quality of life and sense of well-being.

Underlying this proposition is the increasing awareness that the emergence of the networked economy will entail fundamental structural change at all levels of society, which in turn presents major threats and opportunities for all concerned.

I sense that the changes will be very profound and that they will come very quickly. The following are some of the issues that need to be considered.

For individuals – employed knowledge professionals

Faced by the opportunities and threats that have been raised above, the individual wishing to succeed in the networked economy needs to be asking the following questions about him or herself and his or her situation:

- How do the current changes affect the competitiveness of my employer and therefore how secure are my long-term prospects?
- What is my level of desktop competence and how willing is my employer to support me in fully developing the technical skills required to maximize my productivity?
- Where do I stand in terms of psychological development? Assuming that I am in Kegan's institutional stage, am I at the holding on, contradiction or staying put for reintegration stage?
- If I am at the holding on stage, to what extent is my employer encouraging me to stay there or to what extent is he encouraging me to let go and move on, especially in relation to the development of my knowledge-sharing skills?
- Do I want to become an independent knowledge professional as described above, and if so, what support and encouragement am I likely to get from my employer? What structural changes would I have to make in my life to make myself globally competitive?
- If I made a strategic decision to become self-employed, how could I make this transition in such a way that both I and my current employer get the maximum benefits?

For organizations employing knowledge professionals
- What is the level of desktop competency in our organization?
- Do our desktop end-users have access to high-quality business information, both from fee-based information providers and from the Web? Do they need more training to let them know what is possible and how to get the best advantage?
- Do we think that our internal information sources are better than information that can currently be obtained from public service providers? If so, have we recently conducted an audit to check whether this is the case?
- How good are our systems for knowledge-sharing both within and outside the organization? Are they better than knowledge-sharing systems currently available to users over public networks? If so, how much better and for how long?

- Do we think of our knowledge resources in terms of 'intellectual capital', and if so, have we put into place steps to measure and monitor it?
- Have we considered our key knowledge professionals in terms of 'psychological capital'? With respect to the pressures outlined above for individual empowerment in the emerging networked economy, what strategies are in our best interest? Should we support or discourage our employees in this respect?

Notes

1. Tapscott, D. (1995) *The Digital Economy: Promise and Peril in the Age of Networked Intelligence.*
2. Ratti and Westbrook (1973) *The Secrets of the Samurai.*
3. Kegan, R. (1982) *The Evolving Self: Problem and Process in Human Development.*

Chapter 34

Tomorrow's company

John McIntyre

Transformation

Threshold of a new world

Apart from being one of history's great milestones, the new millennium will usher in something even more profound and far-reaching. Peter Drucker, the leading management thinker, observes in *Post-Capitalist Society* that we are now in the middle of one of Western civilization's periodic transformations.[1] From such a period of change emerges a world so different in basic values, in social and political structure, in art, and in its world view that its people cannot even imagine the world in which their grandparents lived. Drucker believes that this transformation may take until 2010 or 2020 to be completed, and although the world which emerges 'will be different from anything anyone today imagines' he is clear that some of the basic shifts – in society and in its structure – have already happened.

Two major changes are already very visible, though we probably cannot imagine where they will lead: the dawning of what some refer to as the Information Age and the almost unbelievable advances in information technology, the term used for the convergence of computer and communications technologies. Although massive changes are also occurring in almost every other aspect of life – in population, in social structures, in the environment, in energy, in new materials and so on – these two above all will literally transform society and the way it operates.

Until recently, natural resources, labour and capital have

been the economy's critical resources. Not any more. The primary
resource now is knowledge: about needs and desires, sources and
resources, design and processes; materials, markets and money;
about knowledge itself – in fact about everything. Twenty years
ago bankers knew that, to them, information about money was
more valuable than the money itself. Ten years ago supermarket
management knew that in merchandising, information was more
valuable than merchandise. Now information, the raw material
of knowledge, is potential treasure, and IT is the new world's
defining technology.

What are the implications for organizations? Drucker gives
a typically direct answer: 'Because making productive use of
knowledge requires an organisation, the emerging society will be
a society of organisations.' However, the new organization will be
quite different from the traditional model which has dominated
the industrial age. Birchall and Lyons of Henley's Future Work
Forum observe that: 'We are witnessing the end of the predomi-
nance of the large business organization in its present form. The
only question that remains is: how long will it take?'[2] The answer
is likely to be determined far more by man's willingness or ability
to change than by the limits of technology, the capabilities of
which have in recent years far outstripped the demands we have
placed on it.

A brief history of work

To get some idea of what the organization of the future will look
like it helps to look at what is already happening and consider
some of the likely effects of the domestication of IT, typified by
the PC and the Internet. A quick glance at what has happened
over the last 200 years shows an interesting pattern, with a
modern trend which looks like a return to a version of an earlier
model (see Figure 34.1).

The left side of Figure 34.1 shows the workplace of the eighteenth century. Most working people lived in villages, and the
units were small firms – butcher, baker, cobbler, thatcher – or
couples like the proverbial farmer and his wife. The wife played
a critical role in running the business – she hired and paid the
hands, planned the crops, made sure the produce went to market
and kept the accounts. Apart from obvious other factors, IT is

making it increasingly practical for woman to return to her vital role in business while leading a portfolio life – an interesting echo of earlier times, and one which has enormous importance for the organization of the future.

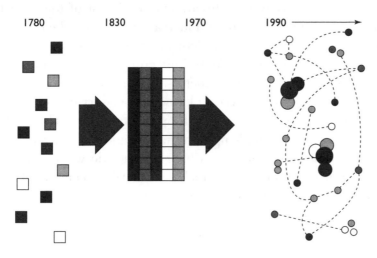

Figure 34.1   From village to worknet

With the march of industrialization came the migration from the land, and the emptying of the village into the town, with its factories and offices. The organization began to develop. As shown in the centre of the diagram, large, centralized factories and offices required by the production-line approach replaced the small, dispersed units of the village. The model was machine-like and the management system was command-and-control. Gradually we became a nation of employees, and by the late 1970s 93 per cent of the UK's workforce were on someone's payroll. Then followed a phenomenal shift away from payroll employment, as companies fragmented and downsized. The result will be that by the year 2000 some 50 per cent of the work-force will be owner-managers or self-employed. In parallel is another sea-change as traditional factory work is replaced by knowledge work. The blue-collar population is declining from being half of the total workforce in the 1950s to only about 15 per cent early in the next century – the same as in the late 1800s.

We have now arrived at the kind of organization shown on the right of Figure 34.1, which looks more like a biological organism than a machine and is the model for increasing numbers of organizations. In order to survive, they have to develop chameleon-like ability to adapt rapidly, keep a 360-degree look-out at all times, and be able to transform their capabilities as they respond to opportunity and threat. The fixed cost of the payroll has to be kept at a minimum and increasingly work is being done on a pay-as-you-go basis by independent specialists and service workers on contract. These loose-knit groupings of workers get work done in the same way as doctors, lawyers, cleaners and gardening contractors do, delivering know-how or services on an as-required basis to agreed standards for predictable fees. The model of the organization is made up of a nucleus and a set of relationships with other organizations, which together do what is necessary to fulfil its purpose. The nucleus, like DNA, consists of the minimum number of elements needed to define the organization's identity, purpose, values, core capabilities and essential relationships. Needless to say, the technology which enables this type of organization to work effectively is IT.

These changes in the nature of organizations have resulted from several huge shifts on a global scale over the past few decades, the common denominator being what has happened in IT. In less than twenty years computing has moved from the corporate computer room to the desktop, the home, the laptop and even the pocket; while communications have spread from telephone and telex (remember that?) to mobile telephone, fax, e-mail and services like CompuServe, AOL and, of course, the Internet. In parallel with the development of the hardware and software technologies have been relentless reductions in costs and prices, and massive increases in functionality and ease of use. Despite that, we have seen only the beginning of the advances which will continue to revolutionize the 'person–machine interface' and further integrate the technologies.

As a symptom of the rate of change, children at an early age are more computer-competent than their parents, who in turn are daily buying far more technological capability than they can possibly use. Even a relative power user of a modern notebook computer can probably only make use of a small fraction of the staggering capability routinely supplied in 'office suites' software. This unexploited potential represents an opportunity for new and more advanced uses of the facilities and applications yet to be defined. However, even with what the lay user can make use of, organizations are being transformed rapidly.

The death of distance

Imagine what becomes possible when information can be stored anywhere in the world, can be accessed, retrieved, manipulated, distributed, updated – what you will – in seconds at any time of the day, by anyone you wish (and even some you may not wish). Since the information content is more and more the important part in any transaction, it matters less and less where client and supplier, company and government office, teacher and student, user and support staff, buyer and seller, are located. For information and communication 'distance is dead' is now a reality.[3]

The future is all around you

Why not change the way we work?

British Telecommunications plc (BT) has been exploring, experimenting with, and now promoting the potential business improvements possible with new communications technologies. As well as that, as a giant organization in a competitive global marketplace, BT must search relentlessly for ways to improve its own costs, flexibility and responsiveness. The company has proved the effectiveness of dispersed operations in several of its own services, notably in the Highlands and Islands of Scotland, where it has had the support of Highlands and Islands Enterprise, eager to attract other businesses to its remote regions. British Telecom's telesupport centre at Thurso in Caithness started from a pilot project involving twenty people and is now fully established with 400 staff providing services ranging from dealing with public queries about BT's Internet services to implementing 18,000 remote software changes a month throughout BT's organization. Other successful operations include the Cellnet 999 call handling centre and the Directory Assistance service, both based in Inverness. In none of these cases is the user of the service aware of the physical location of the provider, apart perhaps from a telltale Highland accent. Many factors are important in the success of these operations, but distance is not one of them.

Highland Telematics, managing 200 teleworkers scattered throughout the Highlands; Lochaber International, a technical translation company servicing BMW, Mercedes-Benz and others; and Lasair, an electronic publishing firm working between Stornoway and San Francisco, are just three from many other examples of the irrelevance of distance to organizations whose business is knowledge and information based.

Guildford firm's biggest client is in Texas

Not long ago, the sales manager of a graphics design company in Austin, Texas, had to explain to her CEO how they had just lost their biggest client to some outfit in Guildford, England. As she said, the competitor just was not visible in the local market, she had never heard of them, and wondered how their ex-client had found them. The answer was that someone had been 'surfing the Net' and had found the Guildford firm's Web page. He found out that they could do the same kind of work as his company had been getting done locally, could match local prices and deliver in much less time – as much as 50 per cent less.

They used a combination of the oldest and the newest technology – the Earth's rotation and high-speed telephone lines. Taking advantage of the six-hour time difference between Texas and Guildford, the design company drafts an initial response to the client's statement of requirement and uploads it to the client's computer system. The UK firm go home leaving the client most of the day to review the work and send back comments and changes. Then, while Texas sleeps, Guildford goes to work and by the time the client gets to the office, the next draft of the design is ready for review. There is an overlap of two or three hours when both client and supplier are in their offices and can discuss things over the phone.

IBM software: the eagle and the dragon chase the sun

IBM's mirror-image software laboratories in the USA and China provide a good example of what can be done nowadays with IT to be competitive in a knowledge-based industry. This case combines a global view of things, an understanding of the cost/performance of information and communications technology and an appreciation of China's world-class software talent and competitive manpower costs. Using the sixteen-hour time difference between China and the USA, IBM can get two eight-hour shifts of programming done within a twenty-four hour day while working only single shifts in each country. The entire systems analysis and programming work of the site is stored in computer files which are transferred by high-speed communications links from the USA round the world to China, and back again at the end of the respective shifts. By this means IBM can develop software at less cost and, more importantly when time to market is crucial, in half the normal elapsed time.

Better margins at half your price – and you say we have a problem?

When the owners of a computer systems agent based in a Surrey town decided to go into the 'business continuity' business ('disaster recovery' to older hands), they set the whole operation up using the latest information and communications technology. The management team had ISDN phone lines to their homes, and mobile telephones, faxes and notebook computers. They ran the business from wherever they happened to be, which was mostly near their clients' businesses. Except for modest accommodation for a few finance and administration people the only office space they had was for customers' use, and that was sublet whenever possible, usually to training companies which could free up the space at short notice in an emergency. The result of all this was a dramatically smaller cost base, allowing them to offer their services at half the price of their two main competitors and still make healthy margins. When the competitors, both large companies, took issue with what they perceived to be ill-considered 'skimming' tactics they realized that they had the problem, not the new entrant. When they had first started out, the owners of the new company had asked themselves what was possible with new technology, and had come up with an organization in a completely different league in terms of cost and responsiveness. Only by major restructuring could their competitors come close to getting their cost bases anything like the same.

These are just a few examples from a fast-growing catalogue of new-style success stories. Their variety shows that there is practically no type of organization which cannot take advantage of IT to improve, not just its performance, but its flexibility and responsiveness as well. Any new venture, whether start-up, merger, acquisition, new department or subsidiary should start with a blank sheet of paper and write the heading 'IT' and the questions: 'What is possible?' and 'Why not?' The one certainty is that if you do not do it, someone else will, and they are probably a competitor.

Tomorrow's organization, today

Mainframe power for under a pound?

In a previous chapter of this book Bill Gates, co-founder and leading light of the global personal computer software giant Microsoft, observed that the cost of computing today was a million times less than twenty years ago, and that in the next twenty years the cost would be one millionth what it is today[4]. What does that mean? Such galactic figures in themselves do not tell us much, but in practice it means that computing has become accessible to a mass of people in terms of both cost and simplicity. Gates made another very important point. Contrasting computing with the example of the radial tyre manufacturers whose market shrank as the products lasted longer, he underlined the fact that the computing market expands as the efficiency of the products improves, and IT becomes cheaper and easier to use.

Trying to guess at the implications of that trend even five years ahead is hard – twenty years is impossible. But as Peter Drucker says: 'Trying to foretell the future is a waste of time.' Better observe what is already happening, perhaps on quite a small scale and extrapolate the effects of its being widespread. Using that kind of thinking suggests that things which are today only possible with giant computing and communications systems will be comfortably within the reach of the tops of desks and laps in twenty years. Since few people can imagine wanting big mainframe applications for themselves, we have to translate the capability into something which is relevant for the individual and the common enterprise. That suggests being able to seek out, assemble, manipulate and model, transmit, store and retrieve information of all kinds worldwide, as easily as we can use the global telephone system today. In fact of course, the telephone is still mostly used for one application – the conversation. Though useful while it lasts, once over, the conversation is gone for good. Imagine if all information – data, graphic and sound – were digitized and captured; it could then be stored, retrieved, etc. That will soon be a commonly available facility.

The organizations of the future?

The implications of these kinds of possibilities for the organization of the future are immense. Almost any degree of aggregation or dispersion can be chosen. Any combination of capabilities and capacities can be arranged, over any sensible duration. Several models or approaches to organization are evolving to reflect the needs of the modern enterprise, as the following examples show.

Organizational trefoil – Handy's shamrock

As long ago as 1989 Charles Handy coined the term 'shamrock organization' to describe an organization model consisting of three lobes: (1) a core of management and essential staff supported by (2) long-term contractors and (3) temporary workers. While observing that this was not new – it is the model used traditionally by builders, farmers, newspapers and others – he pointed out that it was being adopted by large corporations. Handy concluded that, 'All organizations will soon be shamrock organizations'.[5] Information technology is a natural technology for the shamrock organization, enabling simple intra- and inter-organization communication and information management, anywhere, anytime.

Four square – Bridges adds the customer

William Bridges extends Handy's shamrock naturally to a four-segment square that includes the customer or client.[6] Again this model, common in supermarkets, DIY store and petrol forecourts, is not revolutionary. In fact, as we all know, the customer may even have to do less pleasant work (filling the car in a freezing February gale) than the firm's employee (taking the payment in a warm shop). In any case the customer is an essential component in the workings of the firm. Of course, large companies have included their customers in discussions about new products, even developed products jointly. The difference again is the scale of this inclusion.

Future organizations that fail to integrate their customers' thinking and effort into their way of business life will find themselves at a disadvantage, perhaps even hearing that most feared sound – the silence of the departed customer. Bridges also highlights the increasing trend to spin out non-core activities as independent businesses, leaving the parent as major client. The results can be startling when a previously peripheral activity becomes the core of a new business. A minor division can be transformed overnight into a specialist supplier which not only does a better job for the parent, but may rapidly become an industry leader in its own field – IBM UK's Procord is a classic case in point. Procord was originally the Estates and Construction department of IBM's UK operation, responsible for everything from changing light bulbs to planning major real estate developments. In a computer company it was never going to be a front line division. Spun out as an independent company, the frog turned into a handsome prince and, under enthusiastic and dedicated leadership, acquired a new sense of identity and purpose and an excitement about its potential. The company was soon hiring super-qualified specialists in everything from ergonomics to the wired office, offering strategic space planning services, running full facilities management contracts, and numbered several household names in its client list. They were spun out from IBM United Kingdom Limited and consisted of IBM's Estates and Construction division and their General Services and Building Services functions. Set up as an independent company, they now handle everything from janitor services up to strategic building design – the 'wired office' – with all the ergonomics, environmental, communications, etc.

Plus education makes five – the maple leaf

From Handy's shamrock through Bridges' four-segment square I would suggest we have to progress to a maple leaf, the fifth element being added for education. As organizations condense down to their essence the training facility may become specialist and non-core. Increasingly units will stay small individually, even when they form parts of vast agglomerations like ABB. They will need access to externally provided education and training. In a knowledge economy with an increasingly rapid rate of change, lifelong learning needs to be translated into something more than 'life-learn longing'. All the talk about learning organizations, skill acquisition, 'learning how to learn', and so on, needs to be supported by the equivalent of a Procord of learning and teaching. It will be vital for organizations to have constant access to specialists in education and training, and the new processes possible with IT. Delivery systems are increasingly becoming IT-based, and new materials are being developed in virtually every field of knowledge and skill. This is a major growth area for the education and training industry, and should be the province of the UK's colleges of further and higher education and its universities. Locally based, nationally spread and very much 'in the business' they should be present and future organizations' permanent partners.

Orderly chaos – Dee Hock and the chaordic organization

Who owns Visa? Where is its headquarters? How can I buy its shares? These are some of the questions that Dee Hock, retired architect of that organization, likes most to ask his audiences, because the answers do not conform to any traditional concepts. The Visa credit card is one of the best-known brands in the world – anywhere in the world. The organization consists of some 20,000 fiercely competing financial organizations who at the same time collaborate in handling each others' card transactions. In aggregate they process 7 billion transactions annually, worth $650 billion. Organizational cooperation on a grand scale.

Hock describes the underlying principle as 'chaordic' a combination of order and chaos, and likens it to such biological organizations as the mind, and the immune system. He makes the point that these natural systems are vastly superior to our traditional organizations in efficiency, power, sophistication, self-repair, self-regulation and self development, and yet they have no leadership structure nor any of the other attributes of our mechanistic, predictive, command-and-control based organizations. They represent a model for future organization, where its essence is defined by its function, its behaviour by a code of values and its operation

by the relationships occurring at its periphery, and based on its
interdependence with its environment. Could such a system hope
to function without superior IT? Hardly. Are we likely to see
'virtual' organizations of that sort evolving around the interconnection possibilities of the Internet? Absolutely – they already are,
however informally. Do not watch this space – get into it!

Tomorrow's company and the inclusive approach

In 1990 Charles Handy, then Vice-President and Chairman of
the Royal Society for the Encouragement of the Arts,
Manufactures and Commerce, seeking to stimulate debate about
Britain's relative decline in long-run economic performance,
delivered a lecture asking, 'What is a company for?' The event
turned out to be the touch-paper for a major business-led study
involving the leaders of twenty-five of the UK's top organizations.
The study concluded with a report describing what it termed the
'inclusive approach' – a philosophy of business leadership based
on the deliberate and constructive management of all the organization's key relationships, typically the stakeholders. This con-
trasted starkly with the then (and still, in the minds of many)
popular notion that the principal concern of the leaders of public
companies should be shareholder value. However, there was substantial evidence that the best way to maximize shareholder
value was in fact to achieve success for all stakeholders and,
further, that concentrating only on shareholder value actually led
to less than optimum performance in that area itself.

The stakeholder management model embodied in the inclusive approach provides the leaders of organizations with the
means to deal effectively with several topical concerns and maximize the performance of the organization by harnessing the collective energy, creativity, enthusiasm and support of its interested
parties. Ideal practice of this approach includes all employees,
customers, suppliers, shareholders and members of its communities in the organization's commonwealth, generating a two-way
flow of contribution and reward.

In order to implement the inclusive approach effectively in
an organization requires comprehensive measurement and continual communication. Again IT will be the crucial enabling technology and will support inclusive activity, however dispersed the

organization and its constituencies. In fact the facilities for trans-ferring information of all kinds, including multimedia, and for comprehensive communication between the interested parties will be a major determinant for the adoption of the inclusive approach in complex organizations.

How boldly dare you dream?

At one level, the structures of organizations now evolving reflect what IT makes possible. Conversely, the new forms of organization required for effectiveness and even survival in a knowledge economy cannot exist without IT. The management of an organization's knowledge assets is crucial to its survival and success, and the technology of survival is IT. We are seeing organizations fragment an amazing rate. The fully integrated organization is in full retreat in the face of the forces of change. Disaggregation is in, whatever its pseudonym: outsourcing, downsizing, reinvention, whatever. Organizations are seeking their organizational 'absolute zero', the lowest fixed-cost entity which can fully define the organization's identity, purpose, values and relationships. Ultimately, like a benign version of the 1950s Mekon of Dan Dare infamy (who was all mind and very little body), the perfect organization may evolve to a 'mind and heart' organism which forms relationships with other compatible organisms in order to fulfil their mutual purposes – the ultimate in organizational symbiosis. This would be a sophisticated meta-organism which at every level would have to have matching information systems analogous to biological systems such as the nervous system, the blood stream, the lymphatic system and so on.

We are seeing glimpses of such possibilities today as the individual members of organizations begin to disperse around the world, working alone or in small groups, now as colleagues, now with customers, with suppliers, with part-time competitors, with prospective clients, with business partners; but without the daily commute, without the factory, without the drawing office. No offices. 'The office is you.' What enables them to work effectively? It is the portable or pocketable computer, the modem, the global database, the mobile telephone, the videophone and the rest. It is the definitive enabling technology of the knowledge society. It is IT.

Notes

1. Drucker, P. (1993) *Post-Capitalist Society*. Butterworth-Heinemann.
2. Birchall, D. and Lyons, L. (1995) *Creating Tomorrow's Organization*. Pitman.
3. Cairncross, F. (1997) *The Death of Distance*. Orion Business Books.
4. Microsoft CEO Summit. Remarks by Bill Gates, Seattle, May (1997).
5. Handy, C. (1989) *The Age of Unreason*. Random House.
6. Bridges, W. (1996) *Job Shift: how to prosper in a workplace without jobs*. Nicholas Brearley.

Chapter 35

The global village: today and tomorrow

Nelson Thall

In human communication there is neither neutral media, nor pure observers. In short, there are no 'undistorted facts' – for facts, like fakes, are artefacts, and the intent of the maker may be either to enlighten or deceive.

'The user is always the content' of any medium, just as the programme, which modulates it, is always another medium (e.g. movies or plays broadcast on television; speech or music played on radio).

If the programme is affected by conceptual bias, due to our personal 'values' or abstract philosophy, its effect will be simply to hold (or lose) the attention of our audience in reference to the actual medium we are studying. This is because the visible programme is always 'another medium.' (For example, the electric light created an entire environment of services and disservices – the electric utilities, electrified equipment and 'electrified' people are its ultimate message.)

Each user forges individual meaning out of what the medium does. But its 'programme,' whether in traffic signalling or advertising, is yet another medium.

Nevertheless, there are classifiers who still demand a clear, unequivocal answer – yes or no – as to whether a particular medium (like radio, for example) is 'good' or 'bad,' or even whether percepts are better than concepts – or vice versa.

The universal human condition today in a period of rapid innovation is necessarily that of alienation. Every culture now rides on the back of every other culture. The extremely mobile individual consciousness of the print-oriented man now reverses into the tribal inertia of multiconsciousness. It is rather similar to what happens when countries demobilize at the end of a major war.

Since Sputnik and the satellites, the planet is enclosed in an artificial environment that ends 'Nature', and turns the globe into a repertory theatre to be programmed, just like the computer. We are entering the age of implosion after 3,000 years of explosion. The electric field of simultaneity gets everybody involved with everyone else. Sputnik put the globe in a 'proscenium arch' and the global village was transformed into a global theatre. The result, quite literally, is the use of public space for 'doing one's thing.' A planet parenthesized by an artificial environment no longer offers any directions or goals to nation or individual. The world itself, has become a probe. 'Snooping with intent to creep' or 'casing everybody else's joint' has become major activity. As the main business of the world becomes espionage, secrecy becomes the basis of wealth, as with magic in a tribal society.

The result of living inside a proscenium arch of satellites is that the young now accept the public spaces of the Earth as role-playing areas. Sensing this they adopt costumes and roles and are ready to 'do their thing' everywhere. In the older fragmented and mechanical world of specialism, we tended to use only a part of our faculties at any one time. This was called 'work'. When, like the artist, we use all our faculties at once, we are recognized to be playing and are at leisure. A man must work very hard at his hobby, but because he uses all his faculties when playing, he is thought to be at leisure. Looked at in the rear-view mirror this leisure takes on the illusory form of unemployment and joblessness and vacancy.

As a society, we have been made to become peculiarly vulnerable.

As Narcissus fell in love with an outering (projection, extension) of himself, humankind seems invariably to fall in love with the newest gadget or gimmick that is merely an extension of his own body. Driving an automobile or watching television, we tend to forget that what we have is simply a 'part of ourselves' hanging out there. Thus disposed, we become 'servo-mechanisms of our contrivances,' responding to them in the immediate, mechanical way that they demand of us.

The point of the Narcissus myth is not that people are prone to fall in love with their own images, but that people fall in love with extensions of themselves – which, ironically, they believe are 'not' extensions of themselves. This provides, I think, a fairly good model of all our total relationship with technologies and it directs us toward a basic issue – the idolatry of technology as involving a 'psychic numbness'.

We are machines serving machines – and not vice versa. To survive today, we must strive to understand the power of technologies to isolate the senses and thus, to 'hypnotize' society.

All technologies hypnotize the user. Our tools and technologies are closed systems incapable of interplay. Every new technology further diminishes sense interplay and awareness for that precise area ministered to by that precise technology. Computer banks dissolve the human image. When most data banks come together into a reciprocating whole as a result of the Internet, our entire Western culture will turn turtle. Visualize an amphibian with its shell inside and its organs outside. Internet-person wears his or her brain outside the skull and his or her nervous system on top of the skin. Such a creature is ill-tempered and eschewing overt violence. Internet-person is like an exposed spider squatting in a thrumming web, resonating with all other webs. He or she is not flesh and blood but an item in a databank, ephemeral, easily forgotten and resentful of that fact.

It would be hard to imagine a state of confusion greater than our own. As Marshall McLuhan said, 'Literacy gave us an eye for an ear' and it succeeded in detribalizing that portion of humankind that we refer to as the Western world.

In fact, we are now engaged in an accelerated programme of detribalization of all 'backward' parts of our world by introducing them to our own 'ancient' print technology – at the same time that we are engaged in retribalizing ourselves by means of the new electronic technology.

I envision this process as becoming 'conscious of the unconscious,' and of 'consciously promoting unconscious values' by an ever clearer consciousness.

When we put our central nervous system outside ourselves, we returned to the primal nomadic state. We have become like the most primitive palaeolithic man, once more global wanderers, but now 'information gatherers' rather than food gatherers.

Humankind in the electronic age has no possible environment except the globe and no possible occupation except information-gathering. By simply moving information and 'brushing information against information,' any medium can create vast wealth. Look at Bill Gates!

The richest corporation in the world, American Telephone and Telegraph, has only one function: moving information about. Simply by talking to one another, we create wealth. Any child watching a television show should be 'paid' because he or she is creating wealth for the community.

This wealth is not money. Money is 'obsolete' because it stores work (and work, as we have seen, is itself obsolete). In a workless non-specialist society, money is useless. What we need is a credit card, which is really only information.

When new technologies impose themselves on societies long habituated to older technologies, anxieties of all kind result. Our electronic world now calls for a unified global field of awareness; the kind of private consciousness appropriate to 'literate humans' can now be viewed as an unbearable kink in the collective consciousness demanded by electronic information movement.

In this impasse, suspension of all automatic reflexes would seem in order. I believe that artists, in all media, respond soonest to the challenges of new pressures. I would like to suggest that they also show us ways of living with new technology without destroying earlier forms and achievements. The artist is our 'lifeline to tomorrow'.

Today, electric technology increases the speed of action of everyday life and daily events to the point where ordinary people cannot make sense of their world. Twentieth-century people are not awake, but 'walking asleep'. They have had too many novelties thrust at them. These have made them numb and unaware.

The great artists of the past hundred years have been trying to communicate this fact to society.

Communication speed-up has created an 'identity crisis.' It

eliminates the very image of one's self. The 'non-person' is the inevitable result of communications speed-up.

How ironic that when all barriers of private consciousness are overcome, the resulting collective form of awareness is a 'tribal dream'. The patterns of such a 'dreamworld' become invisible to the old perceptual process. It is in this dreamworld where electric illusions result – and where patterns of 'conspiracies' appear to exist where they are not, and then disappear where they actually do exist.

This electric illusion stems from the computer's ability to create the impression of a multitudinous environment and to make the walls invisible. We programme our environment to appear the way the 'managers of the global theatre without walls' wish it to appear. Someone else creates 'reality' for you.

We have evolved into a 'complete subliminal projection project.' Electric technology has turned us into images without a body – literally. Humanity is now able to be in two or more places at the same time. This is very difficult for Westerners' twentieth-century literate mind to visualize. We lost our bodies, and became 'no-bodies' – and thus without identity. The identityless person also lost the image of themselves as individuals, and became part of a 'collective body of no-bodies' all in cyberspace.

This gave rise to the so-called 'out of body' experiences, as well as the feminism movement of the 1960s. Also the macho movement of the 1970s, unisex of the 1980s and generation X of the 1990s – all fashions of thought and images of the times.

We are about to extend the consciousness of humankind into a new state. But first we must study the effects of 'electrified waiting' on 'Waiting'. We rediscover ourselves in a post-angelic collective 'unconscious' state while the machines are becoming more and more conscious. The computer is the first component of that hybrid of video-related technologies which will move us toward a world consciousness. It steps up the velocity of logical sequential calculations to the speed of light, reducing numbers to body count by touch. When pushed to its limits, the product of the computer reverses into simultaneous pattern recognition by eroding the mechanical processes in all sequential operations. It brings back the Pythagorean occult embodied in the idea that 'numbers are all' and at the same time it dissolves hierarchy in favour of decentralization. Any business corporation requiring the use of computers for communications and record-keeping will have no other alternative but to decentralize.

The very nature of the computer will push logical maturity to the point of breakdown. Most logical sequential calculations can easily be driven to the speed of light. As this process evolves, it will bring back and accentuate an ancient preoccupation with the mystical quality of numbers in a sensuous tactile mode. At this stage of greatest intensity of development there will be an unanticipated reversal. The simultaneous will emerge from the sequential, the mythic from the historic, acoustic from visual space. The old ground rules of point-to-point logic will breakdown. And holism will then emerge as a dominant form of thinking, governed by a considerably smaller group of management élite.

A perceptive prophet can predict how human culture will retune humankind's mind; for by recognizing the dominant process patterns he or she can anticipate the interplay both with the body and with any society inherited or invented. Such a prophet can foresee ever widening and deepening conflicts between devotees of the old literate and the new tactile cultures. Today normal scientists are trapped in the paradigms of normal science – the model problems and solutions recognized as scientific achievements by a community of scientists. However there is no universally acknowledged 'scientific method,' only paradigms that communities of scientists accept for their own separate disciplines. Science organizes knowledge through concepts that reinforce existing disciplines whereas art organizes existing ignorance through percepts that discover new disciplines. That is why discovery has been the role of amateurs who explore without bounds, while development has been the job of the professional who work within limits. Any seer can plainly see that providing logical answers has become the indispensable job of computers just as discovering relevant questions will remain the irreplaceable role of people. Art will always anticipate science because percepts always precede concepts.

Everything will disappear.

Chapter 36

Staying human in a machine-dominated world

Susanna Opper

Imagine that it is the year 1151 and you live in a walled town in France. Consider how you would get information. You cannot read. Except for a few clerics, neither can anyone else. All the information you gain in your entire lifetime you either see with your own eyes or hear about. Before you die, you will have no more than 200 to 300 encounters with information outside your village. You depend on occasional visits from troubadours, travelling knights, pilgrims and other visitors, and listen with rapt attention to their tales late into the night. That is it. No television, no newspapers, books or magazines, no telephones, no airplanes and, of course, no Internet.

Now fast forward to today. Consider how our ability to be in touch and to obtain information has transformed our lives from a simple, tedious, isolated existence to one that is rich, exciting and global. But we are paying a price for this richness that leaves us vulnerable both as individuals and as business entities. Somewhere along the way we have lost touch with a part of our humanity; we will need to reclaim it in the years ahead.

'Too much'

The sense of overwhelm that most businesspeople experience today cannot be sustained into the future. Frequently voice-mail in-boxes refuse new messages before their owners arrive at the office in the morning. Some of these same workers face 300 e-mails a day.

A senior executive recently related the favour she did for a subordinate who returned from vacation to 500 unanswered e-mails. The executive persuaded the head of information systems to delete all the messages. The subordinate, deeply grateful, thanked the executive profusely later that afternoon.

An 'antidote' is defined as a remedy to counteract the effects of poison or of anything noxious taken into the system. We need an antidote to the 'too much' of our lives today. There are simply too many choices, too many results in our Internet searches, too many possibilities, too little time.

Some of this overwhelm will be mitigated by the very technology that spawned it. Our information systems will learn our needs and scan themselves to isolate and present only critical information to our desktop. Like automobiles before them, our computers will become nearly trouble free. We relate to our computers today as automotive pioneers did to their cars in the early twentieth century. In those days a simple trip of twenty or thirty miles could take a day and might require one or several tyre changes. Today automobiles are reliable with minimal maintenance for at least 100,000 miles.

Our technology is allowing us to work at home today as people have for most of human history. As more people telecommute and our entrepreneurial home-based business economy expands, families will again dine together. Children will be raised with a clearer understanding of work and their parents' vocation. These are all positive contributions our technology is making to the quality and humanity of our lives.

The shadow side is that we no longer have space between our work and our home. Faxes churn out into the night; e-mails pile up; cell phones seek us out on weekends; pagers call no matter where we are. Technology has increased not only the pace of external demands, but more importantly, the intensity of internal expectations. We believe we should respond to 500 e-mails. Did deleting the e-mail messages really free the overburdened employee? Will he, in the end, be more stressed as he struggles to explain why he did not respond to the missing e-mails?

Our enmeshment with technology has transformed us into entirely different beings than we have been historically. We look to machines to solve our problems. Our machines have become our beasts of burden. Laundry, washing dishes, cooking meals – activities as necessary today as in 1151 – are made simple by machines.

In the 1950s and 1960s, Americans got lazy. Automotive transportation caused lack of exercise, which was eventually proved harmful by numerous medical research projects. So exercise was reintroduced – but this time largely by machine. We invented stationery bicycles and treadmills to challenge our muscles with fictitious hills. We still walked or jogged outside, but usually with a tape machine setting the pace with music or the persistent voice of a recorded instructor.

Back to basics

The keys to retaining our humanity in our machine-dominated world lie in those areas that have not changed since humanity began. Back in 1151 babies learned to walk and talk just as they do today. At night in 1151, people dreamed when they slept. We know little more today about those dreams than they did; perhaps, in our overstimulated world, we may even know less. We still do not fully understand how we learn or how memory works or what inspiration causes an artist's creation or a scientist's discovery. We understand hardly anything more about our emotions – why we fall in love or out of it.

We will begin to regain our humanity by returning to more primitive behaviour.

We can see how this trend will work in the future by considering how we have adjusted our attitude toward childbirth in recent years. In the 1940s mothers bore their children under heavy sedation in an antiseptic environment which eradicated any emotional experience – either for the mother or the father (who paced back and forth in the hospital waiting room). Today children are often born at home again; fathers usually are present at the birth and have a role to play. Breast feeding – eschewed for decades – is common practice again today.

The Information Age is a leveller. The Internet allows everyone access to information so that many products and services are becoming commodities. The only way business entities can achieve and maintain success is to discover a sustainable competitive advantage. In most industries that advantage cannot be totally technology driven – it must be fuelled by creativity, by reflection, by the freedom to dialogue and invent. These very qualities are being squeezed out in our intensely competitive, infomationally stressed business environment. In the race to stay current, many companies are allowing no time to invent their futures.

The rapid pace at which we conduct our business and our lives today has made a fundamental shift in the coin of the realm. Until a few years ago, costs were measured monetarily. Today time has become equal to money in evaluating costs. Free events are as difficult to sell as sessions requiring a fee because the knowledge worker's time is as valuable, or more so, than money.

The conundrum is that in order to be creative, it is necessary to spend time. As any artist will testify, you cannot know in advance how long creativity and innovation will take. While inspiration, by definition, occurs in an instant, it is impossible to know how long it will take for that inspiration to present itself.

Turning the tide

Anaesthesia and hospital births altered our experience of the fundamental human process of birth. Similarly, our current dependence on electronic communication coupled with our fear of spending time threatens to change how we experience human connections. E-mail allows greater ease of communication, but can lessen face-to-face conversation. Soon new technologies will provide us visuals and video clips to put a face on our now faceless electronic conversations. But none of this will provide us with the relationship-building quality of a human connection in the same place at the same time.

In order to truly be creative about our business challenges, we need to take a fresh look at information. In order to be fresh, we need to clear our desks and our minds of the clutter and demands of daily business and escape to a purer environment. In that place we can reclaim some of our essential humanity. While we do not need to turn the clock all the way back to 1151, we will do best when we escape from the concrete modernity most of us work in.

IBM CEO Lou Gerstner knows this:
Every six weeks he takes his top 40 managers off-site for a two-

day retreat ... dedicated to management learning in non-traditional areas. Each session features an outside speaker who addresses a topic that is peripheral to the immediate concerns of IBM's leadership ... Gerstner personally leads these sessions; his objective is to give his executives practice in stretching their thinking and developing new perspectives on IBM's business.[1]

Similarly, the Shawenon Centre provides an unconventional environment in which strategic business issues can be discussed. Here participants explore using contemporary tools in a non-traditional setting. My husband, Will Ryan, and I founded the centre to link state-of-the-art technology with a serene natural setting. Working with computer-based meeting facilitation technology, we provide an environment in which business people confront key issues. The objective is to collaborate on creating an action plan everyone present can commit to. Along the way we encourage participants to invent unconventional solutions by tapping into the inspiration of poets and artists – trees, water, grass, insects, birds and other animals.

The collaborative technology we use helps uncover the basic values of the group by exploring the beliefs and commitments of team members. A clear statement of the problem or challenge and practical knowledge of resources are also key. Creative business solutions occur in this environment.

Getting creative

Creative solutions are possible even when it is not practical to travel off-site. Both changed attitudes and different behaviour are key to creating this state of mind.

Inner adjustments include recognizing that none of us can expect to read everything, visit every relevant Website and respond to all the outside requests of our business and personal lives. These inner adjustments call for great clarity of purpose. We need to be clear about our values – what really matters and what can be pushed off, perhaps indefinitely. We need to be aware of the inherent seductiveness of our burgeoning information environment. We cannot pursue every tasty morsel of information. We also need to recognize that 'no' is sometimes the right answer.

Most of us were raised in a traditional educational environment in which we were expected to know it all. Success in school meant that you did your homework – read the chapter and did the exercises. Then we were tested on what we managed to remember. This educational concept, which assumes there is a finite amount of information, is inappropriate in today's work environment. Still, most of us have the vestigial expectation that we can know it all. We need to give that up.

Behaviour changes foster creativity when we learn how to maintain balance at work and at home and, most importantly, at our home office where the two come together. While not everyone can visit a serene rural environment, everyone can take time to walk in a nearby park. One Wall Street executive we know jumps on the ferry to Staten Island when he needs a break. In slightly over an hour, the water, the seagulls and the calming motion of the boat refresh him.

We need to allow ourselves some empty time to just think and find creative solutions to our business issues. How often a brilliant resolution to a nagging problem arrives while we are in the shower or behind the wheel driving to work. There is a reason for this. When we leave our minds alone, they often produce amazing results.

We need also to commit time to the things we love doing. How many people who used to love to paint, play an instrument or indulge in a hobby have given that up? Taking the time to do the things we love seems an enormous indulgence in our overworked lives. But perhaps these actions that keep us human actually contribute to our ability to solve problems and meet our daily work demands.

Sometimes it is just as efficient to let the strong hand of serendipity do the work:

Until one is committed there is hesitancy, the chance to draw back, always ineffectiveness.
Concerning all acts of initiative (and creation) there is one elementary truth, the ignorance of which kills countless ideas and splendid plans: the moment one definitely commits oneself, then Providence moves too.

All sorts of things occur to help one that would otherwise never have occurred. A whole stream of events issue from the decision, raising in one's favour all manner of unforeseen incidents and meetings and material assistance, which no man could have dreamed would have come his way.[2]

Years from now we will look back at the end of the twentieth century and wonder how we did it. How did we manage all the unsorted information, the uncertain software and the cranky hardware? How did we make the transition from technology being the focus of some to technology being the way of all?

In time, our technology will mature so that we can depend on it to make our lives easier. If we also pay attention to our humanity – to relationships, to discovering who we are and what we want to be – we will have richer and more productive lives both as individuals and as members of organizations. The power of human commitment and focus has not changed since 1151. We expect it will still be essential for getting things done in 2151.

Notes

1. *Fortune*, 24 November 1997.
2. W. N. Murray, The Scottish Himalayan Expedition.

Chapter 37

Symplectics: weaving world views

Robin Wood

Scene 1: a collaboradome on the Concorde Space Station in Earth orbit, 2010

Professor Jay Forrest just finished doing a learning review with some colleagues on Earth of their latest collaboration about community building in extraterrestrial environments, called 'Communextra'. He cast his mind back to the days when he was a young Java programmer in Silicon Valley.

During the final years of the twentieth century, the groupware and internet communities were still dominated by technophiles, but a new and substantial minority was beginning to assert itself – the 'symplectics', who understood the importance of the human dimension in any conversation or dialogue.

Looking back at 2,000 years of recorded human history, Professor Jay Forrest was convinced that the next ten years would see major breakthroughs in humankind's ability to create virtual presence in both a non-local quantum way, as well as using the technological infrastructures such as the Web to facilitate the 'tuning-in' process required to get non-local quantum communication going.

When Roger Penrose (Stephen Hawking's collaborator on the theory of Big Bang and black holes) and Stuart Hameroff finally won the Nobel prize for their work on Evolutionary Quantum Computation in 2001, following their breakthrough research on conscious events as orchestrated space-time selections, it had become clear to a number of adepts that non-local communication was not only possible, but very effective. This was particularly important in space travel and in orbit, as travellers could not always be interfacing with one another via technology.

But for most of the human race, NetMeetings were still the easiest way to communicate across space-time. What had become increasingly important, however, was the understanding of different world views, cultures and personality types, as new communities were being thrown together in an extraterrestrial melting pot, often under high-risk and dangerous conditions. This understanding had become embodied in a new field of knowledge called: 'Symplectics', which provided a set of frameworks, methods, models and tools which could be used to bridge the distances between people with very different backgrounds and life experiences.

In the late twentieth century there had been many myths generated by clever left-brained people which took hold across left-brained communication media such as the Internet. What began to happen was the myth that technology would solve everything and that increased global trade, electronic communication and organizational techniques would bridge cultures and resolve conflicts, became widespread among a technophilic extreme, who dominated the investment in new technologies with the wealth they had earned from putting the new electronic backbone in place.

In the meantime, personal, organizational and social conflict continued to accelerate. The pace of change between 1990 and 2005 had left very large numbers of people 'future-shocked', and there were increasing numbers of young and old people marginalized by the technological élite. Forrest was reminded of a quote from Marshall McLuhan, whose words came back to him now with great force, as he remembered how his own family had suffered through the 'bifurcation':

The medium, or process of our time – electronic technology- is reshaping and restructuring patterns of social interdependence, and every aspect of our personal life. It is forcing us to re-consider and re-evaluate practically everything. Everything is changing – every thought, every action and every institution formerly taken for granted.

You, your family, your education, your neighbours, your job, your government, your relation to the others, and they are changing.

The suddenness of the leap from hardware to software cannot but produce a period of anarchy and collapse, especially in the developed countries.[1]

On the downside, this had produced a great split between information 'haves' and 'have nots', at individual, corporate and country levels, creating massive tensions and conflicts which had erupted in the global showdown of 2002 over Tibet and the regionalization of China. Luckily a major peace facilitation initiative headed by Bill Gates at the UN using symplectics resulted in a superpower non-aggression treaty between Russia, China, the USA and Europe in 2003. The symplectics movement had realized its first major triumph and became a mandatory part of the curriculum in most developed countries.

Despite scientific and technological breakthroughs resulting in 10 Ghz 1 billion transistor Intel chips and gene cancer therapy, the world was still a dangerous and unpredictable place. E-voting was resulting in more instability in the political systems of the Organization for Economic Cooperation and Development and this translated into much more volatility in the global network economy, where private and corporate program trades were also moving markets much more rapidly than ever before. As the complexity and chaos theorists had predicted in the late 1990s, the interconnectedness of the global economic and political systems was now resulting in greater uncertainty and volatility.

This had led to the emergence of a new social movement founded by the Plexis Institute, which focused on the social and human implications of the new sciences such as chaos, complexity, fractals, artificial life, evolutionary biology and cognitive science. 'Putting people first' was its credo, and through its work in symplectics it had evolved a method for working with different personally and socially constructed realities, which accelerated collective learning and intelligence. Forrest liked the methods and used them daily in his interactions.

To do this, one had to start with the ability to diagnose oneself, people and situations, and then place oneself in the right state with the appropriate tools to be effective. Much of the pioneering work had been done in NLP and similar techniques, to help individuals be more resourceful in managing themselves and others. But the sheer complexity of people, cultures and technologies one might have to deal with required more.

So, Forrest had used his background in psychology and anthropology to integrate four levels of science:

- the personality differences in individuals
- the cultural differences between people, groups, organizations and nations
- the different modes people prefer to interact in from different world views
- the challenges of making technologies such as the Internet and groupware sensitive to their users and their differences.

The key to all of this had been the 'culture grid', which complexity science had demonstrated was the key to maintaining a dynamic balance between order and chaos in any system. Such a dynamic balance enables the system to maintain its coherence while adapting and innovating at the 'edge of chaos', a place where the only thing one can predict are surprises.

It had come to be understood that starting a change process to resolve an issue without taking into account a person's world view leads to a great deal of pain. In fact, much of the corporate and social re-engineering, transformation and change programmes launched in the late 1990s were seen, in retrospect, as the equivalent of a gross pun being introduced into a serious dialogue. (Puns are an odious form of humour that threaten conversation with systematic ambiguity.)

The threat that there will be another pun puts the audience on the defensive, generating defensive routines against a flood of new contexts entering the conversation. Puns inflict new meanings from an alien world view, offending our realities with ambiguity and confusing our ability to make distinctions. Sometimes puns, and change, if pursued relentlessly, can drive you crazy, ultimately denying the world view of the recipient and thereby denying their rationality. No wonder 'change agents' and the makers of puns are not the most popular people!

Symplectics started right here to address how one could bring a recipient or listener along by establishing a context, rather than 'shocking' or 'punning' them into change. Forrest and his team had begun to develop a method which presented the course of change in ways which integrated the histories and visions of those involved, and the cultures they had created with the new realities that must be encountered in the change process.

This required the:

- co-creation of an environment in which those involved can encounter new ideas and ways of thinking and being, safe from the demands of the particular realities of their own day-to-day world
- co-design and co-development of a path of resolution which enables all the stakeholder groups to realize their aspirations while managing their anxiety and excitement about change
- use of a variety of appropriate methods and tools for working with mental models, mindsets, deep-seated needs and feelings in the change process
- ability to diagnose (a) the balance of different culture and personality types in an organization and its network of relationships, (b) the perceived need for change along the several dimensions in which the organization operates, (c) the capability of the organization to change, and where the change potential is strongest and/or most appropriate.

Forrest settled back in his chair with a strong mug of Colombian Mocha, and chatted idly with his colleagues while they waited for their 11.00 web-weaving session with some folks down there in the Himalayas.

Scene 2: Inside a small geodesic structure somewhere in Northern Tibet

Hieronymus ('Harry') Hochauser was preparing for his meeting with Professor Forrest, together with a small group of Tibetan community leaders. They were about to enter their local collaboradome to contribute to the Communextra project.

Hochauser had been living in Tibetan communities for decades, studying their unique culture and community structures. In his own way he had become something of a post-modern mystic in the process. Harry had been a brilliant, if introverted, student, and was an early convert to transcendental meditation back in the 1970s. This led him on a journey into human consciousness and a study of the mind.

What had always fascinated him was how, out of the several thousand documented cosmologies discovered on Earth, there appeared to be, at most, fifty or so basic creation myths. His study of Jung had also led him to explore the common origins of the human psyche, some aspects of which can be intuited through frameworks for exploring personalities such as the Myers Briggs Type Indicator and the Belbin team stereotypes. Other frameworks for understanding different world views, mindsets and cultures such as McWhinney's Map of Alternative Realities, had become very useful in helping different people gain an understanding of different cultures and mindsets, and how those world views influenced the values and behaviours of individuals, groups and organizations.

The Tibetans and Hochauser all donned their 'WaveGuides', headsets which contained small brainscanners and indicated the nature of the brainwaves being emitted by the participants. WaveGuides enabled their users to get instant feedback on their current state of mind, using biofeedback to enter the most appropriate state for the situation in hand. The workings of emotion, intuition and their role in cognition and behaviour had become much better understood in the early part of the twenty-first century. It was now possible to design interfaces between people and technologies which facilitated and harnessed emotional and practical, as well as intellectual, intelligence.

Hochauser greeted the Tibetans gathered in the Collaboradome: 'Tashi Dillek – Welcome!' Lama Wangdor Rimpoche, scholar Chonchok Sumon Khenpo and other Tibetan leaders were gathered together in the interface room, surrounded by a 270-degree three-dimensional wall-screen running from floor to ceiling. At the prompt, Hochauser activated the dialogue with a softly spoken, 'Begin'. The interior walls of Concorde's dark blue Collaboradome hove into view, with Professor Forrest's plaid shirt, twinkling blue eyes and white beard coming sharply into focus, in contrast to his more soberly dressed colleagues.

'Hey there, Forrest. How're things goin' in that high altitude spam can?' said Hochauser. The Tibetans chuckled quietly to themselves with their hands over their mouths.

'Okay, thanks Harry', Forrest replied, using Hochauser's nickname. 'We are still working on the Level 3 protocols for Communextra. We've had some difficulties with the auto-translator units, but otherwise we're more or less on schedule. The Biosphere 5 results are also just in.'

Hochauser turned to the Tibetans: 'Well, Lama Wangdor, could you continue from where we left off last week- you were telling us how you negotiated the Treaty of Lhasa.'

Lama Wangdor, a wizened holy man, spoke softly and carefully: 'At the height of the battle for Lhasa we realized that we would not win the war, let alone the peace. Our symplectics advisers helped us map the alternate realities we were confronting in the Red Army, so that we could map the paths of change between our own mystical traditions with the strongly sensory/unitary world views of the Chinese generals.'

Wangdor paused, then continued: 'Those generals viewed us as a primitive culture, needing modernization, which was not helped by the extremists in our cause. We got the ruling council of lamas and scholars together and agreed, after much meditation, to reconsider the United Nations proposal. It was hard for us to accept that we needed to open up Tibet to the world, but this was the only avenue which could satisfy our economic needs with the requirement that we negotiate some taxation revenue for the Chinese which would enable them to view us as an autonomous state.'

'We offered General Xinjiang a settlement during our dialogue, which they could live with, and did not feel threatened by. Dalai Lama was allowed to return, and the dialogue teams set up between the Chinese authorities and our leaders began to develop a shared understanding of our future together as neighbours. This vision required much effort and understanding on both sides, in which the first release of Communextra played an important role for us.'

As the orb on Wangdor's WaveGuide glowed deep purple, Professor Forrest was listening intently, the twinkle in his eyes now replaced by a deeply reflective glow echoed in the deep blue colour of his WaveGuide. Forrest spoke tentatively: 'That shift from the Mystic to the Sensory world view is a pretty big one, Lama. In moving from your world of deep truths toward the autocratic/sensory world of the Chinese generals, you enabled the realization of new creative ideas around you. We call this "inventive change", and that will no doubt offer great benefits to burned out materialists like us who need a retreat to explore the higher realms of consciousness.'

The exploration of this profound shift in world views continued, until the Communextra team had all the evidence they wanted for their case study. Forrest and his team were now in the final stages of development of the Level 3 protocols for Communextra, which integrated the eight paths of change into the group dialogue system.

It was becoming clear that all the multicultural groups being assembled for extraterrestrial exploration needed shared protocols to establish some form of collective intelligence. The speed at which things happened in space and on planetary expeditions meant that intimate mutual understanding was needed to react quickly together and take life-or-death decisions. In settling into a way of life together on a distant planet, it was also clear that a strong sense of shared destiny and enjoyment of each other's company was crucial to effective community operations in such diverse groups.

Author's comments

If we cannot predict the future, then we can at least develop a heightened sensitivity to the different possible structures of the future and the different logics and paths of change by which they emerge. We can also become more aware of how the world views we and others hold and the actions we take as a result, influence the kinds of futures we set about creating.

Jay, Harry, Lama Wangdor and General Xinjiang, all represent archetypes which emerge from the different ways in which we construct our personal and social realities. From each of their perspectives, they are all 'right', and whenever any change is proposed which stresses their conceptions of self and their value systems, they will experience a personal learning challenge which can often degenerate into conflict, if badly handled.

Paths of change and transformation emerge from the different threads of

- belief systems and cultures
- individual personalities and mindsets
- situations and opportunities

unfolding together in novel and unpredictable ways. The more conscious we can be of this process and its elements, the better we can facilitate the sustainable outcomes we would like to see emerging from the personal, business and organizational change agendas of the late twentieth century.

Note
1. McLuhan, M. (1995) *Mind Grenades*, Wred.

Index